HOW WALT DISNEY CHANGED ANIMATION FOREVER

To Andrea:
I am glad you have been by my side,
to always press the final keystroke.

Happy fifteenth anniversary.
I love you.

HOW WALT DISNEY CHANGED ANIMATION FOREVER

ANDREW STANLEY KISTE

WHITE OWL
AN IMPRINT OF PEN & SWORD BOOKS LTD.
YORKSHIRE – PHILADELPHIA

First published in Great Britain in 2025 by
PEN AND SWORD WHITE OWL
An imprint of
Pen & Sword Books Ltd
Yorkshire – Philadelphia

ISBN 978 1 39905 508 6

A CIP catalogue record for this book is available from the British Library.

Typeset in Times New Roman 11.5/14 by
SJmagic DESIGN SERVICES, India.
Printed and bound in the UK by CPI Group (UK) Ltd, Croydon, CR0 4YY.

The Publisher's authorised representative in the EU for product safety is
Authorised Rep Compliance Ltd., Ground Floor, 71 Lower Baggot Street,
Dublin D02 P593, Ireland.
www.arccompliance.com

For a complete list of Pen & Sword titles please contact

PEN & SWORD BOOKS LIMITED
George House, Units 12 & 13, Beevor Street, Off Pontefract Road,
Barnsley, South Yorkshire, S71 1HN, England
E-mail: enquiries@pen-and-sword.co.uk
Website: www.pen-and-sword.co.uk

or

PEN AND SWORD BOOKS
1950 Lawrence Rd, Havertown, PA 19083, USA
E-mail: uspen-and-sword@casematepublishers.com
Website: www.penandswordbooks.com

NOTE

Everything that I have written is factual. Any piece of actual information has come directly from some sort of primary source, whether book, newspaper article, video, telegram, scientific study, or peer-reviewed article. I also use photographs and interviews to flesh out the conversations and thoughts that various individuals had, interspersed with quotes and dialogue pulled from interviews and primary source material. None of this is historically or factually inaccurate, but rather a narrative representation of actual events that happened based on individuals' recollections of specific events. A select bibliography of sources can be found at the end of this volume.

The Author has taken reasonable steps to trace the copyright holders to obtain permissions for use of images and quotations but, despite their best endeavours, has been unable to do so. The copyright holders, or the late copyright holders' estates, are advised to make themselves known to the Publisher.

CONTENTS

ACKNOWLEDGEMENTS

Oftentimes, the cover of a book like this features only the name of the author, the person who thought of the concept for the book and put words to it. In many ways, this idea is similar to how Walt Disney's films often started out: a title card which identified the animated short as "A Cartoon by Walt Disney." However, as you will find upon reading this book, there was so much more that went into the crafting of this book than just the sole efforts of myself.

For example, it was the great folks over at Pen & Sword and White Owl who pitched the idea to me of writing a book series about the life of Walt Disney in the first place.

As I began to try to wrap my head around this colossal task, I began to map out what a research trip around the United States might look like to "follow in Walt's footsteps." This required a 'research assistant' of sorts. My incredible wife, Andrea, became my Roy Disney, graciously loosening the purse-strings of our family and encouraging me to travel and acquire books – some rare – for the purpose of accumulating source material. She also was my Lillian Disney, following me around southern California as I traced the life of Walt: peering through the bars of the Griffith Park's Los Angeles Live Steamers Railroad Museum (and caring for me after I got attacked by a bird doing so), wandering around as I aimlessly wandered Forest Lawn Cemetery searching for Walt's gravesite, sitting at a table for hours in the Tam O'Shanter restaurant while we waited for the 'Disney table' to become vacant for pictures, and more. There is no way I could have done any of this without her.

As my book project came to a close, it needed to be honed and edited akin to a film's ink-and-painting and trimming. For this, I get to thank Melanie de Clegane, who spent tireless hours correcting my awful American grammar and making it more palatable for global audiences. I am also ever thankful to Laura Hirst, who helped ensure that the proper permissions had been acquired, answered my questions with patience and grace, and advocated for my book and I along the whole way. Finally, a great thanks to Pen & Sword/White Owl, my distributors, who have taken my work and are ensuring that it is spread around the world, posted online, and finding its way onto bookstore shelves for public consumption.

All of these people and more should really be the ones with their names on the cover of this book. I am just the one who got the honor and pleasure of putting their work into the words resembling a story.

Andrew Stanley Kiste
September 10, 2025

CAST OF CHARACTERS

Babbitt, Art: animator who established artist-training classes at the Walt Disney Studios, animated characters including the Big Bad Wolf and Donald Duck, and later helped lead the 1941 studio strike.

Belcher, Marjorie: ballerina who was hired to be a visual reference model for Snow White and *Pinocchio*'s Blue Fairy.

Blair, Mary: inspirational sketch artist whose unique and unconventional focus on colour played an important part in determining the look and feel of Disney's features throughout the 1940s and 1950s, including *The Three Caballeros, Cinderella, Alice in Wonderland,* and *Peter Pan.*

Blank, Dorothy Ann: member of the Story department who used volumes in the studio's research library to write treatments of various animated shorts and features; Blank also provided visual reference for animated characters, including the Evil Queen from *Snow White and the Seven Dwarfs*

Borgfeldt, George: agent hired to contract licensing of Disney properties for consumer goods: primarily responsible for licensing and marketing the Mickey Mouse dolls created by Charlotte Clark.

Caselotti, Adriana: voice of Snow White.

Clampett, Bob: young man who helped design first Mickey Mouse doll for his aunt, Charlotte Clark; would later go on to animate and direct Warner Bros.' *Looney Tunes* shorts.

Clark, Charlotte: local woman who created the first Mickey Mouse plush doll and would later be hired by the studio to oversee doll production.

Colvig, Pinto: an ex-circus clown who was hired on as a voice actor for shorts at the Walt Disney Studios; he brought vocal life to characters including the titular Grasshopper of "Grasshopper and the Ants," as well as Grumpy from *Snow White and the Seven Dwarfs,* but most famously served as the vocal actor for Goofy.

DeForce, Helen Josephine: head librarian of the Walt Disney Studios' research library; DeForce and her staff would often provide reference material, story treatments, and help storyboard for animators.

Disney, Diane: Walt and Lillian Disney's oldest daughter.

Disney, Elias: Walt Disney's father.

Disney, Edna: wife of Roy Disney and sister-in-law of Walt Disney.

Disney, Flora: Walt Disney's mother.

Disney, Lillian: wife of Walt Disney.

Disney, Roy: brother of Walt Disney and the co-founder and Chairman of the Board of the Walt Disney Studios.

Disney, Sharon: Walt and Lillian Disney's youngest daughter.

Disney, Walt: co-founder of the Walt Disney Studios and executive producer of the studio's animated films.

D'Orsi, Ugo: member of the studio's Special Effects department, leading alongside Cy Young.

Edouarde, Carl: former conductor at New York's Capitol Theatre who would later help compose soundtracks for many Hollywood films. Edouarde would be chosen by distributor Pat Powers to help arrange and conduct the synchronised soundtrack for "Steamboat Willie."

Ferguson, Norm "Fergie": artist who helped develop personality animation at the Walt Disney Studios; best known for his work on the Big Bad Wolf and Pluto.

Garity, William "Bill": technician at the Walt Disney Studios; Garity helped develop Disney's synchronised sound system, the multiplane camera, the air conditioning system at the Burbank studio campus, and Fantasound.

Gottfredson, Floyd: former inbetweener and artist who helped develop the backstory of Mickey Mouse through the syndicated comics.

Graham, Don: former faculty at the Chouinard Art Institute and artist and instructor of the in-house animator training program at the Walt Disney Studios.

Grant, Joe: Head of the Story department at the Walt Disney Studios, who helped develop and write a number of Disney's animated films including *Dumbo* and *Lady and the Tramp.*

Iwerks, Ub: close friend and fellow artist who helped develop Mickey Mouse and the early Silly Symphonies alongside Walt Disney. After the closure of his own studio, Ub returned to the studio, where he helped solve technical challenges including the combination of live action and animation, assisting Bill Garity in the development of Fantasound, and the realistic depiction of enemy aircraft in shorts during the Second World War.

Jackson, Wilfred: early animator at the Walt Disney Studios who helped develop a synchronised soundtrack for "Steamboat Willie" and would later direct various shorts.

Huemer, Dick: member of the studio's Story department at the Walt Disney Studios, who helped develop and write a number of Disney's animated films including *Dumbo* and *Lady and the Tramp* alongside Joe Grant.

Hurter, Albert: inspirational sketch artist and member of the studio's Story department who helped provide concept sketches for "Three Little Pigs". Hurter was also responsible for designing buildings and fixtures for *Snow White and the Seven Dwarfs* and *Pinocchio*, giving the films their old-world feel.

Kamen, Herman "Kay": Executive responsible for licensing characters and properties of the Walt Disney Studios.

Kimball, Ward: animator known for his sense of humour and pranks throughout the studio. Kimball's zany and humorous personality often came out in his work, as in the musical "The Three Caballeros" and *Alice in Wonderland*'s Mad Tea Party sequences.

Lessing, Gunther: company lawyer of the Walt Disney Studios who helped dissolve partnership with Pat Powers and attempted to negotiate a truce in the 1941 studio strike.

Marcus, Mike: early cameraman at the Walt Disney Studios who helped secretly photograph "Steamboat Willie."

Mintz, Charles: a previous partner to Walt and Roy Disney who once distributed the Oswald the Lucky Rabbit shorts; Mintz would later "steal" the production and distribution rights of the Oswald character and films in the late 1920s.

Moore, Fred: animator who was primarily responsible for defining the "look" of Mickey Mouse, as well as his personality. Moore also valued personality and realism in his work, as evidenced in his work on "Three Little Pigs" and Mr. Stork from *Dumbo.*

Nash, Clarence: milkman and voice actor who performed as Donald Duck for the Walt Disney Studios.

Powers, Pat: New York film distributor who worked alongside Walt Disney in distributing the early Mickey Mouse cartoons. Powers also assisted the Walt Disney Studios in developing an early synchronised sound system.

Sears, Ted: inspirational artist and member of the Story department who helped write "Three Little Pigs" and define the character and personality of many of the studio's characters including Mickey Mouse.

Sewell, Hazel: sister-in-law of Walt Disney who served as the first head of the Ink-and-Paint department.

Smith, Webb: artist and member of the Story department who helped develop the mainstream use of the storyboarding process.

Stalling, Carl: friend of Walt Disney and musician who helped compose soundtracks for many of the studio's early animated shorts. Stalling was also responsible for suggesting and helping develop the Silly Symphonies series.

Stokowski, Leopold: world-renown conductor of the Philadelphia Orchestra who would help develop and perform in *Fantasia*.

Tenggren, Gustaf: inspirational artist and member of the Story department who completed background paintings and helped give an old-world feel to films including "The Old Mill," *Snow White and the Seven Dwarfs,* and *Pinocchio.*

Tytla, Vladimir "Bill": animator responsible for animating many of the studio's important characters including Grumpy from *Snow White and the Seven Dwarfs* and Chernabog from *Fantasia.*

Wallace, Oliver: Academy Award-winning composer who wrote songs for many of the studio's films during the 1940s and 1950s, including *Dumbo, Alice in Wonderland,* and "Der Fuhrer's Face."

Weber, Karl Emanuel Martin "Kem": architect and designer who helped to develop the layout and plans for both the Walt Disney Studios located in Burbank, as well as the furniture used at the Walt Disney Studios.

Young, Cyrus "Cy": member of the studio's Special Effects department, leading alongside Ugo D'Orsi.

PREFACE

When I began my journey into the past back in 2019, I had no idea how much the world would change in five short years: new presidents would come and go, wars that echoed around the world would break out, and a global pandemic would rage through communities and homes, leaving a striking impact on culture, daily life, and collective memory. I also had no idea how much my world would change: we would welcome a new member to our family in 2021, move across the country in 2022, and I would completely change careers. But just as significantly, I would come to know on a personal level a person who had completely altered not only American – but global – culture and who had become something of a cultural myth himself: Walt Disney.

Twentieth century author Robert Brault once wrote that "[i]n the end you don't so much find yourself as you find someone who knows who you are." While I have certainly learned a lot about myself over the past five years, I believe this quote is also applicable to the experiential knowledge acquired when one is intentional in spending time getting to know another person. So was the case with me as I have spent the last five years of my life immersing myself in the person and businessman of Walt Disney. I have stood in the room he was born in Chicago, enjoyed dessert in the parlour of his childhood home in Marceline, and climbed the wooden steps he would have trudged up after a bitter cold day delivering newspapers in Kansas City. I have eaten in the exact same spot in restaurants he frequented, ducked into the barn in Los Angeles where he first animated, stood on the site of the now demolished studio where Mickey Mouse was born, and gazed in awe around the office he worked in for nearly thirty years. I spent countless hours poring through newspapers nearly a century old, as well as numerous biographies, monographs, and cultural histories to understand the various innovations, achievements, and accomplishments of the Walt Disney Studios. And I have sat on a small bench in a small, enclosed garden, quiet orchestral music playing, gazing at a plaque marking the final resting place of this man I had spent so long getting to know on a deep professional and personal level, shedding silent tears of both gratitude and loss.

My previous book, *The Early Life of Walt Disney*, provides a sort of origin story for the burgeoning artist. It traces the story of young Walter from his humble beginnings as the youngest son of a working class family which moved from industrial Chicago to agricultural Marceline, Missouri to suburban Kansas City. As he grew, Walter found solace from difficult situations in the artistic pursuit of drawing, finding his talent improving through the adversity of being relatively isolated in a country farming town; recovering in bed from the chicken pox, a foot injury, or the Spanish Flu; or even spending time helping rebuild a war-torn Europe in the days following the First World War. After numerous failures attempting to find success in the young industry of film animation, Walt joined his older brother Roy in Los Angeles where together they created the studio which has changed the mediums of film, animation, family entertainment, theme parks, technology, city planning, and more.

While it is important to tell the entirety of Walt Disney's story, this has successfully been done dozens of times by accomplished biographers and documentarians, as well as celebrated by the Walt Disney Company itself. Rather, this volume is self-explanatory based upon its title: *How Walt Disney Changed Animation Forever*. While anecdotes about Walt's life are sprinkled throughout and we continue our discovery about the life of the man, Walt Disney and the studio became relatively synonymous with the "birth" of Mickey Mouse in 1927, mainly because so much of his life revolved around his work and vice-versa.

Walt Disney, and by default his company, was a trailblazer in the film industry, the field of animation, and popular culture. In addition to creating one of the most successful cartoon characters of all time – which according to a study conducted in 2008 identified Mickey Mouse as having a "97% recognition rate in the US [which] even edges out Santa Claus" – the Walt Disney Studios premiered the first cartoon with synchronised sound, the first animated short and cartoon series synchronised to and revolving around a musical score, the first animated short in full colour, innovations in animation and film techniques and technology including dimensional animation, the first to implement a successful in-house training program, the progenitor of imbuing personality upon animated characters, the one who risked everything – including his reputation – by introducing the feature-length animated film, and more. It is safe to say that without Walt Disney's boldness, courage, vision, and creativity the world, and Hollywood, would be a very different place today.

PART 1

IT ALL STARTED WITH A MOUSE 1928–1929

BORN OF NECESSITY

Walter Elias Disney, aged twenty-six, couldn't believe he was back in this predicament. As he sat on the New York Central Cannonball bringing him home from New York City to Los Angeles, he realised that the path of his life was much like the Dips Coaster he used to ride at Electric Park in his childhood home of Kansas City, Missouri.

After spending his first few years in Chicago, Illinois, his family moved to the small agricultural town of Marceline, Missouri where his father, Elias Disney, purchased an apple farm. The family, which also included Walt's mother Flora and his three older brothers and younger sister, often struggled to bring in a profit as a result of meagre agricultural harvests on their farm. While their time in Marceline was short-lived, the simplicity of small-town life and its focus on the importance of building a family-like community made a large impact on Walt Disney's personality and nostalgic musings for the rest of his life. As he came to the end of his elementary school years, Walt and his family relocated to Kansas City, Missouri, where Elias had decided to purchase a delivery route for *The Kansas City Star*, one of the local newspapers, relying on Walt and his older brother Roy to deliver the twice-daily subscriptions.

Unfortunately, once again this scheme was not one which brought Elias Disney success. After learning about an opportunity to invest the family savings, Elias moved his family back to Chicago, where he took a position first as a handy-man for O-Zell's, a factory which produced jellies and sodas to provide respite to thirsty Americans in the days of prohibition. While Elias pursued this new opportunity which turned out to be a scam, teenage Walt worked a number of odd jobs in the Windy City, including on the city's elevated train system and as a postman.

In the young man's sixteenth year, international events brought a dramatic turn of events to Walt Disney's life. With Europe embroiled in the Great War, young Walt was inspired by his older brother Roy's service to enlist for the trenches of France. After a number of false starts due to his young age – he was legally unable to enlist until he was seventeen, something that a good forgery couldn't fix – the patriotic young man joined up with the American Red Cross to support the Allied Forces in France. However, while participating in training in Chicago, he fell victim to the influenza epidemic, which almost took his life. He soon learned to his dismay that his group had been called off to war while he lay recovering, and shortly thereafter an armistice had been declared. Luckily, he was given a second chance when it was announced that the Red Cross would be supporting recovery efforts in Europe postwar for affected communities and injured individuals alike. Over the next several months, Walt worked at a number of Red Cross hospitals throughout France and served as a truck and ambulance driver, transporting the injured, VIPs, and supplies.

Throughout his formative years, Walt Disney occupied himself by drawing. This hobby was encouraged by his Aunt Margaret Disney, who regularly provided the boy crayons and a Big Chief writing tablet to help keep him out of trouble on the farm in Marceline, but was discouraged by his father Elias, who believed that drawing was a distraction and would never amount to anything. In school, Walt was inspired by his artistic hero, Carey Orr, a cartoonist for the *Chicago Tribune*, and imitated his hero's style by creating his own editorial cartoons for his school newspaper. While serving in the Red Cross in Europe, the young man attempted to cheer up wounded servicemen by drawing on the canvas sides of his ambulance and painting German helmets as souvenirs for soldiers returning home.

Upon his arrival back in the states, Walt was determined to pursue a career in art in Kansas City. A friend of Roy's recommended he apply for a job at Pesmen-Rubin, an agency where Walt would go on to create advertisements for businesses throughout greater Kansas City, including for the local Newman Theatre. While employed with Pesmen-Rubin, Walt met another aspiring artist, Ub Iwerks; after being laid off from the ad agency, the two young men created their own business as freelance illustrators. While this was great experience for the young men, they weren't as successful as they'd hoped, and instead found jobs at the Kansas City Slide Company, which created advertisements to show on screens between films in the city's theatres. In an effort to improve the quality of advertisements, the owner of the Kansas City Slide Company,

A.V. Cauger, began to implement the use of animated advertisements rather than static ones. This required Walt and Ub to learn new skills, incorporating their artistic style of caricature and humour into the archaic animation of Cauger's animated advertisements.

Fascinated by this growing medium, Walt and Ub began to experiment with animation in the evenings and on weekends, using the small garage located behind the home of Elias and Flora Disney – who had relocated back to Kansas City – as their workshop. Walt began to create animated advertisements and editorial cartoons, selling them to Frank Newman, the owner of Kansas City's Newman Theatre, who agreed to show these "Newman Laugh-O-grams" on-screen between films. The relative success of these seconds-long advertisements led to Walt branching out to create gag-driven animated fairy tales, partnering with a handful of Kansas City artists, including Hugh Harman and Rudy Ising. However, these short cartoons were more experimental than anything, allowing the artists to learn more about the craft of animation while continuing to do work for the Kansas City Slide Company.

In 1922, Walt Disney decided to go out on his own to focus primarily on creating animation like his Laugh-O-grams and experimental animated films. The young entrepreneur began building a staff of artists, and together they soon established a studio in an office building a few kilometres from the centre of Kansas City. A number of shorts began to emerge from this studio, including Laugh-O-gram fairy tales and Lafflets, or gag reels which served as fillers between feature films in the theatres. Unfortunately, Pictorial Clubs, Inc., the distributor of Disney's Laugh-O-grams, folded, resulting in the loss of profits guaranteed to the studio and the inability to pay debts owed. Artists began to leave, and the assets of the studio were frozen. With nowhere else to go, Walt Disney, who had enjoyed such big dreams of being a successful artist, lived essentially homeless in his empty studio, eating beans and chilli out of a can, bathing in the public bathroom of nearby Union Station, and with no friends nearby except the handful of mice who also called the office building home.

Unwilling to give up, Walt continued to do odd jobs here and there, such as directing an educational film for a local dentist and directing and performing in a Song-O-Reel, a film which featured musical lyrics along the bottom for audience members to sing along to. Walt collaborated on this job, set to the song "Martha: Just a Plain

Old-Fashioned Name," with the organist of the nearby Isis Theatre named Carl Stalling.

A few weeks later, while sitting in a darkened theatre, Walt saw an advertisement for a bread company featuring a little girl. A stroke of genius hit him like a thunderbolt: why not put a live-action girl into an animated world? This idea would spawn a series of films known as the Alice Comedies, which found a distributor in Margaret Winkler, a New York executive who offered Walt a film deal.

In an effort to escape his string of bad luck and debt in Kansas City, Walt followed Roy – who had gone to California on the advice of his doctor after contracting tuberculosis – and decided to pursue a career in animated film. Over the next few years, the popularity of the Alice Comedies would wax and wane, as a number of little girls would play the titular role of Alice. However, one significant effect of the Alice Comedies was the start of a new relationship with one of the employees working in Walt's new venture: Lillian Bounds. Over the next several months, Walt would begin to court Lillian, eventually joking with her that the best way for the studio to save money would be to marry her so he no longer had to pay her. As a result, the young filmmaker found himself in love with the girl of his dreams, and she with him.

Unfortunately, America had not yet decided that it was in love with Walt Disney. By 1927, Winkler's new husband, Charles Mintz, had taken over the distribution of the Disney shorts and had decided that the Alice Comedies were not as successful as he'd hoped. Instead, he charged Walt and Ub with creating a new animated character to compete with Koko the Clown and Felix the Cat. This character, Oswald the Lucky Rabbit, was picked up by Universal, ultimately resulting in twenty-six films made by Disney during its run of the series. Unfortunately, Mintz repeatedly changed his contract with Walt, promising lower payments per film during each renewal of the contract.

Fed up by Mintz's unwillingness to negotiate a fair contract, Walt and Lillian travelled to New York City to meet with the distributor in person. However, in his absence from the Los Angeles Studio, Mintz had instructed his brother-in-law, George Winkler, to sign away Disney's artists, making them his employees rather than Walt's. Upon the studio executive's arrival in New York, the distributor informed him that he owned Oswald, not Disney, and that unless Walt accepted a drastic reduction in payment for each Oswald film, he would be out of a job.

Incensed, Walt Disney and his bride returned to the train station for their return trip to Los Angeles. Before embarking, they stopped by the Western Union office and sent a telegram to Roy in California: "LEAVING TONIGHT, STOPPING OVER IN KANSAS CITY. EVERYTHING OK." But as the train departed toward the setting sun, he wasn't sure he believed the reassurance he had sent to his brother. At first, the young artist was discouraged, gazing out the train window at the scenery flashing by. It reminded him of animation printed on a film strip which, when moving quickly past a lit projector lens, created the illusion of life through the principle of persistence of vision. As he contemplated the memories of his past failures, which likewise flashed through his mind, he thought of the people who had stuck by him in the hard times: his wife Lillian, his older brother Roy, his friend and coworker Ub Iwerks…and a handful of mice who kept him company when he was homeless and living in the Laugh-O-gram studio in Kansas City.

Mice. No one had created a mouse character before. At least not a mouse character who starred in his own series. Sitting up in his seat, he turned away from the film strip-esque window which served as an allegory for his failure towards his wife, and began to animatedly describe his new idea. Speaking almost too quickly for Lillian to understand, he finally explained that this new mouse character should be named Mortimer. Lillian scoffed, explaining that the name for a cartoon character felt wrong, that it was a "sissy name." Instead, she suggested the name Mickey.

"Mickey," Walt said aloud, testing the name in his mouth like his favourite Scotch Mist. "Mickey Mouse." A grin spread across his face: maybe everything would be okay after all.

When Walt and Lillian arrived in Los Angeles, Roy met them at the train station to give them a ride home. The younger of the Disney brothers had a look on his face, which signalled to the elder not to ask many questions. Upon arriving at the Disney homestead on Lyric Avenue – Roy had built a home right next door to Walt – Roy sat his brother down.

"Alright, kid," he began. "Tell me what kind of deal you made."

"No deal," Walt explained. He went on to describe how Charles Mintz had made off with Oswald while George Winkler had signed away their artists.

But there was a catch, Walt explained. "This time, we are going to own our character – a mouse." As Lillian unpacked their bags from their trip east, Walt and Roy spent several hours excitedly planning their new mouse series, with Walt talking about his ideas and Roy sketching out preliminary financial figures to make the cartoons work in spite of no future guaranteed income.

The following day, Walt made his way to the small whitewashed complex which housed Walt Disney Studios located at 2719 Hyperion. He coolly but politely greeted his artists, some of whom were sheepish for abandoning their friend and boss for Mintz, while others were indifferent or even indignant about their change in loyalty. Under the stipulations of the previous contract with Mintz and Universal, Disney was still required to finish the final few instalments of the current Oswald series before the studio's artists changed hands. Only a few studio employees were loyal to Walt and Roy and had decided to stay on: Ub Iwerks, Johnny Cannon, Les Clark, and the recently hired Wilfred Jackson. New to animation and the studio system after attending the Otis Art Institute, this young man was fascinated to discover the artists constantly clowning around and laughing, noting that it didn't seem that much work was being accomplished. However this illusion was shattered on Saturday afternoons when, after work was completed for the week at 1.00 in the afternoon, the artists packed up their supplies, assumed a serious countenance, and made their way for their cars, suspicious that their colleagues would steal their supplies or take credit for their work.

Making his way into his office suite, Walt got the attention of Roy, Ub, and Les Clark and together the group retired into an empty office. Walt described his idea for a new mouse character to his friends. As he talked, Ub sketched out a concept for the character, drawing inspiration from the mice supporting characters in Paul Terry's series, *Aesop's Fables*, as well as those drawn by artist Clifton Meek in his syndicated comic strips in the early years of the twentieth century. Taking characteristics from Oswald, Mickey had a similar shape to his predecessor, albeit in a more compact manner. Designed to encourage ease in animation, Mickey featured a pear-shaped torso and was made up primarily of circles. After completing his quick sketch, Ub turned his pad around and showed the group, who all agreed this would be the studio's new star. Like a protective, proud papa, Walt vowed that Mickey Mouse would be copyrighted, trademarked, and wholly owned by Walt Disney and his studio so that another situation akin to the theft of Oswald the Lucky

Rabbit would never happen again. Walt was true to his word: Mickey Mouse was trademarked in Walt Disney's name on 21 May 1938.

With Mintz now in control of the remaining Oswald films and undercutting Walt on his profit, the Walt Disney Studios needed to produce its own animated shorts – and quickly – if it planned to stay in business after the final film was submitted to Mintz. Walt wrote out a storyline for the first Mickey short, inspired by Charles Lindhberg's fateful crossing of the Atlantic Ocean in May 1927.

Contrary to the expectations of many experts and ordinary individuals alike, Lindbergh defied all odds, completing his solo flight from New York City to Paris in thirty-four hours while navigating the single engine *Spirit of St. Louis*. The pilot became an instant celebrity. Newspapers and movie theatre newsreels extolled his feat. Upon returning to the United States, he participated in a tour of the country, making stops in ninety-two cities and becoming a recipient of both the Distinguished Flying Cross and the American Medal of Honor. Even popular culture bowed down to the altar of Lindbergh, with more than two-hundred songs hailing his accomplishment, while *Time* magazine made him their first "Man of the Year."

Much like "Lucky Lindy," Walt Disney took a gamble in his attempt to introduce a new character – whom he described as an amalgamation of Charlie Chaplin and Douglas Fairbanks Jr. – to the existing pantheon of animated personalities. In "Plane Crazy", Mickey converts an automobile into an aeroplane, inspired by a book titled "How to Fly" which features an image of Lindbergh himself. It is soon revealed that Mickey does this to woo an enamoured female mouse, who would later be known as Minnie, named after a former patron of Walt's, Minnie Cowles.

Walt was too busy running the studio to take an active part in the animating of the film. Instead, he assigned Ub to work exclusively on the short. However, the staff was still under contractual obligation to produce Oswald films for Mintz, and this contract stipulated that anything produced in the contractual period belonged to the New York distributor. As a result, Ub animated "Plane Crazy" in secrecy, making sure to have sketches of Oswald near: if one of the disloyal artists walked in, Ub could quickly cover the frames of the Mickey film with the latest Mintz cartoon to avoid suspicion. Produced at a cost of $1,772.89, Ub single-handedly animated the entirety of the film's frames, sometimes completing seven hundred drawings in a single day. Due to the pace at which the film was animated, and the exhausting work of doing it alone, Ub employed a number of tricks to make the process easier for himself, including cycling, in which a number of frames of action are repeated in a series of "cycles." This is particularly evident when Mickey, in the aeroplane, is chasing a cow down the country lane or when the barnyard animals are attempting to construct a plane for the intrepid pilot at the start of the film. However, he and Walt injected their own special touch into the film as well, such as pioneering the concept of giving a character a distinct personality and successfully animating crowd shots featuring those who have gathered to see Mickey off on his flight.

After Ub had finished hand-drawing each frame, Walt snuck them out of the studio and into the makeshift workshop he had set up in the garage and kitchen table of his Lyric Avenue home. After the line drawings had been traced on the transparent cels by loyal employee Mary Tebb and Lillian's sister Hazel Sewell, they were opaqued by Lillian, Roy, his wife Edna, and Kathleen Dollard Smith. They were then snuck back into the studio, where they were secretly photographed by Mike Marcus under the dark cover of night. A few hours before the rest of the artists returned to the studio for the day to work on the Oswald shorts, Marcus and Walt hastily cleaned up the studio's drawing rooms, inking studio, and photography lab to eliminate any suspicion of their clandestine work. With their whole attention focused on "Plane Crazy", the film, which was comprised of approximately eight thousand individual drawings, was completed in a mere two weeks.

Walt was thrilled that he had completed this new cartoon. But a film sitting in a canister is worthless unless audiences see it. Refusing to utilise an agent after Mintz's betrayal, Walt began reaching out to his contacts throughout Los Angeles, hoping a local theatre proprietor would be willing to screen his short to paying customers. Eventually, Walt convinced the owner of a theatre located on Hollywood's Sunset Boulevard to show the film, premiering on 15 May 1928 to an organ accompaniment and resulting in an enthusiastic response from theatre-goers. Walt did not take long to revel in his success: on 29 May he pitched his idea for the next Mickey film by gathering his artists together and acting out the basic storyline for what would become "The Gallopin' Gaucho".

Life for Walt and Lillian was just as difficult at home as it was in the studio in the days after losing Oswald and developing Mickey Mouse.

The couple attempted to live as frugally as possible with no guaranteed future income due to the end of the Oswald contract in August 1928. Stew and pot roast became regular rotations in the couple's meals because they were relatively inexpensive options. Even their wardrobes were impacted by their reduced income: in one instance, Lillian tripped on the garage stairs, ruining her last pair of silk stockings.

While the trappings of everyday life were limited, Walt and Lillian still felt as though they lived like royalty in their home at 2495 Lyric Avenue located in the Franklin Hills neighbourhood north of Los Angeles. With its yellow-tinted stucco exterior, wrought iron and plated glass windows, and red brick steps up to the round top front door, the Disney home was not only opulent when Walt had it built in 1926, but it was located in an exclusive neighbourhood full of brand new homes.

In 1926, a new bridge measuring 79.5 metres was built over a ravine through which ran the Sacatela Creek, connecting East Hollywood to the Franklin Hills neighbourhood. While many of the hills for which the neighbourhood was named were undeveloped prior to the bridge's construction, this new ease of access allowed for an influx of new residents as the area became developed. While visually appealing with its eight steepled towers reminiscent of Gothic-style architecture, the bridge was relatively controversial, as an increase in local taxes required pre-existing residents of Franklin Hills to pay $60,000 for its construction.

This didn't deter the Disneys from relocating to the neighbourhood, however. The nature of Walt and Roy's relationship – with the interconnectedness of their lives with work – led to them constructing homes next door to each other with Roy and Edna's a mirror image of Walt and Lillian's. The close-knit community nature of their living arrangements expanded when, shortly after moving in, Lillian's sister Hazel Sewell and her thirteen-year-old daughter Marjorie moved in with Walt and Lillian after Hazel and her husband divorced. Luckily, Walt seemed to enjoy this living arrangement, doting on his niece, and playfully bantering with his sister-in-law who described he and Roy as "two crazy guys who will never amount to anything drawing cartoons", while still working tirelessly blackening the animation cels for the Oswald, and later, Mickey cartoons.

Back at the studio, work continued on "The Gallopin' Gaucho." Trusting his loyal artists to continue production, Walt decided to return to New York City to find a distributor for his new Mickey Mouse series, carrying a print of "Plane Crazy" with him to his meetings with executives. Wary of his failed relationship with Charles Mintz, Walt was determined to request a $3,000 advance for each of the twenty-six films in the first Mickey series, as well as retain all rights and ownership of Mickey Mouse and his films. Because of the radical nature of his contractual demands, Walt was unable to find a company to distribute his films. MGM refused to distribute the Mickey Mouse films, and when film agent EJ Denison offered to help, he was unable to find someone willing to gamble on the new Disney series. Even more disheartening, all of the distributors Walt met with agreed on the fact that film money was not in animation: "Cartoons are dead!" they derided.

Walt was undeterred, though. Upon returning to Los Angeles, he and Ub brainstormed to determine what would make their cartoons more appealing to distributors and audiences alike. Luckily, technological developments in the film industry provided the answer they were looking for. Once again, Walt Disney was going to make a gamble, this time with nothing to lose: the Walt Disney Studios would produce the world's first cartoon with synchronised sound.

A MICKEY MOUSE SOUND CARTOON

Animated films weren't alone in being at risk of obsolescence. Vaudeville theatre – both local and travelling shows – were maintaining their popularity throughout the 1920s in spite of the presence of motion pictures playing in American cinemas. The nature of these variety shows, which featured acts including acrobatics, comedy, musical numbers, burlesque, and more, meant that every show would be new and exciting. Not only that, but a number of popular performers including Abbott and Costello, Edgar Bergen, Jack Benny, and Will Rogers found new exposure to a wider audience when their acts began being broadcast on the radio. American listeners could now enjoy the jokes, radio dramas, songs, and commentaries offered by performers in their own homes – something that a silent film with an organ accompaniment couldn't provide.

Hollywood producers realised that innovation was necessary if their industry was to survive. While studios had experimented with synchronised sound beginning in the 1910s, this was often through the use of a separate soundtrack recording playing via phonograph, which required precise synchronisation with the film projected on screen.

During the mid-1920s, a group of theatre owners who were also brothers – Harry, Albert, Sam and Jack Warner – began to experiment with recording dialog and musical performance on records to accompany the films of Will Hays and a performance of *I Pagliacci* in an effort to save money from paying Vaudeville troupes visiting their theatres. After a few more successful experiments, the Warners decided to attempt a feature accompanied by a synchronised soundtrack and dialog. Thus, it was on 6 October 1927 that their film, *The Jazz Singer* starring Vaudeville performer Al Jolson, made history when it premiered at the brothers' New York theatre located at Fifty-Second Street and Broadway.

American audiences were entranced, while the film industry was inspired. Fox Film Corporation and RCA independently moved to innovate synchronised sound from the system used by the Warners. Rather than record a film's audio onto a phonograph record to play in synchronisation to the film as it sped through the projector, this new technology converted sound waves into light waves and printed the visual representation of the film's soundtrack onto the film strip itself. This ensured exact synchronisation and, should a film need to be edited, ensured that both the visual and audio portions of the film matched up.

The major film studios quickly moved to install the new sound technology in their partner theatres throughout the United States, with smaller, independently-owned theatres opting for a cheaper system so they could compete with the larger movie palaces. This forced the hands of studios and producers to phase out silent films in favour of those with recorded music and dialog, known as "talkies". Soon, feature films, operas, and newsreels featured sound, amazing audiences. Live orchestras and organists, who had been employed at theatres to accompany the action on screen, soon found themselves out of a job, replaced by a soundtrack that was standard for all audiences throughout the United States.

Walt Disney had already experienced failure and bankruptcy several times in the four years he had been on his own in the film business. With the relative success of "Plane Crazy" in local cinemas and audience enthusiasm toward his new mouse character, Walt recognised that the best way to stay relevant, compete with more successful animation studios like the Fleischer Brothers and Paul Terry, and secure distribution for his Mickey Mouse series was to adapt synchronised sound to his animated shorts. Unfortunately, when Walt and Ub Iwerks had written the concept – including plot and gags – for "The Gallopin' Gaucho," they had done so without any plan or concept that a soundtrack, dialog and sound effects would be possible.

A new short would need to be developed – one planned around making use of music and sound effects that would drive the story rather than the story driving the music as was the norm with the live orchestral accompaniment for silent films. This presented a challenge, however: while the voices, sound effects and music created by live action actors and musicians recorded naturally onto a film's soundtrack, this was not the case with an animated character who was created by the nub of an artist's pen on paper and celluloid. It soon became obvious that synchronising action performed by Mickey and his supporting characters with accompanying sounds and music would be challenging.

Walt gathered a small team of his trusted artists in the living room at Roy's house one evening to propose his idea of introducing a sound cartoon. Over the next several hours, the small group of men developed a plot for the short, as well as dozens of gags that could make use of the new medium of sound.

Work quickly began on this new short film; animators soon discovered that it was nearly impossible to establish a regular rhythm of sound in the standard animation format of eighteen frames per second. Instead, an adjustment was made to twenty-four frames per second, which allowed for a more natural rhythm. However, the challenge of synchronising sound to the picture on screen remained, until artist Wilfred Jackson discovered that a metronome could be used to establish a beat, accenting the animation every eight seconds with a sound effect. This regular beat could be notated on an exposure sheet, a technical document which showed both a thumbnail of the animation and its accompanying sounds and dialog, aligned with timing, and used by the animator when drawing the cartoon.

This film, "Steamboat Willie", was a satirical Disney version of the recently released film, *Steamboat Bill, Jr.* starring Buster Keaton. Walt's newest short featured Mickey Mouse as the first mate of a steamboat piloted by an imposing and impatient cat character that would later become Pete, the perennial villain in future Mickey Mouse cartoons. After being caught attempting to drive the steamboat by his captain, Mickey gets to work loading supplies and animals from a dock onto the boat, picking up a passenger – Minnie Mouse – along the way. Musical gags commence after a goat devours Minnie's ukulele and sheet music; drawing upon physical humour, Mickey turns the goat into a music box, cranking its tail as "Turkey in the Straw" begins to play out of its mouth. Mickey begins to accompany this tune by treating a cow's teeth as a xylophone, a duck as a bagpipe, and pots and pans as drums.

With animation complete in May 1928, it was time to consider the soundtrack for the film. Walt, Wilfred Jackson, and Ub decided that the best way to plan the soundtrack that they wanted included was to screen the short while performing the music and sound effects live to see if they would work with the animated action. Walt drove around to some local stores, where he purchased an assortment of items: tin pans, cowbells, washboards, slide whistles, and other seemingly random objects.

One afternoon, Walt invited the wives and girlfriends of several of his artists to the studio after dinner to "see something new". When the women arrived around eight o'clock, they were ushered into a room featuring a few chairs and a bedsheet hanging from the ceiling. Outside the window, Roy was fiddling with a projector, which he had pointed through the pane toward the bedsheet. Not sure what was going to happen, the women – Lillian, Edna, Hazel Sewell, Wilfred Jackson's girlfriend Janie, and Mildred Iwerks – sat patiently, hearing the muffled voices of Walt, Ub, Johnny Cannon and Wilfred Jackson on the other side of the sheet. Finally, Walt came out from behind the sheet and explained that they would be screening "Steamboat Willie" while the three men played the music and sound effects live in synchronisation. The excited director stressed that they wanted honest input from the women before scurrying back behind the sheet, an excited smile on his face.

The whir of the projector came from outside the window, and as if on cue, a grainy, black-and-white picture appeared of a steamboat chugging along a river. The women jumped as a scraping sound came from behind the sheet, in time to the smoke billowing from the steamboat's funnels. The view changed to show Walt's new character, Mickey Mouse, at the wheel of the steamboat. As Mickey puckered his lips to whistle, a mouth harp behind the screen began to play "Steamboat Bill, Jr.", followed by slide whistles which mimicked the steamboat whistles hooting when Mickey pulled the cord. Over the remaining seven minutes of the film, the sound of washboards, ocarinas, and deep and falsetto voices added to the realism of the cartoon, accompanied by Wilfred Jackson's rendition of "Turkey in the Straw" on his harmonica. While the concept was impressive, several of the women had been working alongside the men in the animation business for several years, so the novelty of the medium soon wore off. After a few minutes, they began to chat about their friends' babies and which hairdressers they had recently been to.

When the film ended, the only light was that of the projector sans film illuminating the screen. Walt, Ub, Jackson and Cannon came out from behind the screen beaming.

"How was it?" Walt asked expectantly.

"Huh?" The conversation paused as the group of ladies looked toward the men. "Oh – it was nice." The audience quickly resumed their conversation, unaware of the dejection on the men's faces. Shaking their heads in disappointment, the group of artists ducked back behind the makeshift screen, taking their places to try again as soon as Roy finished respooling the film for the next attempt. To the women's disappointment and slight frustration, this process repeated itself over the next six hours, with the men giggling like children behind the sheet as they experimented with different objects in an attempt to perfect the sound effects. When the group called it quits around 2 am, Lillian and Edna in particular found "Steamboat Bill, Jr." and "Turkey in the Straw" bouncing around inside their heads.

Because of the studio's limited funds and available technology, Walt decided to take a print of "Steamboat Willie", as well as the score developed by he, Jackson and Ub, to New York to find someone to help record the soundtrack. On the way, Walt had a slight layover in his native Kansas City, Missouri, and met up with old friend and colleague Carl Stalling, an accompanist for silent films with whom he had done some work prior to moving to Los Angeles. Walt explained to Stalling that he had decided to produce cartoons with synchronised sound, and asked Stalling if he would be willing to retroactively develop a score for "Plane Crazy" and "The Gallopin' Gaucho" for release should "Steamboat Willie" find success. Stalling agreed and suggested that Walt let him know when he secured a deal to record the soundtrack for "Steamboat Willie" in New York so he could join his friend to assist in the recording process. After giving Stalling prints of "Plane Crazy" and "The Gallopin' Gaucho," Walt embarked for New York City, encouraged by the task that lay ahead.

While the technology which allowed for recording sound for films was relatively new, there were a handful of companies who had proprietary systems, requiring Walt to determine which would work best for the Walt Disney Studios and its animated shorts. Armed with specially printed business cards which identified him as a maker of "Sound Cartoons", Walt made appointments with the studios that held the industry-leading sound technology. Unfortunately, he was relatively unimpressed with Fox's Movietone and RCA's Photophone, especially after screening Paul Terry's cartoon *Dinner Time*, whose soundtrack he determined was poor quality and was limited in its sound content. Even more surprising to Walt was the high price tag attached to the use of the subpar Photophone, which included a $3500 deposit, a $600 usage fee, taxes, and a fee paid to the recording orchestra, as well as royalties paid to RCA for theatrical showings of the Disney films using its technology. RCA's sound men made Walt's decision easier when they insisted their system should be utilised and were unwilling to budge when Walt requested they add sound to his films the way he requested.

Undeterred, Walt decided to reach out to New York film executive and distributor Pat Powers for help, arriving in the Big Apple on 4 September. By 1928, Powers had become an integral part of the film industry during its infancy and growing adolescence. After finding relative success as the founder of the Powers Moving Picture Company, he decided to combine his studio with Carl Laemmle's Independent Moving Picture Company, which would later become Universal Pictures. Unfortunately for Powers, his partnership with Laemmle and Universal would be short-lived: when his partner insisted on looking at the ledgers due to some shady accounting, Powers threw the books out of the building's twelfth-story window. However, he had anticipated the conflict with Laemmle, and had stationed an associate with a truck on the road, who scooped up the books and trafficked them out of state.

Looking for new opportunities, Powers became a distributor as part of the Film Booking Office of America and Associated Exhibitors. He also invested his money in dying businesses in an attempt to consolidate his hold on New York's film industry, including DeForest Phonofilm, which sold technology to theatres in the process of converting to sound films. DeForest failed, resulting in a liquidation of its technology and employees.

Ever keen on an opportunity to advance both the film industry and his own career, Powers recruited Bill Garity, a former employee of DeForest, to reproduce the Phonofilm, despite the fact that its patents were now owned by RCA, making the Powers version an "outlaw" or illegal copy. This new opportunity for the New York film executive became the Powers Cinephone, which he licensed to numerous film studios interested in beginning to produce sound films. This system converted sound waves into optical impulses and printed them onto the edge of the film reel which, when read by the sound head of a projector, converted the visual representation of the soundtrack into an electrical current, reproducing the sound from the corresponding speaker.

Powers understood that animated cartoons were the next frontier in making sound film popular, and recognized Walt Disney by reputation.

He agreed to licence the Cinephone to Disney for $1,000 in addition to helping him to find a distributor for his new Mickey Mouse series. As owner of the sound technology, he maintained proprietary rights over the recording process, including where and by whom the soundtrack was recorded. However, the crafty businessman, always willing to use others to further his ambitions of wealth and success in the world of film, scoffed at this new deal's likelihood of success: he merely planned to use Walt Disney's films as sample reels to sell his technology to other animation studios.

The two film executives set up a meeting whereby Powers introduced Walt to Carl Edouarde, who had recently left his profession in composing soundtrack accompaniments for films to break into the new industry of recording music for synchronised films. As a professional musician and the former conductor for Capitol Theatre in New York, Edouarde was used to finely and professionally composed and performed musical pieces. Thus, he and Powers were shocked when Walt showed them the composition that he and Wilfred Jackson had written to accompany "Steamboat Willie", which was full of cues for the mouth harp, washboard, and the exclamations of pigs, cats and ducks.

To take the place of the metronome used in the initial animation process, Ub had drawn a mark every twelve frames of animation in India ink to signify the beat. When run through a projector, these marks would cause a flash on the screen to be used to time the orchestra. Walt explained this to the seasoned conductor so the man understood the process the artists used. Edouarde explained that he had been conducting films "for years" and that he knew what he was doing without the filmmaker's help. Powers sided with the conductor, telling the young artist that he could sit in on the recording session, but that he should sit quietly.

Edouarde got to work, converting Disney's unpolished score into something that could be read and performed by professional musicians. At the same time, he began to select those who would record the soundtrack, which ultimately included a seventeen-piece orchestra, three trap drummers, and a number of men assigned to sound effects. The first attempt to record the film's soundtrack took place on 15 September, less than two weeks after Walt arrived in New York. However, both Walt and Edouarde were exasperated – after several hours of performing – that the musicians were unable to fully synchronise the music and sound effects to the animation. Walt was silently disappointed, as he had noticed that some of the musicians had arrived at the studio intoxicated or exhausted after working an overnight shift recording soundtracks for other films.

The film executive and the conductor sat down to discuss what they perceived to be the problems of the recording, with Powers as intermediary. Edouarde claimed that Walt's method of synchronisation was incompatible with proper orchestration. Walt pleaded with Edouarde to reduce the number of musicians, claiming that twenty people making music for his cartoon was three times too many, which made synchronisation more difficult. More privately, Walt was concerned about how much money this process would cost him, recognising that he would still be responsible for paying the musicians even in this failed attempt. After one recording session, he was required to pay $1200 to the musicians alone, and that didn't even cover the sound effects men or conductor. Walt was so afraid that this process would cause the studio to go under due to the extravagant costs associated with the recording process, that he was unable to eat or sleep.

Luckily for him, Walt had been down this road before. During his time in Kansas City, he had partnered with Carl Stalling in the production of an experimental film called a Song-O-Reel. This film, called "Martha, Just a Plain, Old-Fashioned Name", combined live-action film with music, while lyrics to the song ran across the bottom of the screen for the audience to sing along.

After insisting as the creator of the film that he knew what he was doing, Edouarde agreed to try Walt's solution. Inspired by his work on "Martha," Walt devised a plan to project the image of a bouncing ball onto the conductor's sheet music. This would ensure that Edouarde would stay in time as he conducted his musicians.

With a solution in mind, Walt was feeling encouraged about Edouarde and his orchestra performing a second attempt at recording the soundtrack for "Steamboat Willie". Short on cash to pay the musicians for their additional time, Walt wired Roy, instructing him to take out a second mortgage on the studio and sell his beloved Moon Cabriolet Roadster. Edouarde and his orchestra performed their second attempt at recording the soundtrack on 30 September, satisfied with the results after a three hour session.

With the animation and its accompanying soundtrack complete, Walt's next task was to find a studio willing to distribute "Steamboat Willie" to theatres. Powers agreed to set up appointments on Walt's behalf with the different film studios and their executives. Most of the studios and independent distributors – including Paramount, Metro, and the Film Booking Office – were uninterested in inking a deal with the Walt Disney Studios. Only Universal showed interest in taking on a new animated series, but they soon withdrew their offer when they realised it would conflict with agreements made with Charles Mintz, who was finding success with animated series starring Oswald the Lucky Rabbit (after Walt had lost the rights) and Krazy Kat.

Walt found himself once again very discouraged until he was approached by Harry Reichenbach, the manager of New York's Colony Theatre who also had experience promoting films. Reichenbach, who had been present at one of the screenings of "Steamboat Willie" for film executives, was intrigued by the small, spunky mouse, and was willing to give Walt Disney a chance. Walt, who was worried that showing his film on Broadway would hurt the possibility for national distribution, agreed when Reichenbach reassured him that the press and public's reactions would have the potential to attract big distributors. It also helped that the theatre manager offered the studio $1000 for the opportunity to show "Steamboat Willie" exclusively for a two-week run.

Mickey Mouse was introduced to the world on 18 November 1928 alongside the Film Booking Office's *Gang War*. Audiences were amazed at how the action on-screen was accompanied by the folksy tunes produced by harmonica, fiddle, and mouth harp, as well as steamboat whistles, the yoo-hoo of Minnie, and the cackle of a parrot. But even more importantly, they fell in love with the mouse who was a hero to the "little man," who was a little bit Charlie Chaplin and a little bit Douglas Fairbanks, Jr. *Variety* described the effects of "Steamboat Willie", noting that "giggles came so fast at the Colony that they were stumbling over each other," while *The New York Times* lauded the animated short as lauded the animated short as ingenious.

ACTION DRIVEN BY THE MUSIC

Over the next two weeks, Walt Disney sat in the back row of the Colony Theatre at each showing of "Steamboat Willie," listening as the chuckles, laughs, chortles and guffaws echoed throughout the darkened room. This experience confirmed to the young producer that his gamble to marry sound and animation had paid off and that more Mickey cartoons should be made. Pat Powers' gamble to partner with Walt had paid off as well: the early success of the first theatrically released Mickey Mouse cartoon had led to several other studios approaching Powers to lease the use of Cinephone. Recognising that this good fortune was due to the work of the Walt Disney Studios, Powers offered to become Disney's distributor, promising Walt $2500 for each subsequent Mickey Mouse cartoon as long as the studio covered ten per cent of distribution cost. The contract stipulated that Disney would produce twelve shorts in a calendar year. This new deal would also require Disney to exclusively use the Powers Cinephone for the next ten years, netting its owner an additional $26,000 per year. There was one thing, however, that Walt Disney demanded in whatever deal was struck: he and his studio would maintain complete control and ownership over Mickey Mouse and the content of his films in perpetuity. Powers agreed that this would not be a problem. Walt was so excited that he had found a distributor for his new films that he didn't bat an eye at the cost and immediately signed his name.

Roy Disney, on the other hand, was not nearly as excited as his enthusiastic younger brother. He reminded Walt that they had scraped for funds to pay for Carl Edouarde's second attempt to record the orchestration for "Steamboat Willie," and was unsure whether the studio could survive a deal like this if the mouse cartoons did not perform well. Roy was especially concerned that Powers was unaffiliated with a major film studio, and as a result planned to utilise states' rights distribution for Disney's newest animated short.

While major film studios of the time, such as RKO or Metro-Goldwyn-Mayer, owned their own theatre chains which guaranteed nationwide distribution, smaller studios and distributors – which included Pat Powers – resorted to the process known as states' rights distribution. This system was one in which a film, or in this case an animated short, would be licensed to a regional chain of independently owned theatres for a set period of time. This resulted in a much slower exposure of a film or short to the American public, as the theatres that typically booked states' rights films were in smaller towns that otherwise wouldn't make studios as much money on a blockbuster release. Thus, Roy's fears of Powers' state's rights distribution were well founded, as it could potentially result in less exposure for their films and thus, less profit to continue to increase the size and scope of studio productions.

Luckily, the shores of the Atlantic Ocean didn't stop the spread of Mickey's reputation. Powers negotiated the international distribution of "Steamboat Willie" in European markets, which began in February 1929. With this newfound popularity came the opportunity for more exposure due to his likeness produced as consumer goods. Later that year, a licensing agent from New York contacted the studio, requesting that Mickey Mouse be featured on notebooks marketed to children in the United States. When the agent offered $300 to purchase licensing rights, Walt accepted, opening the floodgates to merchandisers looking to cash in on the national fascination with the cartoon mouse.

Walt and his team had been preparing for additional instalments in their new series even before the premiere of its inaugural film. While working alongside Powers and Edouarde in New York, he had reached out to Ub in Los Angeles and dictated plot ideas for the next cartoon to animate, "The Barn Dance." Ub and Les Clark immediately began working on the film – which was complete by December – and Carl Stalling was asked to compose the score, in addition to his work on "Plane Crazy" and "The Gallopin' Gaucho". Upon completing his work on "The Barn Dance", Stalling arrived in New York City on 26 October with all three scores on hand, ready for them to be recorded using Powers Cinephone. When Walt finally left New York to return to California, Powers arranged to have Cinephone equipment shipped to the California film studio for the recording of future scores.

The first four Mickey films had all been plotted and animated prior to the writing of Stalling's scores, which resulted in gag-oriented films, where the music and sound responded to and were results of the action. However, Walt was interested in making full use of the new medium of synchronised sound, and the next Mickey Mouse short would showcase what the studio could do with the Cinephone technology. Work began on "The Opry House", which would feature the first pre-synchronised score for a Mickey Mouse film. Always one to incorporate popular culture in their films to make them as accessible to the masses as possible, this film featured a number of well-known folk and classical songs, all of which were wonderfully incorporated into Stalling's score.

While Carl Stalling appreciated the work of developing scores for the new Mickey Mouse series, he found himself frustrated that his compositions played second fiddle to the action on-screen. If Walt was going to develop "sound cartoons", the composer argued, then the action should be driven by the music rather than the other way around. What if, he suggested, a second series of animated films were developed where the action fit the mood and rhythm of original music? These new films could serve as an opportunity for Walt's artists to experiment and improve their craft by featuring inanimate objects coming to life in response to the music and accompanying sound effects, as well as determine the ways they could manipulate the emotions of audiences.

Walt Disney was a man of action. If someone had criticism of how he or his studio were doing things, he expected that an accompanying solution was provided rather than mere arbitrary criticism. As an introduction to the new series, Stalling suggested a short taking inspiration from a jointed skeleton toy he owned as a child, as well as novelty films featuring skeletons and ghosts in the early days of cinema. This film would combine original music in the style of a Fox Trot with Edvard Grieg's "March of the Dwarfs", which would be accompanied by the fantastical dancing of graveyard skeletons. Stalling had thought through the concept so completely that he had even conceived of a name for this short film: "The Skeleton Dance".

But what would this new series be called? Because music was meant to be the focus and driving force of each short, the composer suggested that the word "symphony" be included in the series title. True to form, he also believed that the title should feature a humorous adjective in the style of Disney whimsy. Believing that alliteration would help with brand recognition, it was decided that the shorts would be called *Silly Symphonies*. These films would find inspiration in ghost stories, fables, mythology, legends and fairy tales while incorporating original musical compositions, all the while encouraging experimentation and the development of new animation techniques, technology, and special effects.

With Walt's approval, Ub Iwerks began the process of animating "The Skeleton Dance",which took a total of six weeks. Eager to speed up the process of developing the short, Walt encouraged his friend to draw key frames of animation and using other animators to do the "inbetweening", or drawing the secondary and tertiary frames of animation. The driven and master animator that he was, Ub refused. He did, however, allow Les Clark to animate a scene where one skeleton plays xylophone on another's ribcage.

Walt believed that Ub's relentless work of animating the film almost singlehandedly was resulting in a less-than-desirable quality, and often watched over the artist's shoulder, offering suggestions and, occasionally, criticism. The biggest issue, the film producer believed, was that Ub's timing was off, resulting in animation that was not perfectly synchronised to Stalling's score. When Ub refused to make the corrections his boss suggested, Walt snuck a seat at Iwerks' desk after he had left for the day and retimed the film's exposure sheet – a document which provided an outline to the animator for how to animate the film and for the camera operator on how to photograph the drawings. Upon returning to the studio the following day and discovering what Walt had done, Ub was furious, arguing that these corrections messed up his idea of the characters' timing and movements.

With animation complete in March 1929, it was time to find a theatre to exhibit it to audiences. Walt had the film photographed and printed, then shipped to Pat Powers in New York, who showed it to several different managers. None were very impressed. Frustrated, Powers sent feedback to the studio in Los Angeles: "MORE MICE!"

Undeterred after nearly three months, Walt decided to try to find a place to have "The Skeleton Dance" screened in southern California instead. A friend recommended that he send the film to Fred Miller, owner of the Carthay Circle Theatre, located on San Vicente Boulevard in West LA. Miller was impressed, and he premiered "The Skeleton Dance" on 10 June alongside the film drama, *4 Devils*. Proving to Powers that there was a potential audience and that Los Angeles theatre owners were interested, Walt requested that the distributor find a theatre in New York City to exhibit his film. Columbia Pictures agreed to release "The Skeleton Dance" at its Roxy Theatre on 22 August. Periodicals including *Variety*, *The Film Daily* and *The New York Times* praised the film for its gags, but warned parents to keep their children at home due to the morbid and "macabre" nature of the animated short. The early praise of this unique and groundbreaking film resulted in Columbia agreeing to distribute the *Silly Symphonies* for the next two years. Walt and Roy, with the counsel of attorney Gunther Lessing, decided to use this offer as an opportunity to dissolve their contract with Pat Powers, paying the corrupt distributor $100,000 for the difference of the films remaining per their annual agreement, as well as dissolve the agreement to use Powers' Cinephone and begin using its own sound technology instead.

With two relatively successful film series coming out of the animation studio, decisions were made to continue to expand to ensure that deadlines and contractual obligations were met. Experienced animators, including Ben Sharpsteen, Norm "Fergie" Ferguson, and Jack King, were hired from competing studios in New York, while a number of young men who were new to animation – such as Bill Cottrell, Jack Cutting, and Roy Williams – were brought on board with the intention of training them up in the "Disney style".

Unfortunately, his zeal to keep improving upon the medium of animation and to release the best animated shorts in the market led him to continue criticising and correcting the work of his best artist, Ub Iwerks. Having worked alongside Walt for the better part of a decade and as the only one, other than his brother Roy, who had stuck by the producer's side through his bankruptcies and the loss of Oswald, Ub was hurt by what he perceived as a lack of faith and a betrayal of his skill and hard work.

Things came to a head between the artist and the dreamer one evening at a dinner party they both attended. Upon learning that Walt Disney, the "creator" of Mickey Mouse, was in attendance, a young boy ran up to him and asked the studio executive to make a drawing of Mickey Mouse and add his autograph. Walt, who recognized that Ub was better at illustrating their popular character, handed Ub a piece of paper and instructed him to draw the mouse, explaining that he would add his signature before returning the sketch to the boy. Ub was incensed: shoving the paper and pencil back into Walt's hands, he demanded that Walt "draw your own Mickey" and stormed out of the party.

Thus, the temptation was strong when, in Walt's absence, Ub was approached by an associate of Pat Powers, who encouraged him to leave the Walt Disney Studios with a promise of a salary of $300 per week and guaranteed distribution from MGM if he developed a new character and series of his own. The lure of creative independence and being in charge of his own studio was irresistible. Ub Iwerks, the artist who had helped create Oswald the Lucky Rabbit and Mickey Mouse and who had brought Mickey Mouse and a quartet of musical skeletons to life, tendered his resignation by letter to Roy Disney on 21 January 1930.

The departure of his close friend, longtime associate, and arguably the one who had made happen Walt Disney's dreams of creating a successful animation studio made the film executive simultaneously frustrated and discouraged. To add insult to injury, Carl Stalling soon left Disney to compose for the Van Beuren Corporation's *Aesop's Fables* in New York, leaving a vacancy in scoring the short films; luckily for Walt and his team, Stalling had composed nearly twenty scores for a number of animated films in the works. However, the Disney brothers were determined to not only keep film production going, but to continue to innovate to effectively compete with this new adversarial studio. Animation veteran Bert Gillett was quickly moved into the director's chair for the Mickey Mouse series, while Wilfred Jackson, Ben Sharpsteen, and David Hand split up the *Silly Symphonies* unit amongst themselves.

In the early days of animated short films, cartoon studios focused on entertaining audiences through the novelty and humour of the medium. Extensive experimentation was conducted to determine the different ways to stretch and contort characters' bodies, how to effectively anthropomorphise inanimate objects, to create animated realism, and establish as much depth and dimensionality of field as possible while still remaining cost effective. However, all of these artistic goals were secondary to creating a wave of laughter that would sweep through the rows of the theatre, created through the implementation of gags, or jokes which played upon slapstick humour, visual puns, or fantastical or unbelievable events.

The artists and directors of the Walt Disney Studios recognised that films which focused on a string of gags had the potential to cause Mickey Mouse and the *Silly Symphonies* to get lost in the world of animated film series of the late 1920s and early 1930s, which included popular characters like Oswald the Lucky Rabbit, Koko the Clown, Betty Boop,

Felix the Cat, and Ub Iwerks' Flip the Frog. Instead, it was believed that a focus on plot and the development of character personality would set Disney apart from its competition.

With more time devoted to the development of story, the animation process itself needed to be streamlined to establish a division of labour, akin to the scientific management system employed by Henry Ford in his Dearborn plant and other centres of industrial production. In other words, rather than a single animator doing the work for an entire short – as was done by Ub Iwerks for "Steamboat Willie" and "The Skeleton Dance" – it was decided that it would make more sense to establish a hierarchy of skill, which would ensure a quicker and more masterful development of the animated cartoon.

Conceptual ideas for instalments in the *Silly Symphonies* and Mickey Mouse series were typically introduced by Walt, who had the primary vision for the kind of stories he wanted the respective series to feature based upon their respective purposes. From there, a visual outline of the film – represented by sketches of the major plot points, gags, and actions – would be pinned in order on a bulletin board known as a storyboard. This process, which was innovated by Disney animator and writer Webb Smith, allowed for the production team to plan out a film in detail before taking the time and expense of putting it on paper and celluloid. This procedure would soon become standard practice for animated and live action film studios across Hollywood and New York City, and later throughout the global film industry. This innovation allowed for Walt and his directors to see the progression of the entire plot of a film, allowing drawings to be taken down and rearranged to improve the storyline, or removed entirely if a sequence was deemed unnecessary to advancing the plot.

A number of processes also became procedure at the Walt Disney Studios to improve the efficiency and workflow of top animators, many of which had been used sporadically before, but were often disdained by Ub Iwerks. The first of these was developing the new role of inbetweeners. While some of Walt's best artists, such as Wilfred Jackson and Les Clark, would draw the key frames of animated action, they would pass the frames "in between" to assistant animators called inbetweeners to complete the action that would be seen in the final film. For instance, the animator might draw a ball bouncing with frames one, five, and nine showing the ball at different heights and spinning. The inbetweeners would then draw frames two through four and six through eight to show the ball progressing in its descent between those key frames.

After the animators and inbetweeners had finished their sketches of the action, the sketches would be passed along to a cleanup artist, another new role established at the Disney studio.This artist would take the rough sketches drawn by the lead animator and inbetweeners and clean up the drawings so that the lines were crisp before being inked onto celluloid.

But Walt Disney wasn't satisfied by merely creating the animation-equivalent to Henry Ford's assembly line: he wanted excellence. In an effort to save time and money, he instituted the process of reviewing the day's work, providing feedback to the directors and lead animators in case a character's movement needed to be adjusted or a scene needed to be reworked. Drawings would be photographed and printed onto a film strip, then run through a Moviola machine which was typically used for checking film during the editing process. Walt would stand at the Moviola, and sometimes project the day's work – called Dailies – in a small projection room for lead animators and directors to review. The term "Sweatbox" was coined to describe this process of reviewing the Dailies as a result of the cramped quarters around the Moviola and the high stress animators felt, especially when Walt might give brutal and honest criticism – and he often did.

With the implementation of these new processes and a deeper commitment to producing excellent animated short films, the staff of the Walt Disney Studios continued to increase, and with it the size of the studio campus grew as well. Buildings were added to the front and side of the existing studio facilities on Hyperion and departments were often occupying the same room with partitions separating the workspace. The increased space and size of the staff didn't change the amount of effort the artists exerted, however: on particularly hot days, the animation staff was known to strip off their shirts and draw bareback, attempting to avoid dripping drops of sweat onto their sketches.

One department who received its own dedicated space, however, was the Inking, Tracing and Opaquing Department. Supervised by Hazel Sewell, this department became one of the studio's fastest growing due to the two increasingly popular film series produced by Disney. This led to an "all hands on deck" approach, with every available female artist being employed in transferring the animators' drawings onto celluloid in preparation for photography. By 1931, a new two-story animation building was completed on the studio lot, giving Sewell's girls a devoted place to perform their work in the newly vacated space, free of dust and the distractions caused by men looking for a date.

This devotion to excellence also worked in the studio's favour by helping to secure a more reliable film distributor. On 27 December 1930, a contract was signed with United Artists to serve as distributor of the Silly Symphonies after the conclusion of the Columbia contract in 1932. Studio executives were pleased by this deal, as it promised a $15,000 advance on each Silly Symphony short in the series, as well as guaranteeing nation-wide distribution. With this new partnership with UA, the studio anticipated that Americans would flock to their local cinemas to partake in the latest Silly Symphony or Mickey Mouse cartoon, making them a vibrant part of the flourishing American culture of the late 1920s.

However, it would be a national – and global – tragedy that would catapult Disney's cartoons into the spotlight and make its characters household names.

PART 2

TRICKS OF OUR TRADE 1929–1937

A GOOD AMERICAN

New York City's weather in October 1929 was a seasonable average of the upper 60s, warm enough for the bankers and businessmen to walk the streets without their suit coats. Like a foreboding oracle of things to come however, a series of storms raging throughout the United States brought troubles, including destructive winds in Cincinnati, a wrecked steamer on Lake Erie and a boat in distress on Lake Superior, and the incessant poundings of waves along the Chicago lakeshore, which brought flooding through the Windy City's streets, stranding many inside of highrises and hotels. As these storms blew eastward toward New York, they brought with them a cold front, with temperatures plunging from a balmy 74 degrees on Sunday 27 October to a chilly 49 degrees on Tuesday 29 October, accompanied by overcast skies.

The streets of Manhattan weren't the only dark and dismal part of the city on that Tuesday: as the day came to a close, darkness and the chill of death had descended upon the rooms of the New York Stock Exchange and cavernous teller halls of the city's banks as a result of the crash of America's stock market. This day – later known as "Black Tuesday" – had been long coming, with erratic spending, the overworking of soil on American farms, an unhealthy dependence on credit for purchasing consumer goods, and speculation on America's stock exchange leading to the impending disaster which cascaded during the final week of October 1929. In the coming days, millionaire misers would become dependent on soup kitchens, banks would close due to the loss of all liquid assets, millions of Americans would become homeless, and several millions more would lose their jobs.

The economy and culture of America – and soon the world – was in crisis. Many quickly lost faith in the ability of the federal government to ease the symptoms of what would soon be known as the Great Depression, with President Herbert Hoover refusing to acknowledge that the American economy had a problem, calling a "lack of confidence in the economic future or the basic strength of business in the United States…foolish." He went on to say that the solution to the nation's economic problems would be solved through "hard work and intelligent cooperation" amongst Americans, believing that any assistance necessary should be provided to the citizenry by local businesses and state governments rather than the federal government. When his constituents began clamouring for change and even at times led to open protests and riots against his presidency, Hoover implemented higher taxes and tariffs, believing that this increase in money would stimulate available resources for business and government alike. Instead, this led to higher unemployment, the foreclosure or bankruptcy of approximately 750,000 farms, and astronomical difficulties for millions of Americans.

In March 1933, Franklin Delano Roosevelt became president of the United States after a landslide win over the incumbent Herbert Hoover. Almost immediately, Roosevelt enacted his domestic policy change to get the nation and its citizens back on track, which he called the "New Deal." This plan included the provision of new government assistance for those hardest hit by the financial strain such as Social Security, put new government-operated watchdog agencies into action to monitor and protect the economy including the Federal Deposit Insurance Corporation (FDIC) and Securities and Exchange Commission (SEC), and even created programs to help Americans get back on their feet in light of unemployment including the Works Progress Administration and National Recovery Administration. While the American and global economies had a long way to go, FDR's New Deal went a long way to help the United States recover from the worst economic blight of American history to that time.

The Great Depression in America was particularly hard on children, many of whom were impacted in physical ways by a lack of food or housing, or psychologically and emotionally due to the stress of unemployed parents. According to some sources, twenty percent of children in New York City suffered from malnutrition, while in the more rural regions of Kentucky, Pennsylvania and West Virginia, the statistic was as high as ninety percent. For many, childhood was nonexistent due to the scarce family savings being put toward food and rent rather than toys and clothes. Feeling a particular sense of guilt, many young people attempted to support their families: many adolescent girls turned to prostitution, while several boys participated in pickpocketing and other petty crimes. Some children and adolescents recognised the financial strain their existence was putting on their families and left home, feeling that homelessness and travelling in the boxcars of the rail system would ease the burden of their parents feeding an additional family member.

While waiting for relief and with little help from their leaders, the middle and lower classes of the United States turned to each other for a panacea to stave off the ills of the Great Depression: a flourishing of culture, which was aimed at providing a sense of escape from the day-to-day problems caused by the Depression, a rallying cry against its symptoms, and an opportunity to unite Americans and families together into a stronger, cohesive whole. Radio programmes – complete with a variety of voice actors, sound effects, and musical accompaniment – provided in-home entertainment on a nightly basis. These shows, which included early Soap Operas, provided some of the only continuity in many listeners' lives, as the audience could return to their favourite show each evening to learn what would happen to the characters in the newest episode. Many of these programmes depicted characters who were down-and-out, but through hard work, good luck, and by relying upon relationships, could overcome struggle and become successful.

Contrary to the trends of the time, American cinema actually succeeded and even excelled in the years of the Great Depression, leading many to dub this era the "Golden Age of Hollywood". Because the films being screened provided escape for audiences, in the first year of the Great Depression alone, eighty million Americans (or approximately sixty-five percent of the nation's citizens) attended the movies weekly. With nearly ten thousand films released each year of the early 1930s, Americans had their choice of film genres depending upon their moods: Marx Brothers screwball comedies which made fun of the Depression, feel-good movies like Jimmy Stewart's *Mr. Smith Goes to Washington* which depicted the cast overcoming the Depression, horror/sci-fi films like *King Kong* which depicted the conquering of the Great Depression, and musicals including Busby Berkeley's *Footlight Parade* which showed Americans working together and joyfully singing through the Great Depression.

Parents and national and cultural leaders alike also recognised the dangerous effect the Depression was having on the lives of children in America. The federal government under President Roosevelt instituted educational reform including free school lunches and free nursery schools to ensure that children were fed, educated, and had somewhere to go rather than wandering the streets during the weekday. Programs like the Civilian Conservation Corps hired young men to restore the nation's wilderness by planting trees, creating parks, and participating in soil conservation.

Cinema was also considered beneficial to children by offering a low-cost escape through a full day's entertainment consuming the latest newsreels, comedy or musical feature, and of course, animated shorts. Recognising that a key demographic visiting the theatres was children, studios began to produce content geared toward the younger audiences. Film series including the Dead End Kids and Little Rascals soon became favourites, featuring the hijinks of children competing with each other and outwitting adults. Both series featured low-income kids who through grit, cooperation, and a never-give-up attitude, overcame their difficulties. Even films with more grown-up themes for adult audiences showed children and adolescents like Shirley Temple and Jackie Coogan exhibiting great endurance in the face of worldly troubles and finding happiness in spite of a nationwide depression.

Animation studios also began to produce more shorts and new series. The Fleischer Brothers introduced two new characters in the late 1920s and early 1930s who would become celebrities in their own right: Betty Boop and Popeye the Sailor. Warner Bros. also established its own animation plant to compete with Disney in 1930. Like Disney, Warner Bros. also produced two animated series: Looney Tunes to compete with Mickey Mouse shorts and Merrie Melodies – which focused on animation accompanying classical and original music and was composed by Carl Stalling after 1936 – to compete with Silly Symphonies. But while cinema was an escape for America's youth, the escape didn't accompany them through their front doors: it ended as soon as they exited the darkened theatres and stepped into the blinding light of the real world.

American companies quickly sprang into action to redeem the lives of American children at home. Toy companies and marketing teams began to create goods specifically targeting children, hoping to appeal to their fleeting characteristics of wonderment and innocence. Shirley Temple dolls, tin toys, and clothing items lined the shelves hoping to entice the children who had been impacted by the financial crisis most. New board games were developed, including Monopoly, which would allow for families to spend time together and cooperate on something while also instilling morals and ideas like healthy spending habits. Collectively, these new marketing strategies attempted to play off the idea of a "democracy of goods", or the concept that by purchasing these new consumer goods, poor children and families would be equal to those who seemed untouched by the Depression.

One such syndicated comic which became incredibly popular in the throes of the Great Depression and was soon printed for individual purchase was "Superman". Symbolic of middle-class Americans' fight against the villainous forces which caused and resulted from the Great Depression, the Man of Steel was nearly immediately popular, selling a half-million monthly copies by its seventh issue, resulting in a fascination with and increasing number of titles of comic books for purchase at department stores and drug stores.

The publishing world also attempted to assist in acting as a balm to the pain of financial stress. Syndicated comic strips began to become popular in newspapers around the country, bringing printed humour into the home both daily and weekly. Readers could follow along with the narrative drama in "Detective Dick Tracy" and "Buck Rogers" or one-off jokes told by Popeye the Sailor in "Thimble Theatre" (prior to his film debut by the Fleischers) and the relational humour depicted in "Blondie". As these comics increased in popularity, many of them were published in collections and sold to consumers at low prices, which was justified by being printed on an inexpensive, high-acid paper, giving them their name, pulp magazines.

In July 1929, a few months prior to the Great Stock Market Crash that October, Joseph Connolly of King Features Syndicate approached Disney via Ub Iwerks to propose a comic strip for newspapers around the United States. Mickey Mouse made his debut in print for the *New York Mirror* and the *Oakland Post-Enquirer* of California on 13 January 1930. Much like his on-screen adventures, this new medium depicted Mickey as an adventurer who matched wits with the intimidatingly villainous Peg-Leg Pete, ultimately overcoming his adversary with cleverness and humour, inspiring readers to approach the Depression in the same way. While Walt initially wrote the story and dialogue for the strip and Ub illustrated, the explosive growth of the Mickey and Silly Symphonies series took their attention away from the page and onto the screen. With Americans clamouring for more Mickey, the job soon went to Disney inbetweener Floyd Gottfredson, who developed the story, characters, and universe in which Mickey inhabited. The new comic artist's work was so popular that throughout the 1930s, the syndicated Mickey Mouse strip was enjoyed by 2.8 million readers every week. Mickey comic strips quickly spread overseas with a daily strip appearing in British papers on 17 March. Much like its contemporaries, the Mickey Mouse strip became a pulp magazine, with the first *Mickey Mouse Annual* appearing on store shelves in time for Christmas 1930.

Comics weren't the only Disney merchandise marketed to children and adolescents as a method of dispensing joy and encouragement during the financial struggle. With the burgeoning of Mickey's popularity, Walt began to explore the idea to capitalise by creating Mickey-inspired consumer goods. After being sung in the 1929 short "Mickey's Follies", "Minnie's Yoo Hoo" became the theme song of the Mickey Mouse series of shorts and was published as sheet music. Writing tablets bearing Mickey's likeness were designed by studio artists, as well as other small items available to purchase by families. In order to manage the growing desire to purchase Mickey-inspired merchandise, a contract was signed with New York's George Borgfeldt Corporation, which would handle the licensing of Disney properties for consumer goods.

Mickey Mouse was even invited into arms and bedrooms to provide tactile comfort to children facing the uncertainty of the early 1930s in the form of a plush doll. As an aspiring artist and puppeteer, 16-year-old Bob Clampett – who would later go on to animate for and direct Warner Bros' Looney Tunes series – brought his sketchpad to Glendale's Alexander Theater to sketch Mickey while enjoying one of the mouse's latest cartoon releases. His aunt, Charlotte Clark, was impressed with Clampett's sketch and used it to design and produce a Mickey Mouse doll. Clark reached out to Walt and Roy, showing off her new creation and requested permission to sew dolls and sell them for profit.

The Disney brothers provided Clark a counter-offer: they proposed contracting with the seamstress to produce and sell the dolls on behalf of the studio, even going as far as setting her and a small team up with a workshop in a bungalow on studio property, which soon became known as the "Doll House." After a photograph of Walt posing with several of her dolls was published in the periodical *Screen Play Secrets*, orders for her Mickey Mouse doll began pouring in, resulting in the team of seamstresses sewing nearly four hundred dolls per week in November 1930.

With Clark unable to keep up with demand, Walt and Roy instructed George Borgfeldt to find a manufacturer who could mass produce the dolls; unfortunately, none of the companies selected were able to meet the brothers' standards for perfection or consistency. Instead, in 1932, they turned to the McCall Company, who took Clark's designs and published them as patterns for mothers, grandmothers, aunts, and adolescent girls to create from home.

As the 1930s progressed and America slowly began to emerge from the Great Depression, Disney decided to allow the Borgfeldt contract to expire, and another licensing agent, Herman "Kay" Kamen of Kansas City, Missouri, was signed to help market Mickey products. When watchmaker Ingersoll-Waterbury approached Kamen for the opportunity to use Mickey Mouse on their watch faces in an effort to prevent bankruptcy, Kamen signed off on the deal. Costing $3.75, approximately eleven thousand Mickey Mouse Ingersoll watches were sold by Macy's department store in New York City in one day, saving the company from bankruptcy. Likewise, Lionel Manufacturing Company was saved from a similar fate in 1934 after Kamen brokered a deal for Lionel to produce a Mickey and Minnie handcar. With a price tag of only $1, more than 253,000 units were sold in the first four months on store shelves.

Mickey Mouse had become a national and international celebrity, with his likeness existing in some form in millions of homes around the world. His adventures were read by his fans in several different languages. He and his sweetheart pumped their handcar around thousands of Christmas trees. He assisted both business executives and the common folk in telling time. And in 1935 alone, 468 million people had enjoyed at least one animated short starring Mickey Mouse and his friends.

Newspapers and magazines even featured fan fiction written by and about Mickey Mouse: a 9 August 1930 article in *The Literary Digest* explained that Mickey "is wealthy. He rides in Schootmobiles, lives in a penthouse, and has his own half-acre golf course." The article goes on to explain how the columnist, one "Mr. Hyland," waited around the Disney studio, "waiting for an interview" with Mickey. In his imaginative article, the columnist explains how he talked with Mickey's exasperated personal secretary who described the mouse as "too vivacious, too lively for me," and runs into Minnie who complained that the media didn't interview Mickey as often as it did the human celebrities like

Charlie Chaplin. After finally getting a chance to sit down with Mickey himself, the interviewer learned that Mickey's road to fame with Disney began with disappointment: "I was working on a Felix the Cat picture, and was very discouraged. I seemed to be getting nowhere, fast." He continued by explaining how he met Minnie, who was performing as an extra in shorts at the Walt Disney Studios.

Thus, it was only natural that a homegrown fan club would begin for those who anticipated his latest adventures and desired to celebrate the film culture which had developed around the Walt Disney Studios' golden boy. Mickey mania had swept the nation. A number of businessmen sought to capitalise on the public's obsession with the little mouse, and the public was only too happy to oblige, always looking for an additional way to consume their favourite animated character. In September 1929, California theatre owner, Harry Woodin, began a weekly program centred around the Disney character at his cinemas in Venice and Ocean Park. Hailed as a Mickey Mouse Club, Woodin and his staff provided an assortment of activities themed to the well-loved character culminating in the theatre's premiere of his latest animated adventure.

After several successful meetings with regular increase in attendance, Woodin invited Walt and Carl Stalling to one of the events. Walt was fascinated and suggested that the studio sponsor the theatre owner's brainchild.

"I am sold 100 percent on the idea and would like to see us... put it over in a national way immediately." Walt was particularly concerned that if he didn't begin to utilise Woodin's Mickey Mouse Club model, rival studios would implement similar programs for their animated characters, providing a challenge to Disney's popularity. After conversing with Walt and his team, Woodin offered to personally go on tour throughout the United States, visiting dozens of theatres and assisting exhibitors with establishing their own version of a Mickey Mouse Club. Walt believed this was a great idea, offering the California businessman a position and the title General Manager of Mickey Mouse Clubs. The studio also provided activities and supplies to the clubs at-cost, including buttons, membership cards, and posters and window displays to advertise club events.

Similar to the Boy and Girl Scouts of America, the Mickey Mouse Clubs heralded themselves as not only a juvenile fan club for Mickey

Mouse and his shorts, but also a group that stressed moral, ethical, and behavioural standards, hoping to develop young people into good citizens. Members were expected to ascribe to The Mickey Creed, which encouraged participants to "be a square-shooter in my home, in school, on the playground, wherever I may be. I will be truthful and honorable and strive always to make myself a better and more useful little citizen. I will respect my elders and help the aged, the helpless children smaller than myself. In short, I will be a good American."

Theatres all across America took Woodin's concept of the Mickey Mouse Club and made it their own. Some theatres added vaudeville acts prior to screening the latest film, while others had special buttons or membership cards printed and handed out, identifying the carrier as a member of that theatre's Club. Some cities even hosted Mickey Mouse Club conventions: in June 1931, Milwaukee, Wisconsin hosted four thousand children from thirty Wisconsin cities for a day-long celebration, which included screening of Mickey Mouse shorts, a live show, a parade, and a colouring contest with a $100 prize.

By 1932, more than one million children participated as members at one of nearly one-thousand Mickey Mouse Clubs nationwide. With American children off the streets in the nation's hardest economic times, theatres echoing with joyous laughter, a group holding young people accountable for their attitudes and behaviours, and innumerable new fans of the spunky little mouse, things seemed to be looking up.

The early 1930s was a difficult time for Walt Disney on a personal level. While the studio was producing one successful short after another, it wasn't turning much of a profit; rather, nearly everything that the studio made from a short went into the costs for producing the next. As a result, the Walt Disney Studios was a mere one failed short away from financial ruin.

To ensure that work got done as efficiently, cheaply, and completely as possible, Walt often did a fair bit of work himself, which included reviewing each animator's dailies, conceptual artwork, film proposals and storyboards, and making remarks on edits. Oftentimes, this work did not get finished during the workday, so he would often take Lillian out for dinner and return to the studio for several hours of work afterwards. Even though he encouraged her to return to their home on Lyric Avenue, Lillian would often insist upon accompanying her husband to the studio, falling asleep on the davenport in his office as she often did when they were courting and then newly married.

He also took his work and that produced by his artists very personally. Mickey wasn't just his creation: it was a part of him, a surrogate of a side of his personality he didn't show much. He invested a good amount of his energy and self-esteem upon the success of this company, especially after the several failures, closures, and bankruptcies of his previous studios. He also considered it a personal affront when artists didn't heed his advice on a scene they were animating, which usually resulted in what he considered sub-par work.

In the midst of the darkness of the Depression and the challenges experienced by the studio, a ray of sunshine emerged on 10 January 1930 when, after several failed attempts, Roy and Edna welcomed their first child: Roy Edward Disney. Not long after, Hazell Sewell, Lillian's sister, had finalised her divorce, which resulted in she and her teenage daughter Marjorie moving in with Walt and Lillian. With a new baby living next door and their niece under their roof, the couple began considering parenthood for themselves.

After a few months of trying, Lillian conceived in early 1931 and the couple were ecstatic. With the prospects of further success for the studio and a need to have space for their growing family, Walt and Lillian began searching for a location to build a new home. Unfortunately, Walt's joy was obliterated when Lillian's pregnancy ended in a miscarriage.

The stress of the studio's struggles and the heartbrokenness over the loss of the dream of fatherhood began to impact Walt in an emotional way. As he interacted with his artists and animators, giving them feedback on their work at their desks or in the Sweatbox, he became very irritable, snapping at those around him. While he had always loved his work as an artist and film producer, he began to criticise each film released. He seemed antsy, always wanting to move on to something else, claiming that each film had "too many things wrong with it. I'm sick of it."

Walt began to lose sleep, lying awake all night thinking about his past failures and how the fate of his studio and Mickey Mouse might end up the same way. In the lonely darkness of night, he irrationally blamed himself for Lillian's miscarriage. His immune system became weak, and in the summer of 1931, he ended up in the hospital to have his tonsils removed. Exhausted, perpetually ill, and incredibly stressed, Walt found himself bursting into tears at inopportune and inappropriate moments.

Very concerned and with nowhere else to turn, Walt finally took himself to the doctor. After asking the film producer a few questions about his work and life circumstances, the doctor determined that his patient was having a nervous breakdown. The cure?

"Beat it, Walt. Leave the studio. Drop everything. Go away. Otherwise, there's nothing I can do." He also recommended that his twenty-nine year old charge live a healthier lifestyle, which included daily exercise and the taking up of hobbies. When he scoffed at the idea to Roy, Walt's older brother insisted he listen to the doctor's orders and take some time off, assuring him that he would mind the studio in Walt's absence.

Walt went home and told Lillian to pack her bags. Soon thereafter, the couple enjoyed a journey by train from Los Angeles to Washington, DC before heading to Key West, Florida. From there, they took a steamship to Havana, Cuba for a week, before departing by sea back to Los Angeles by way of the Panama Canal. Lillian watched from a distance as Walt strolled across the deck of the ship and chatted with other passengers. At times, he would stand at the stern of the ship and simply stare for hours at the wake as the steamer progressed, watching the seafoam – like the stress of the past several months – slowly fade into the distance before it dissipated altogether.

A RAINBOW ON THE SCREEN

While the early days of the Great Depression seemed dark and bleak for America and the world, the Walt Disney Studios had decided on its next great innovation: bringing the vivid greens, yellows, blues and reds to the Silver Screen.

The process of portraying film in colour had been in development since the earliest days of film. As early as 1895, exhibitors in vaudeville theatres had been hand painting the glass slides used in the magic lantern portions of their shows. With the introduction of *Le Voyage à Travers L'impossible* in 1904, French filmmaker Georges Méliès also utilised hand-painted images for his live action film; however, while the painted slides of the magic lantern show were merely single still images, Méliès' film required that every frame of action – nearly twenty thousand individual still images – were painted with four hues in at least ten shade and tints.

Inspired by Méliès but recognising how expensive and time-consuming the process of hand painting frames was, filmmakers looked for another way to colourise their live action films. Over the next twenty years, studios began to tint and tone the entire strip of film. This process required the entire film to be run through a bath of dye to provide the desired colour for the duration of the film. These colours were meant to set the tone for the audience regarding how to approach the film's plot. For example, if a film was primarily set at night, the film was tinted blue. For a romantic story, viewers found themselves watching a film that was tinted magenta, while adventures set in nature were tinted green. Unfortunately, with the advent of sound-on-film, a new process was required, as the dye interfered with the soundtrack printed directly on the film strip.

In the midst of the popularity of film tinting, a trio of American engineers and businessmen – Herbert Kalmus, Samuel Comstock, and W. Burton

Westcott – formed a company called the Technicolor Corporation. They recognised that while it had become standard practise, the tinting of film needed to give way to a more realistic colouring of moving pictures. In 1915, they began experimenting to develop a process to bring lifelike colour to film through the use of prisms and coloured filters. This initial process, known as Technicolor Process No. 1, began as action was being captured on camera. As images entered the lens of the camera, the light was split in half with the two images passing through a red and green filter. These filtered images would be captured as negatives on separate film strips. After being printed, the film would be projected onto theatre screens through a corresponding red and green filter which, when combined, would provide a greenish-red tint to the picture, giving a dull semblance of colour.

Unsatisfied with the accurate portrayal of colour and the difficulty of correctly aligning the two filters during projection, Kalmus and his team began to hone the process by developing Technicolor Processes No. 2 and 3. Process No. 2 improved upon its predecessor by printing both the red and green images on a single strip of film, but when projecting the film, it was found that the image lacked the ability to accurately depict blues, purples and yellows. The developing process also led to the film becoming brittle and curling, as well as turning orange over time, leaving Process No. 2 relatively short-lived.

With the development of Process No. 3 in 1927, Technicolor's engineers introduced a new method of producing colour on screen. This new process, while still utilising red and green filters, applied gelatin to the film strip. The areas of the film most exposed to light would end up with a harder layer of gelatin, while the areas less exposed would have a thinner layer which would wash off later in the process. When the strip went through the dye baths, the areas with the thicker, harder gelatin would absorb more dye, resulting in richer colour. It was also discovered that richer colour would occur when the negatives with higher exposure to the green filter were washed in a red-orange bath, while those exposed to the red filter were washed in cyan-green dye. While this process provided the best depiction of colour on live action film to date, it still did not allow for the full spectrum of colours. The novelty of the two-colour process also began to wane as audiences were no longer impressed by the depiction of colours in a non-lifelike manner.

Finally, in 1932, Technicolor honed their craft by creating a three-strip system, known as Process No. 4, which provided the realistic spectrum of colours that filmmakers and the public were hoping for. Similar to Processes 1-3, this new process utilised in-camera filters. However, rather than just featuring a red and green filter during photography, this new three-strip process added a blue filter. As action was recorded, it was printed on three separate strips of film, taking the colour of its corresponding filter. After being printed, the gelatin would once again be applied to each individual film strip and then washed in dye to apply colour. The red print would be washed in cyan dye, while the green strip would carry magenta and the blue negative would absorb yellow. When combined onto a single film strip, the combination of these three colours would create a vast spectrum of colours, hues and tones that were relatively true-to-life.

Not all of the film community were convinced that adding colour to film was good for the industry. Many feared that adding the novelty of realistic colour would distract from the plot and storytelling devices being used, while those on the opposite side believed colour would make films *too* artistic. Those who worked in the film trades – particularly in costume, soundtrack, cinematography and lighting – believed that colour would actually detract from the artistic nature required to produce a black-and-white feature. For instance, a lot of work went into adjusting light and shadows, and designing costumes and set pieces to come out clearly in a black-and-white film. Some who worked in these departments felt that the transition to colour would make the artistic nature of their work obsolete. Not only that, opponents argued that Technicolor operated by making film a scientific process, rather than one focused on "craft-based know-how of a working cinematographer."

The exorbitant cost of producing films using Technicolor also made studios nervous. For example, the higher costs associated with using Technicolor led to the first three-strip film, *La Cucaracha*, costing $65,000 rather than the approximate cost of $16,000 it would have cost to make the same film in black-and-white. By 1937, the amount that a studio would have to pay to partner with Technicolor would increase to $150,000 per feature. Perhaps *Variety* described the hesitancy of the studios well when, in a July 1935 article, it was argued that "[w]hether colour for features is commercially profitable, and will the public pay more and in larger numbers to see such pictures, has the producers guessing."

Herbert Kalmus agreed with his critics regarding the artistic nature of black-and-white films, arguing that an older film shouldn't just be converted to colour simply because the new technology allowed for it: "[i]f a script has been conceived, planned, and written for black-and-white, it should not be done at all in color." Rather, he felt that colour should only be used to enhance a film, writing that "the story should be chosen and the scenario written with color in mind from the start, so that by its use effects are obtained, moods created, beauty and personalities emphasized, and the drama enhanced. Color should…[support] and [give] impulse to the drama, becoming an integral part of it, and not something super-added."

Technicolor responded to these criticisms from an unlikely source. After her divorce from company founder Herbert Kalmus, Natalie Kalmus left the leadership and development team at Technicolor and instead became head of the Color Advisory Service and was later joined by colour consultants Henri Jaffa and Morgan Padelford. In this new role, Kalmus served as an intermediary between Technicolor and production teams of Hollywood's numerous film studios, in which she developed a colour theory which would establish standards for colour as used in film. For example, it was Kalmus who argued that different colours, hues and tones should be used to compliment a film's plot by helping to set the scene's tone, much in the same way as camera angles or the film's soundtrack. This idea of using colour, she argued, could also be used to help with character costuming: by putting a character in a costume using warmer colours such as red, it would characterise them as feisty, while one dressed in more muted colours like grey or blue would give the feeling of being more subdued or repressed. To ensure that colour was used most effectively for every film she advised on, Kalmus even created a "colour score," which would accompany the script and identify which colours should be used for each character, prop, lighting gel, background, and costume in each scene.

Unfortunately, even Natalie Kalmus and her colleagues at the Colour Advisory Service couldn't convince Hollywood of the viability of Technicolor Process No. 4. With the major film studios hesitant to adopt colour universally across their films due to the high cost as well as the stigma that came with using colour in film, Technicolor was in the difficult position of not only progressing their craft but also of surviving as a company. Herbert Kalmus and his leadership recognised that it was critical to prove to Hollywood that films could successfully utilise colour to enhance their films rather than sacrifice the artistic integrity of production and cinematography to tell their stories.

With the prospect of regularly producing live-action films in colour in the seemingly distant future, Herbert Kalmus turned toward the burgeoning medium of animation which leant itself naturally – perhaps more naturally than live-action – to be the proving ground for colour on film. Due to the studio's great success with both the Mickey Mouse and Silly Symphonies series, Kalmus approached Disney to implement Process No. 4, offering an exclusive two-year contract: the opportunity to not only further hone their craft but also the chance to get the one-up on other animation studios led Walt to accept Technicolor's offer. Disney cut the deal close, however: unable to utilise Process No. 4, Ub Iwerks quickly implemented Process No. 3 in his own work, as did other animation studios.

This was not Disney's first foray into producing colour shorts: the studio had experimented with colour tinting in 1930 when they tinted the Silly Symphonies "Night" blue and "Frolicking Fish" green. However, Walt was unsatisfied with the results, believing that the current level of colour technology would "detract rather than add anything from a cartoon". Roy not only agreed, but was also unsatisfied with the high cost required to produce a colour picture. The brothers agreed to stick with black-and-white shorts until something more advanced and fiscally justifiable came along – and it did with Kalmus' offer.

Timing for the Technicolor contract couldn't have been better. When Kalmus made his offer in 1932, Disney was already working on a Silly Symphony that was perfectly suited for the introduction to colour animation. Already animated and photographed by Bill Cottrell, Walt had production on this new short, "Flowers and Trees", halted to convert the film into colour. Roy convinced his younger brother that they should also print a black-and-white version of the film just in case United Artists was unimpressed with Walt's latest experiment.

While Walt's animators were hard at work producing this significant short, Hazel Sewell and her girls in the newly-named department of Ink-and-Paint were also busy. After inking the lines, the cels were painted in blacks, whites, and greys, then photographed to create a black-and-white print of the film. After each cel was photographed, they were rinsed and painted to allow for a colour version of the film as well. While the inking of the animators' lines onto the celluloid remained the same, the process of adding colour to the drawings became more difficult. Completely new paint was purchased for the process of bringing colour to the screen, rather than the several shades and hues of black, white and grey used in previous shorts. Unfortunately, the paint that was used tended not to adhere to the celluloid. Not only that, but because of the lengthy process of photographing the cels, some of the coloured paints tended to fade in the light which led to inconsistent colour in the animated film. Sewell's team began experimenting to find a quick solution, and it was determined that powdered colour could be mixed with gum arabic to create a permanent colour on the celluloid, preventing it from fading or flaking. After solving this problem, new ones would arise: it was also noticed that the colours painted on the cels were different looking on-screen than they were as they were being applied due to lighting, so adjustments were made to account for the inconsistencies. The final, painted cels were sent to the Technicolor facility in Hollywood where they were photographed on Technicolor's three-strip camera.

When Walt was first shown a demonstration of three-strip Technicolor by Herbert Kalmus, he exclaimed "At last! We can show a rainbow on the screen." With the production of "Flowers and Trees", colour was utilised both to drive the emotions of the audience and to demonstrate the marvellous accomplishments of Disney artists. As the short opens, brilliant tones are used to simulate dawn and its corresponding shadows as the forest awakens. Anthropomorphised trees stretch and yawn while rows of flowers perform morning callisthenics. The bright green leaves and browns of the protagonist's tree bark contrast sharply with the dull greyish-brown of the villainous rotting stump who is rapaciously vying for the affection of the film's leading lady, who has the semblance of a slim, girlish figure and has leaves resembling tall hair and muffs. At the film's climax, the old stump attempts to destroy his competition by starting a bright, reddish-orange forest fire which is extinguished by blue rivulets of rain created by blackbirds plunging through a fluffy grey cloud. As the film comes to a close, the valiant male tree proposes to his sweetheart beneath, much to Walt's delight, a rainbow showcasing the full spectrum of colours.

With "Flowers and Trees" nearing completion, Walt set up a private screening of the short with Robert Wagner, editor of *Script*. Wagner was so amazed by what he saw that he recommended that Disney make plans to show the film to his friend, theatre-owner Sid Grauman. Grauman, owner of both the Egyptian and Chinese Theatres, was impressed and encouraged Disney to expedite work on the animated film. "Walt," he exclaimed, "if you make 'Flowers and Trees' in the Technicolor process, you've got a booking at the Chinese."

Originally introduced to show business by his father, Sid Grauman got his start in vaudeville, managing theatres exhibiting the travelling variety shows and early motion pictures in California towns like San Francisco, San Jose, and Sacramento. After the Great Earthquake of 1906 destroyed his theatre in San Jose, Grauman moved to Los Angeles for a fresh start. Over the next twenty years, he opened three movie palaces in Los Angeles and Hollywood, each grander and more opulent than its predecessor: the Million Dollar Theatre, the Egyptian Theatre, and perhaps the most well-known, the Chinese Theatre, which he built with the help of United Artists' owners and Hollywood royalty Mary Pickford, Douglas Fairbanks, and Howard Schenck. Ever the showman, Grauman helped to introduce the film premiere, turning it into a gala attended by hundreds, including celebrities, film critics, and members of the media. It was here that Grauman began a tradition for which he is likely best known: the imprinting of celebrities' hand- and footprints into the concrete in his theatre's forecourt. While he sold his share of the theatre to Fox West Coast Theatres in 1929, he had returned as its managing director by the time "Flowers and Trees" premiered, and would remain so until his death in 1950.

"Flowers and Trees" premiered on 30 July 1932 at Sid Grauman's Chinese Theatre alongside the MGM film, *Strange Interlude*. Audiences were mesmerised by what they saw on screen, as were film critics and the other Hollywood studios, but the fascination was more with the advent of colour than with the story and strength of characters.

The Hollywood elite also recognised the significance of "Flowers and Trees". The Academy of Motion Picture Arts and Sciences, founded by Louis B. Mayer of MGM, invited Walt to its fifth annual ceremony of the Academy Awards to be held at Los Angeles' Ambassador Hotel on 18 November 1932. The Academy had created a new category of awards to be given at the 1932 ceremony, and two Disney shorts were nominated for this award: "Flowers and Trees" and "Mickey's Orphans", which were joined by Warner Bros.' "It's Got Me Again!"

Walt was honoured by the nomination, and wanted to do something special for the banquet. Drawing inspiration from caricatured celebrities depicted in the *Motion Picture Herald*, Walt put into production a full-colour animated short which would recognise and announce those being recognised at the Academy Awards. However, Walt recognised that in order to effectively portray the nominated celebrities, he would need to hire somcone with experience drawing caricatures. Walt personally reached out to the artist who had inspired him in the *Herald,* twenty-four year old Joe Grant, and offered him the opportunity to freelance with the studio during the production of this new short, "Parade of the Award Nominees". After several story and gag meetings with Walt and the directors of the short, it was determined that while Grant's sketches were the style Disney was looking for, they wouldn't be feasible to animate. Joe quickly learned that he would need to adapt his style to Disney's animation style, rather than expect the studio to adapt their process to his art.

"Parade of the Award Nominees" debuted before attendees of the awards banquet, portraying Mickey Mouse, Minnie Mouse, Clarabelle Cow, and Pluto accompanying caricatured versions of Wallace Beery, Lynn Fontanne, Helen Hayes, Fredric March, and Marie Dressler. The audience was delighted as evidenced by the raucous laughter at the exaggerated features of their peers, but Walt was excited by seeing Mickey Mouse in colour on the screen, donning a pair of green shorts rather than his trademark red shorts that would come later.

When it was time for the awards to be given, Walt Disney and his studio won the category for Best Short Subject, Cartoon for their film "Flowers and Trees," primarily due to the technological innovation of successfully using colour in an animated short. However, unannounced in the program, Walt was surprised to receive a second award: a Special Award for the creation of Mickey Mouse.

The technological success of Disney's latest Silly Symphony led to an avalanche of change within the film industry. Production soon began on the first live-action feature in three-strip Technicolor to be released after Disney's exclusive two year contract of Process No. 4, Pioneer Pictures and RKO's *Becky Sharp*. While other animation studios were unable to utilise three-strip Technicolour until the Disney contract expired, Walt was able to convince United Artists to authorise nine more Silly Symphonies in colour, even though they were initially hesitant due to the higher cost of producing them in Technicolor. But it would take a few more successes to prove to Walt that it was safe to let Mickey join the world of colour before the theatre-going public.

Similar to its work on-screen, life at the Walt Disney Studios seemed to become more colourful as well. With the addition of new employees came the opportunity to bolster the culture of the studio. The atmosphere was relatively informal and fraternal, as all members of production worked in close concert every day. Hoping to let off some tension every day during their lunch break, artists would converge on an uneven field across the street from the studio, which was often covered in litter, to enjoy a competitive game of softball. Teams were chosen based upon their relationship status, with one team made up of married men and the other of those who were single. Walt often came out to join in the game, but was known to be uncoordinated and unskilled, hitting poorly and tripping over the bat that he'd tossed in his path on the way to first base. Lucky for him, however, all of the competitors purposely dropped the ball or delayed throwing it, to avoid being the reason that the boss was thrown out. Those not playing softball or other games like badminton or football would often harass or catcall the Ink-and-Paint girls as they ate their lunch in the sun or as they made their way back to their building, nicknamed "The Nunnery" because of its role as the exclusive use for the female employees.

Walt's insistence on informality helped to create the feeling that the studio was one large family. While the employees of many film studios didn't acknowledge each other by their first names and the power held by studio executives led to their being referred to by their courtesy titles, Walt forbade this practice at his studio. Not only did he expect that his employees address each other by their first names, he even refused to be called "Mr. Disney," insisting instead that both visitors and his employees – from his senior animators to the handyman and custodians – call him Walt. This practice helped foster deeper, collaborative relationships between all involved in the production process, especially in light of the long hours and weekend shifts worked by the artists.

The lighthearted nature of the Walt Disney Studios made it a place ripe for antics, shenanigans, and pranks of all sorts, both performed by the artists and those on the other side of the studio walls. Because a tall blue and red neon sign perched atop the studio building featured a waving Mickey Mouse, locals thought the campus would be a great place to deposit their unwanted cats, tossing them over the studio walls. The girls of the Ink-and-Paint department loved it, however, with many of them taking these newly stray cats home.

Perhaps because they were constantly engaged in dreaming up and animating gags for their characters, the pranks perpetrated by the artists weren't as tame. In one particularly unpleasant example, a rotten smell hung in the air of the animation department for a few days, which started off mild and got worse as the morning progressed. Investigations revealed that someone had placed limburger cheese on the lightbulbs placed beneath the surface of the animation desks, which, when turned on, baked the cheese and released the pungent odour into the air.

Looking for a way to communicate with his staff easily and further create a feeling of camaraderie at the studio, Walt instituted a regular newsletter called *The Mickey Mouse Melodeon*, which was subtitled "The House Organ of the Disney Studios." Organised and published by executive secretary Carolyn Schaefer, this newsletter updated staff on events around the studio, gossip notes, jokes, and notes of Disney in the local and national news. For example, when some Disney artwork was featured in an exhibit in Philadelphia, the *Melodeon* reported it to the staff in celebration.

Impressed by the creativity with which his staff used their humour to wreak havoc on each other, Walt was determined to use it to his advantage. A memo began being posted around the studio, open to all employees – including the Ink-and-Paint girls, as well as the service and custodial staff – with a request for gag ideas. At the start of each gag memo was a description of the plot of one of the shorts currently in production. Studio staff were encouraged to submit ideas for physical or verbal gags, with a promise to pay out $5 for an individual gag or a whopping $20 for an entire sequence that made its way into the final cut of the film.

Unfortunately, the cheerful and familial atmosphere at the studio didn't stop the effects of Great Depression from seeping through the bars of the studio gates. One afternoon in 1931, word went out that a meeting for the whole staff would be taking place in the studio soundstage. Over the next several minutes, company lawyer Gunther Lessing spoke to the studio employees, explaining that he had witnessed the devastation caused by the nationwide financial strain during his recent trip to New York City. With Walt standing visibly off to the side, Lessing pleaded with the staff to accept a 15 per cent cut in wages to help the studio during this harsh financial period.

As they were being dismissed, hardly any employee blamed the Walt Disney Studios or its management for this request. Rather, the staff accepted this as symptomatic of the times, resolving to tackle the dark days of the Great Depression by committing themselves all the more to their work. It was their duty, they believed, to save the studio from financial ruin, even if it meant working twenty-four hour shifts. That way, they'd be safe – and not sorry – when the wolf of the Depression came knocking at the studio's doors.

THE MECHANICS OF ACTION

In spite of Walt and Lessing's plea, the Walt Disney Studios was doing alright. Its characters were becoming household names, with many of the nation's families owning merchandise featuring Mickey's likeness. Thousands of the nation's youth were packing moviehouses, not only to see the latest Mickey film, but to celebrate the mouse through day-long events scheduled by local chapters of the Mickey Mouse Club. Even leaders in the film industry had taken notice of the work done by the studio, resulting in recognition, positive reviews and criticisms, and even an Academy Award.

With an increasing number of eyes on his animators' work, Walt recognised that it was important to continually raise the bar on the quality of animation being produced, place an increasing focus on plot over gags, and ensure that his characters – new and existing – were as realistic as possible, both in their portrayal and behaviour.

Despite his big Oscar win for "Flowers and Trees", Walt knew that the award was for the effective development and use of the Technicolor process. Most of his animated shorts to date featured animal characters or inanimate objects come to life, such as toys, flowers, or skeletons. The few examples of human characters were often meant to be humorous or caricatured, such as the beer maid in "El Terrible Toreador," Satan and his demons in "Hell's Bells," or the black-faced tribesmen in "Cannibal Capers." Humour in these cartoons often resulted in exaggerated features of movements of the characters, employing various animation techniques such as squash-and-stretch and rubber hose, by which normal anatomical rules were abandoned in favour of unrealistic flexibility and physical reactions to gravity and disaster. In some cases, characters' body parts were even used as props or to help solve problems, such as when the dachshund became a rope start for the aeroplane propeller in "Plane Crazy". Other instalments of the Silly Symphonies, including

"King Neptune", "Lullaby Land", and "The Pied Piper" depicted its human characters in a nonrealistic, caricatured manner: King Neptune was rotund and seemed more cartoon than realistic, while the infant and juvenile characters of "Lullaby Land", "Babes in the Woods", and "The Night Before Christmas" feature wide eyes and an abundance of baby fat, including chubby cheeks.

Looking toward the future, Walt and his directors realised that there was a plethora of stories that could be developed featuring realistic characters. One topic of interest that Walt and his team considered was mythology. Based upon the myth of Persephone and Pluto, the short "Goddess of Spring" was released on 3 November 1934. While not one of the more popular instalments of Disney's Silly Symphonies series, this short was significant to the studio. While Hades was portrayed as the flamboyant villain and was thus caricatured and exaggerated in his movements and physical characteristics, Persephone was meant to be portrayed in a more realistic manner. Walt and his team of producers lamented that, unfortunately, her drawn anatomy lacked accuracy, with her arms in particular seemingly lacking joints and instead moving in the typical rubber hose manner of earlier cartoons. Her facial expressions also seemed to lack affect, with very little in the way of unique personality conveyed.

Ever one to be overly critical of the work his studio released, Walt recognized that many of the shorts – in both the Mickey and Silly Symphonies series – didn't have much that differentiated the Disney cartoons from those produced by competing studios. The world in which characters inhabited had very few rules, with trees that could duck when approached by a projectile, characters who were unhurt after falling from great heights, and props that simply fell over when collided with. Thus, it became important to Walt and his team that a more accurate representation of physics and movement be embedded into their cartoons to make them more believable to audiences and more complex as compared to those produced by other studios.

Walt also had concerns over some of his new hires. Many of the artists he had hired from art institutes in New York approached their craft through the accurate representation of the human form, looking to solve problems in their craft by utilising art theory, which was not always easily translated to the process of animation. Some of the more experienced artists who came from competing animation studios –

including Fleischer Studios – tended to use time-saving techniques from previous jobs that had daily animation quotas, which often led to poor animation. Rather, Walt wanted his artists to use practical skills to give life to fantasy, creating a caricature of life rather than a drawn reproduction of realism. Walt had such high standards for the artists who worked at his studio, that he created a list of the qualifications of his expectations: "the animator's ability to draw; then, ability to visualize action – breaking it down into drawings and analyze the movement, the mechanics of the action…his ability to caricature action…and see the funny side of it – to anticipate the effect or illusion created in the mind of the person viewing that action…the animator should know what creates laughter – why do things appeal to people as being funny." Because many of his newer artists did not live up to these expectations, in 1929 Walt began encouraging his artists to enrol in art classes to perfect their artistry. The problem was that animation was very different from the subjects that many art schools of the 1920s and 1930s taught. Luckily, a solution to this problem was not located very far away.

In 1921, a new art institute known as the Chouinard School of Art, began accepting students. Its founder, Nelbert "Nelly" Chouinard, who had studied art at the Pratt Institute of New York, had moved to southern California to join a movement of landscape painters in Pasadena, and later became an instructor at local high schools and universities. After the death of her husband Horace, who was killed in action as an Army Chaplain in the First World War, Chouinard opened her new art school in a two-storey house in Los Angeles. Within a few years, Chouinard's institute had outgrown its existing facility, leading to the purchase of land and construction of a new campus, which opened on Los Angeles' Grandview Street in 1929.

The curriculum of the Chouinard School of Art was very attractive to Walt regarding the specific needs of his new animators, particularly the illustration and drawing classes. With money tight at the studio, however, Walt couldn't afford to pay artist tuition, so Nelly Chouinard decided to partner with the studio by offering student loans, allowing Walt to repay the costs when he was able. Thus, in 1931, Walt showed his support for the professional growth of his employees by personally driving his artists to the Chouinard campus for classes every week.

One of the classes that the artists took during their time at Chouinard was Memory Drawing. This course was popular with the Disney men due to the particular challenge that it offered: artists were given a short period of time sitting in a room with a model who would perform a particular action. After a few minutes, the observers were dismissed from the room and were required to recreate the "essence of action" performed by the model in as realistic and lifelike a way as possible. Even more challenging was the fact that the instructor required them to use pen rather than pencil, meaning that any mistakes made had to be adapted into the drawing and that no corrections could be made. When Walt learned of this class, he was intrigued, as an emphasis on the accurate representation of motion was a constant goal for his high standards of animation. As a result, Memory Drawing became a mandatory course taken by all new studio animators and was given a new name throughout studio communications: Action Analysis.

The business relationship between Nelly Chouinard and Walt Disney slowly blossomed into a partnership: Disney would provide students – and thus tuition – to Chouinard, while Chouinard and her instructors would help hone the craft of Disney's artists. Desiring to help create a program specifically to suit the particular needs of the studio, Chouinard even sent some of her instructors to follow Walt around for a few days to learn what specific needs the scores of animators, background artists, and inbetweeners had.

As more and more of his employees began enrolling in Chouinard's art classes, Walt began to realise that it simply was not feasible – both from a logistical and financial standpoint – to continue to have his artists participate in courses and workshops on-campus. He was also alarmed to learn that a group of his artists were gathering at the home of animator Art Babbitt for informal training to study the human form of attractive nude female models from the South California Models Club. Recognising that it would look bad for the studio producing Mickey Mouse shorts geared toward children and families to endorse private parties where naked women were drawn, it was important to monitor and regulate what training was being offered from a leadership standpoint. As a result, Walt was determined to bring art classes to the studio to establish an in-studio program, which became known as the Disney Art School. While animation pioneer Raoul Barré had implemented a similar training program for his artists in the early twentieth century, an in-studio training program like the one Disney offered was revolutionary and relatively unheard of. Because Babbitt had organised these instructional gatherings at his home, he was put in charge of organising these classes with Walt offering the soundstage as a venue for the workshops and providing art supplies for the artists to work with.

While Babbitt had the skills of being a great artist and leader, he lacked instructional skills. Instead, he recommended that Walt contact Don Graham, an instructor at Chouinard, to come to the studio and lead the various classes, which began hosting twenty-five animators twice a week in November 1932. In communicating with Graham his justification for an in-house training program, Walt explained that "[m]any men don't realise what really makes things move. Why they move – what the force behind the movement is. I think a course along that line, accompanied by practical examples of analysis and planning would be very good." In a later memo to Graham, the studio executive explained that "some of our established animators at the present time are lacking in many things, and I think we should arrange a series of courses to enable these men to learn, and acquire the things they lack…I have found that men respond more readily to classes dealing with practical problems than to more theoretic treatment…[I]t would be a good idea to appeal to these men by conducting classes with the practical approach in mind."

The meetings described by Walt became increasingly popular, and within a few sessions, had doubled in size to more than fifty men, leading Walt to offer a job to Graham full-time, rather than freelancing his talents from Chouinard. The workshops covered many different topics, including character performance animation, animal and human anatomy, life drawing, principles of character acting, and a workshop on how to effectively use colour with the implementation of Technicolor. These lectures by Don Graham, as well as guest lecturers like animators Les Clark, Vladimir "Bill" Tytla, and Hamilton "Ham" Luske, and masters of the twentieth century art world including Rico Lebrun, Jean Charlot, and Frank Lloyd Wright were mimeographed and distributed to all staff so that the wisdom and expertise taught could be applied by all, including those who hadn't attended the classes.

With the growth of Graham's art program, Disney realised that the soundstage would not accommodate the needs for space and the variety of classes. A building was purchased across Hyperion Avenue from the studio which jokingly became known as the Don Graham Memorial Institute and was given the motto "Semper Gluteus Maximus" as a result of the prevalence of nude models who bared all for the anatomy classes. More innocently, a patio on the back of the building became fenced in and became a makeshift zoo for artists to study a menagerie of animals for the numerous projects in production. The enclosure held several creatures to be studied as reference models during the 1930s, including penguins for 1934's "Peculiar Penguins", the studio's stray cats for 1935's "Three Orphan Kittens", and later provided space to study parakeets for *Snow White* and a faun for *Bambi.* The space was also used as space to study the movements of animator Eric Larson and the sister of animator Les Clark who both provided reference for Persephone in "Goddess of Spring".

In addition to requiring animators to attend the courses offered, an apprenticeship program with two-week unpaid trial contracts was developed for all new studio artists. Originally assigned under the tutelage of Ben Sharpsteen and Dave Hand, new artists would be assigned as inbetweeners, with the more experienced Sharpsteen and Hand receiving the start and end of an action and the new artists taking the frames that brought that action to completion. Feedback and instruction would be given by the senior animators, providing real-time suggestions and corrections, which was a better system of training than a traditional art institute could offer.

While these apprentice animators completed inbetweening for Sharpsteen and Hand, they were supervised by George Drake, an artist who had animated for both Mickey Mouse and Silly Symphonies shorts, in the Bullpen, a windowless room located in the sub-basement of the studio. Drake was generally disliked by his charges, tending to be harsh, overly critical, and seemingly ignorant of animation technique, which often resulted in the new hires going over his head for help from more respected artists. His autocratic management style also resulted in both open and subversive rebellion and pranks from several of the Bullpen's inhabitants. One of the new recruits, a young artist named Ward Kimball, often took to dressing in unkempt and flamboyant outfits, simply to frustrate an uptight and professional Drake, who often wore a buttoned coat over his Oxford suit. The rebellious Kimball also encouraged the other amateur animators to sing "Song of the Volga Boatmen" as they worked, imitating the depressing drudgery of the chained galley slaves sweating in the holds of a Russian ship.

Walt was constantly seeking to improve the output of his studio. In addition to his training program, he continued to utilise the Sweatbox to review each day's work. He also brought his artists to the local cinemas to screen the newest films and animated shorts, looking for inspiration, seeing what others did well, and looking for tricks to improve their own craft. The studio also partnered with the Alexander Theatre in nearby Glendale, where most of the shorts were offered as early screenings. Walt, the directors, and all of the animators who worked on the particular short would sit in the theatre and take note of audience reactions, including when there was laughter, as well as when a joke seemed to fall flat. After the short finished, the team would congregate on the sidewalk outside the theatre to compare notes and determine what could be improved upon or cut out before the short's premiere.

This self-reflection and willingness to admit that there was room for improvement was what set the shorts of the Walt Disney Studios apart from its competition. Treating lines and paint on a piece of celluloid as actors, improving upon the timing of animation in relation to its corresponding dialogue or soundtrack, and even portraying characters and objects in lifelike realism turned a filmmaking technique previously considered to be frivolous and dismissed by the Hollywood elite into a masterful art form. But it would be the spark of life given to a trio of livestock and their hungry predator which would really make the studio's work a national sensation.

DEPTH AND FEELING

The Walt Disney Studios had become so masterful at depicting their characters in a lifelike way – even those who were anthropomorphised animals or inanimate objects – that their drawings were imbued with what would become known as "the illusion of life". While animal and human characters were anatomically correct and moved in a realistic manner, the early Disney shorts often depicted them as perpetuating, engaging in, and reacting to gags, with a character's particular behaviours or motivations stereotypical in nature. For instance, in the 1931 short "Mickey's Orphans", Mickey and Minnie take in a basketful of abandoned kittens who are depicted as mischievous and destructive because of their juvenile nature and the fact that they are natural adversaries to both Mickey Mouse and his dog, Pluto. In the 1933 short, "The Mad Doctor", the titular character terrorises and experiments on Mickey because that is the nature of the stereotypical crazy scientist, not because of any significant backstory or particular motivation. In the 1930 Silly Symphony "Midnight in a Toy Shop", a marionette performs a silly dance simply because it is assumed that this is what a marionette would do.

While the Silly Symphonies and Mickey Mouse shorts continued to be globally popular – King George V of England refused to attend the movies unless a Mickey Mouse film was shown and United States President Franklin Delano Roosevelt was elected to be the Chief Mickey Mouse for the Birmingham chapter of the Mickey Mouse Club – there wasn't a whole lot that differentiated the use of gags and narrative structure of Disney shorts from that of other animation studios.

Walt had emphasised story over gags in his Mickey Mouse and Silly Symphonies shorts, but realised that there didn't seem to be much motivation behind characters' actions or behaviours. He believed that characters had to be relatable and have realistic and varied personalities like real-life people in order for audiences to truly suspend their disbelief and find the story and its characters relatable. He decided to lend credibility to this pioneering approach to animation by taking advantage of the training program already being offered to his staff.

In April 1933, the studio offered a ten-part lecture series given by Dr. Boris Morkovin, the chair of the Cinematography Department at the University of Southern California. In these classes, Morkovin discussed ideas including the importance of stressing story narrative over a simple string of gags and the importance of strong characters over a focus on technical skills. However, while his students at the studio considered him condescending and "an inexperienced blowhard", it was his teachings on the psychology of cartoons which had a significant impact on Disney's animated shorts moving forward.

Many of the early instalments of the Silly Symphonies series were based upon original concepts, and were often strings of gags tied together to provide a snapshot of a particular theme, such as flora and fauna in "Flowers and Trees" and the underworld in "Hell's Bells". With the new focus on artistic excellence taught by Chouinard and the Disney art program, as well as Walt's desire to concentrate on narrative and differentiating characters, the Silly Symphonies produced as the 1930s progressed began focusing on nursery rhymes, fairy tales, and moral stories, which lent themselves easily to a narrative focus.

In October 1932, Walt introduced the idea of developing an animated short around the story of "The Three Little Pigs", adapting the version found in 1892's *The Green Fairy Book*. In December 1932, Walt began to meet with his team to develop the story of the short, as well as solicit ideas for gags to incorporate into the film. Concepts for the pigs and the film's environments were developed by Albert Hurter, a recent hire to the studio and joining Webb Smith and Ted Sears as one of the members of the newly formed Story Department at the Walt Disney Studios. The titular characters of the short would be depicted as brothers, meaning that they would all resemble each other physically, but the story naturally lent a differentiation between the three pigs due to the particular building material each used to construct their homes. This allowed for the animators to distinguish between the characters in the first half of the film, but the challenge would be how to help audiences determine which pig was which when the trio was together on-screen.

To solve this problem, the story team decided to improve upon what the artists already knew and had recently learned. Between Dr. Markovin's belief in the psychological impact of cartoons on audiences and how various techniques could be used to improve the characterisation of their animated stars, and Walt's emphasis on narrative over a simple string of gags, the studio began to lean towards a new philosophy in telling stories and depicting its characters: personality animation. This technique was intended to bring more life and realism to animated characters by imbuing them with underlying attitudes, ethical systems, and specific personalities which would in turn lead to motivations for their on-screen actions and interactions both with their environments and other characters. Personality could also be portrayed through the design of the characters' outfits, the colours the ink-and-paint team used, the musical themes playing when they were on screen, unique mannerisms and movements such as how a character walked, and even the type of voice that would be dubbed onto the film for character dialog. As Walt had hoped, this would make his films more believable, elicit specific emotions to perpetuate audience buy-in, and justify the suspension of disbelief while watching an eight-minute animated short featuring anthropomorphic trees, musical instruments, or porcine triplets.

In casting his vision for the characters of his newest Silly Symphony, Walt shared with his staff that the story team and artists "should be able to develop quite a bit of personality in [the three pigs]...for things of this sort woven into a story give it depth and feeling. These little pigs…will be more like human characters."

To help audiences understand the three protagonists, each was given a unique outfit. The first two pigs – those who built their homes of hay and sticks – wore costumes which suggested frivolity, which is later confirmed when they preferred to spend their time singing, dancing, and playing the fiddle and fife. Their wiser brother – who built his house of bricks – is instead shown wearing denim overalls and a painter's hat, which suggests hard work and industriousness. Each pig was also given a unique voice: the first two pigs – Fifer and Fiddler Pigs – had high-pitched, sing-songy voices provided by Mary Moder and Dorothy Compton contrasting with the raspy, stern, masculinity of the third brother – Practical Pig – voiced by Pinto Colvig.

The short's villain, the Big Bad Wolf, was also imbued with a personality to help drive the narrative of the film. The wolf's appearance suggested his evil intent for the pigs, with his ears resembling devil horns, his long tongue licking the sharp teeth in his wide open mouth, salivating in hunger for his prey, and even shifty eyes which suggested maliciousness and a conspiring tendency. His unkempt black fur, which suggests that he is a restless vagabond, contrasts sharply with his patched red trousers, suggesting danger and his desire for the pigs. His voice supports his animated depiction, with Billy Bletcher, who had a history providing dialogue for harsh, gruff, and nefarious characters in films, and would later go on to voice Mickey Mouse's rival Peg-Leg Pete, providing the growls, evil laughter, and crafty pleas of the Big Bad Wolf.

Using Hurter's inspirational sketches and the profiles – including voices and outfits – developed by Walt and his team, director Burt Gillett shared his vision for the short with the artists and animation on the short commenced. Norm Ferguson, who animated in a way that suggested passionate emotion and highlighted character personality, was assigned the character of the Big Bad Wolf with the goal of portraying the villain's devious nature through his facial expressions and body language, while Art Babbitt animated some of the wolf's darker and more aggressive sequences. Fred Moore, a twenty-two year old who had learned of the Walt Disney Studios while performing janitorial work at Chouinard Art Institute, was given the role as principal animator of the three pigs, assisted by Dick Lundy. Walt was so impressed with the realism Moore imparted to the movement and emotion of his animated charges that he proclaimed "At last! We have achieved true personality in a whole picture!"

As an instalment in the Silly Symphonies, "Three Little Pigs" needed an accompanying musical score. Studio composer Frank Churchill, who had written the scores of two dozen Mickey Mouse and Silly Symphony shorts, worked alongside Ted Sears to develop the dialog and lyrics for the film's song, "Who's Afraid of the Big Bad Wolf?" Interestingly, while he had been composing for Ub Iwerks, Carl Stalling was hired as a freelancer to help arrange Churchill's score for the piano at the end of the short, even performing the piano solo himself.

Walt Disney's "Three Little Pigs" premiered at New York's Radio City Music Hall on 25 May 1933 alongside the baseball comedy, *Elmer, the Great,* followed by the Los Angeles premiere on 13 July at Loew's State Theatre accompanying Fox's *Arizona to Broadway*. Some initial press reviews of Disney's newest short hailed the cartoon as less than impressive, preferring instead the short's immediate predecessor,

"Father Noah's Ark" because of its modern treatment of a familiar story and excellent depiction of hundreds of moving characters. Other major news outlets didn't even acknowledge the "Three Little Pigs'" premiere at Radio City Music Hall, considering it a footnote in both Disney and general Hollywood news. Even the head of distribution for United Artists was less than impressed when he first saw the film, calling Walt a "cheater" because the cartoon only featured four characters as opposed to the scores usually featured in the Silly Symphonies.

Hal Horne, United Artists' director of advertising and publicity, recognised the potential of Disney's latest Technicolor spectacle. He vehemently disagreed with its critics, arguing that the newest Silly Symphony was "the greatest thing Walt has ever done." Utilising his role as head of publicity for UA, Horne solicited positive reviews and developed advertising campaigns to drive interest. Surprisingly, Horne had an unanticipated ally: the independently-owned theatres of small town America. While the movie palaces that tended to influence national opinion and press criticism in New York City and Los Angeles were wont to recognise the merit of Disney's latest film, everyday Americans attending neighbourhood theatres in rural towns across the nation found inspiration from the three pigs who are successful in their standoff with the Big Bad Wolf.

Slowly, the larger theatres in the big cities began to change their tune about the newest Silly Symphony. Horne was able to convince theatre managers to bill Walt Disney's latest short ahead of its accompanying feature on their marquees. On 4 August, "Three Little Pigs" began playing at New York City's Roxy Theatre for a three week run. However, moviegoers were so enamoured with the film that it received an unprecedented extension, playing for a total of six successive weeks at the Roxy. The theatre's promotional team conducted their own advertising by driving a horse and buggy throughout Manhattan, triplet stuffed pigs propped up in the seats, and a broadside flapping in the breeze reading "We're on our way to the ROXY THEATRE…to see ourselves on the screen NOW. Walt Disney's Original 'THREE LITTLE PIGS'." The popularity of the film would lead to an additional three week run in April 1934.

At another New York cinema, the theatre manager placed hand-painted cutouts of Fifer, Fiddler, and Practical Pigs running away from the Big Bad Wolf to advertise that the short was playing on his screen.

After weeks of a successful run, the manager attached a beard to each of the characters' faces. Each week that the film continued to play in his theatre, the manager placed a longer beard on each cutout, with a caption below explaining that "YOU'VE KEPT US HERE SO LONG WE'VE GROWN BEARDS."

It wasn't only the short that had become incredibly popular. The theme song for the short, "Who's Afraid of the Big Bad Wolf?", became a national sensation after a performance by Don Bestor and His Orchestra, making its way to number 16 on the Top 60 music charts, ahead of popular artists including Bing Crosby, Guy Lombardo, and Mae West. Record albums were printed for consumer purchase, including versions performed by Bestor's orchestra, as well as the soundtrack from the animated short. A deal was signed with Irving Berlin, Inc. for the publication of the song, with additional lines by lyricist Ann Ronell, as sheet music for piano, banjo and guitar, bringing the popular song onto music stands in American living rooms. The popular song had become the studio's first hit song, as well as the first song popularised and published for home consumption from an animated film, even going on to be released in additional languages including Spanish and French, and was later used to accompany foreign language-dubbed versions of the film throughout Europe.

"Three Little Pigs" was more than just a cute fairy tale story depicted in glorious Technicolor with a catchy song. Because the cast was endowed with such personality and that spark of life, Americans were able to see themselves in the plight of the three brothers against an enemy that sought to devour them. With the United States and the world in the midst of the consuming dark days of the Great Depression, the film quickly became an allegory to the plight of Americans and a moral fable of how to address it. Audiences laughed with scorn at the sloth of Fifer and Fiddler Pigs and their failure to take the villain seriously, recognised the wisdom behind the hard work of their more practical brother, and cheered at the defeat of the Big Bad Wolf who had knocked at their doors. The film was an inspiration, serving as an allegory of the times, even if that wasn't the intention of Walt, Burt Gillett, and their team of artists.

However, it didn't matter what their intention was to the Academy of Motion Pictures Arts and Sciences. For the second consecutive year, two animated shorts produced by the Walt Disney Studios were nominated for the Best Short Subject, Cartoon category: "Building a Building" starring Mickey Mouse, and "Three Little Pigs", ironically accompanying Walter Lantz's "The Merry Old Soul" starring Oswald the Lucky Rabbit, which was distributed by Universal. Once again, the Silly Symphony series won the Academy Award, proving the relevance of animation and the superiority of the work coming out of the Walt Disney Studios, this time as a result of imbuing lines drawn in pencil with emotion, feelings, and cognition.

Americans were in love with the three little pigs. In fact, while the film itself had cost approximately $22,000 to produce, it went on to gross $125,000 in its first year. Even United Artists finally came around, sending Disney a memo with a request for a sequel demanding "MORE PIGS". While the studio would eventually go on to produce three sequels to the Silly Symphony – "The Big Bad Wolf" in 1934, "Three Little Wolves" in 1936, and "The Practical Pig" in 1939, as well as a recycling of animation as war propaganda for "The Thrifty Pig" in 1941 – none of them were as popular as their predecessor. Walt knew that this would be the case: when UA had requested a sequel to "The Three Little Pigs", he was hesitant to accept their offer by stating "You can't top pigs with pigs".

It turned out, however, that pigs *could* be topped with another barnyard animal: the duck. Personality animation and its accompanying philosophy had swept the studio, becoming the new standard in portraying characters and driving the story of a short film. This led to an assessment of past films and current characters to determine what needed to be adjusted to fit this award-winning style of animation. Characters who seemed two-dimensional and lacked any kind of prevailing personality, such as Horace Horsecollar and Clarabelle Cow, were cut from Mickey's cast of supporting characters. The personalities and character traits of existing characters, including Mickey, Minnie and Peg-Leg Pete, were honed to make them more lifelike and give them increased believability.

Lucky for the studio, this reassessment of characters took place at the same time as some minor controversy. The Walt Disney Studios had received complaints from the Parent-Teacher Association complaining that many of Mickey Mouse's shorts depicted him engaging in what they deemed morally questionable behaviour, acting mischievously and as a menace. Several examples of this existed over the six years of Mickey Mouse cartoons including when he escaped from prison in "The Chain Gang", when he stole Pluto back from the dogcatcher by stuffing a feral cat down his pants in "The Mad Dog", or when he dresses up as a scarecrow to scare Minnie in "Musical Farmer". While none of these instances were because of any inherent malice in Mickey's character, it made no difference to the PTA. They argued that because so many of America's children flocked each week to their local theatres to enjoy Mickey's latest adventures or participated in the local chapter of the Mickey Mouse Club, these types of behaviours or storylines could inspire America's youth to engage in similar behaviours, especially in the midst of the darkness and lack of structure resulting from the Great Depression. Mickey Mouse, they argued, was a national hero who upheld America's moral well-being.

As the one who had been primarily assigned to animate Mickey over the past several shorts, Fred Moore gave the mouse a redesign, softening his physical attributes and shortening his stature and limb length to give him the subconscious appearance of gentility, approachability, and kindness. Moore also gave Mickey a list of definitive character traits so the other studio artists would know *who* Mickey Mouse was, what he stood for, and how to depict him in the films moving forward: Mickey would henceforth be portrayed as "cheerful, [with a] hopeful underdog attitude…earnest and responsible…kindly and modest."

Working alongside Fred Moore, Ted Sears of the Story Department created a personality profile for Mickey Mouse for other artists to reference. He would be depicted, Sears explained, in a way that demonstrated he was "not a clown…he is neither silly nor dumb…His comedy depends entirely upon the situation he is placed in…Mickey is most amusing when in a serious predicament trying to accomplish some purpose under difficulties, or against time…When Mickey is working under difficulties, the laughs occur at the climax of each small incident or action. They depend largely upon Mickey's expression, position, attitude, state of mind, etc., and the graphic way that these things are shown."

Mickey had become squeaky clean, an "everyboy" who was a hard worker and strong and creative in the face of adversity. But he needed a foil, someone who could add drama, excitement and humour to his shorts and who could act and express emotions in a way that would never be acceptable from Mickey Mouse.

Mickey's opposite was actually introduced as a supporting character in the Silly Symphony "The Wise Little Hen", which was previewed alongside "Gulliver Mickey" on 3 May 1934 at the Carthay Circle Theatre in Los Angeles as part of a benefit gala for the California Commission for the Protection of Children and Animals. "The Wise Little Hen" retold the story of "The Little Red Hen and the Grain of Wheat", who seeks the help of her neighbours Peter Pig and Donald Duck, to plant and harvest corn. However, Peter and Donald, who would rather dance and relax, fake having a bellyache to get out of helping, with Donald shooting a sly wink at the camera from behind the wheelhouse of his boat. After harvesting the corn, the wise hen prepares a feast from her corn, and Peter and Donald suddenly show up to help eat the abundance of produce. However, the Wise Little Hen has a trick of her own to play on her lazy neighbours: rather than giving them a portion of her corn, she gifts them a bottle of castor oil for their "bellyaches".

A number of prominent animators worked on this Silly Symphony, but Fred Spencer was given the task by Walt to develop Donald's look and personality. Art Babbitt and Dick Huemer were given primary responsibility for designing and animating Donald Duck, taking Spencer's concepts and imbuing the character with the personality of an egotistical troublemaker as demonstrated by his frivolous, almost mocking hornpipe dance and corresponding mischievous wink. Learning that the character lived on a boat, Walt Disney and sketch artist and storyman Albert Hurter came up with the brilliant idea of dressing Donald in a sailor's outfit, which would become synonymous with Donald Duck for decades to come.

Inspiration for Donald's behaviour was inspired by the raspy, at times almost indiscernible voice that he is famous for, performed by Clarence Nash. Nash had been a vocal impressionist for *The Merrymakers,* a Los Angeles' radio show on Radio KHJ, where he often mimicked the quacking of a duck, at times providing dialogue in the duck voice. This show gave Nash local fame, leading to freelance employment by other local businesses who wanted to capitalise on his vocal talents. For example, Adohr Milk Company paid Nash – who took on the persona of "Whistling Clarence, the Adohr Bird Man" – to drive a wagon pulled by miniature horses around Los Angeles, drawing attention to the broadside advertisements for Adohr while he gave treats to children who rushed to see the horses and watch his impromptu performances.

Artists at the Walt Disney Studios often worked to music and programmes playing on the radio. One day, while Walt was passing by, *The Merrymakers* caught his ear, particularly Clarence Nash's performance. Looking around at those sitting nearby, he exclaimed "Hey, that man sounds like a duck!" Coincidentally, a few days later Nash pulled his wagon complete with miniature horses past the studio, stopping briefly to leave his publicity sheet as "Whistling Clarence" with the receptionist. Wilfred Jackson, who had begun directing the Silly Symphonies in 1930, made the connection that "Whistling Clarence" was the same person who had performed the duck voices on *The Merrymakers*, and called Nash in for an audition.

During the audition, Jackson connected the intercom to Walt's office so he could discreetly listen in. Nash went through a variety of impressions, including a naughty child and a family of ducks. Walt jumped up from his work and cried out excitedly to those nearby "That's our talking duck!" Clarence Nash was immediately hired, spending a few weeks working one-on-one with Walt to hone his duck voice, learning how to impart emotion and personality into what would become the vocal representation of Donald Duck.

While "The Wise Little Hen" was not even close to having the same popularity as "Three Little Pigs", Disney's Story Department recognised the merits of the character of the conniving sailor-capped duck. A new Mickey Mouse short was in development, which would be the perfect proving ground for Donald Duck. Animator Dick Lundy was given the assignment of completing all animation on the studio's newest character, using Clarence Nash's vocal representation to dictate what Donald's personality would be. In portraying Donald Duck, Lundy determined to portray him as a character who had an "ego [to] show-off. If anything crossed him he got mad and blew his top". Later, animator Fred Spencer further fleshed out Donald's personality, describing him as having a "cocky, show-off, boastful attitude that turns to anger as soon as he is crossed...The Duck gets a big kick out of imposing on other people or annoying them; but immediately loses his temper when the tables are turned. In other words, he can 'dish it out' but he can't 'take it.'"

Released on 11 August 1934, "Orphan's Benefit" featured a number of vaudeville-style acts performed before an audience of distracted and trouble-making orphans. Rather than enjoying the operatic performance of Clara Cluck or the slapstick ballet of Horace Horsecollar and Clarabelle Cow, the dozens of orphans spend their time climbing over the theatre chairs and mocking those on stage. Between the various acts, Donald Duck attempts to recite the poem, "Little Boy Blue". The orphans, however, play pranks on Donald and terrorise him by throwing ice cream, hitting him in the face with boxing gloves, and dropping bricks on his head. In frustration, the duck lets loose his fury, quacking loudly, assuming the fighting position and swinging his arm wildly as became his trademark.

Mickey Mouse had met his match. While he was now able to be on his best behaviour in subsequent shorts, Donald's actions weren't tied to the fate and reputation of the studio. The unfortunate string of events which would befall him led to his blinding rage or diabolical revenge, which was often played for comedic purposes. He was also able to be mischievous, becoming a friendly rival to Mickey, often becoming difficult or obnoxious to frustrate his co-stars' good intentions.

Audiences quickly fell in love with Donald Duck. Writing that his performance "brought down the house" in "Orphan's Benefit", *Stage* writer Helen G. Thompson described Donald Duck as "the bad penny de-luxe. He was called the greatest pest since…chain letters…His persistence was comparable to Jean Valjean's in *Les Miserables.*" In 1935, Richard Tobin, columnist for *The New York Herald Tribune*, wrote that "most audiences squirm in pleasant anticipation of Donald's forthcoming anger. Never in motion pictures has there been such a funny fury as Donald's." Newspapers hailed the merits of Donald Duck as an animated character, with the *New York Times* featuring an editorial about his popularity in celebration of the character's first "birthday" on 9 June 1935. Even Walt recognised the significance of Donald, by explaining that "[h]is towering rages, his impotence in the face of obstacles, his protests in the face of injustice, as he sees it, even though he brings disaster upon himself – have kept him an audience [favorite] from that day to this."

While the humour of Mickey Mouse came from his unfailing perseverance in the face of adversity and Donald's came from his explosive reactions to and subsequent troubles as a result of difficult circumstances, another new character was developed who created humour as a result of his ignorance, clumsiness, and bumbling ineptitude. Inspiration came from Pinto Colvig, a member of Disney's Story Department who had also done some occasional voicework in previous shorts including the Grasshopper in the 1934 Silly Symphony, "Grasshopper and the Ants". As he worked, Colvig would occasionally take on the persona of one of his characters from his days in vaudeville, where he had performed as a clown, to bring humour to various situations. This character, Colvig explained, was based upon an individual from his childhood who was the village "nitwit," a slow-minded, simple man whose voice and mannerisms he had taken inspiration from. In addition to his lanky, clumsy movements, Colvig also imitated the gentleman's slow, lilting speech and gasping laughter, leading to a character whose behaviour would cause humourous gags.

In the 1932 short "Mickey's Revue", Mickey Mouse and his friends put on a vaudeville show featuring an orchestra of pigs, as well as Horace Horsecollar, Clarabelle Cow, and Minnie Mouse performing a ballet. Seated in the audience is a scraggly, bespectacled dog who is loudly cracking open and eating peanuts. Throughout the performance, this character, Dippy Dawg, laughs at inopportune times, guffawing loudly, much to the consternation of those sitting around him. Growing more and more frustrated, those sitting nearby silence him by hitting him on the head with a mallet before imitating his laugh.

This new character would find himself playing bit parts as an extra in the next several Mickey Mouse shorts, finally becoming known as Goofy and joining Mickey Mouse and Donald Duck in "Orphan's Benefit". By 1934, the character had been assigned to Art Babbitt, who was determined to hone Goofy's personality, which was demonstrated through his thought processes, movements, actions, and dialogue. To maintain continuity in Goofy's character and personality for other artists who would work on Goofy shorts, Babbitt created a personality profile on "the Goof", describing him as a "barnyard schnook…a composite of an everlasting optimist, a gullible Good Samaritan, a half-wit, and a shiftless, good-natured hick…He can move fast if he has to, but would rather avoid any overexertion, so he takes what seems the easiest way… Goofy [is] the kind of character that thought very hard and very long about everything he did. And then he did it wrong."

Mickey Mouse had friends, but he was also given a sidekick. As early as 1930, Mickey was accompanied by a non-anthropomorphised dog, who served as a pet, bloodhound, and hunting companion. However it wasn't until 1934 that this character – who became known as Pluto – was also given a personality.

Production on "Playful Pluto" began in 1933, with Norm Ferguson given responsibility to animate the titular character. The story of the short featured a sequence where Pluto, who is curiously following a fly, accidentally gets a piece of flypaper stuck to his nose. Over the next minute of film, he uses every means possible to become unstuck, transferring the flypaper from his nose to his paw to his ear. Finally getting free, Pluto takes a seat to rest from the effort, only to accidentally sit on the flypaper.

Ferguson saw this as an opportunity to develop Pluto's personality by showing how he reacted to the frustrating experience of attempting to free himself from the sticky trap. This was particularly challenging, especially because, unlike Goofy, who was an anthropomorphism, Pluto was meant to be portrayed as a dog with animal, rather than human, behaviour and characteristics. As such, Pluto did not speak, and this required Fergie to find a different way to convey emotion and cognition.

To solve this problem, Ferguson brought in a common mirror, placing it alongside his animation desk. When he needed to show Pluto – or any of the characters he worked on – emoting, he would make a face in the mirror and simply draw what he saw, using himself as a model. This made the feelings of Pluto more believable, conveying the character's joy, sorrow, or frustration. He also realised that although Pluto was unable to speak, he still needed to communicate the animated dog's thoughts. One way he successfully did this was by showing Pluto "break the fourth wall", making eye contact while looking at the camera to elicit commiseration or celebration from the audience.

Up to this point, United Artists and Walt Disney had been hesitant about producing Mickey Mouse shorts in colour, fearful that the reputation and dominance of Disney's golden boy could be destroyed if their foray into Technicolor was unsuccessful. However, as the studio's exclusive contract with Technicolor came to an end, Walt was willing to take a chance in order to get a leg-up on competing animation studios who had been preparing to produce successful cartoons after watching how Disney did it over the previous two years. On 23 February 1935, the studio released "The Band Concert", which, while a part of the Mickey Mouse shorts series, was part Silly Symphony due to the adherence of its animation to its soundtrack.

The film opens with a small band directed by Mickey Mouse and featuring Goofy, Horace Horsecollar, Clarabelle Cow, Peter Pig, and an assortment of animated extras playing on a pavilion in a wooded park, while an audience listens to the music. As they play the *William Tell Overture,* Donald Duck walks through the crowd selling ice cream out of a makeshift wagon. True to his nature, his mischievousness emerges, and he purposely tries to distract the band by playing "Turkey in the Straw" on a flute he has handy, and the band follows suit. Mickey, getting frustrated, takes away Donald's flute, breaking it in half. But Donald quickly produces another flute from his shirtsleeve and continues to cause trouble. Mickey once again appropriates the flute, leading Donald to pull another from his sleeve. The band begins to become irritated, with the trombonist strangling the rascally duck with his trombone slide, shaking dozens of hidden flutes from his clothes. After some gags featuring Mickey and the band responding to a troublesome bee, the song transitions to the next movement of the overture, "The Storm". As though the music creates reality, a tornado sweeps across the landscape, sucking the band into the whirlwind, unaware of the maelstrom around them. As the storm dissipates, they are dropped into the limbs of a tree, getting caught up on its branches along with the debris from the storm. As the short comes to a close, Donald reappears and once again produces a flute from beneath his sailor cap and plays a few notes from "Turkey in the Straw", dodging instruments thrown at him by the band, before being trapped in the bell of an upturned and dented tuba.

The anxieties of Walt Disney and United Artists were soon dashed after the film's release. Magazines and film critics alike praised the short for its artistic achievement, proving that Mickey Mouse and his new co-stars *were* still relevant in colour. Even globally-renowned Arturo Toscanini, who was resident conductor of the New York Philharmonic, was a fan of Disney's newest Mickey Mouse short: he reportedly saw the short six times in New York cinemas and even invited Walt to his home as an admiring fan.

With the success of "The Band Concert", this ever-expanding cast including Donald Duck, Goofy, and Pluto caused the popularity of Mickey Mouse to wane. To keep him relevant, it was decided that he would always be accompanied by one or more of the other characters in the Disney pantheon, creating what would become known as the "Fab Five": Mickey Mouse, Minnie Mouse, Goofy, Donald Duck, and Pluto. While audiences seemed to enjoy shorts where Mickey was accompanied by Pluto (such as "The Moose Hunt") or Minnie Mouse and Pete (including "Barnyard Olympics" and "Building a Building"), it was the films that featured the trio of Mickey, Donald, and Goofy together that were the most popular. These films, which included "Mickey's Service Station", "Mickey's Fire Brigade", and "Moving Day", resembled other popular comedy troupes of the time, such as The Three Stooges: Mickey was straight-man who was good-natured, Goofy was the bumbling character who often caused problems due to his ineptitude or ignorance, and Donald Duck was the one who reacted to difficult circumstances with an anger which usually backfired on him. While the team often started the short together with a common task, they would usually split up and work on different tasks separately before finishing the short together, often with disastrous results.

Walt Disney and those around him quietly believed that Mickey Mouse was an animated surrogate of his creator, if not an extension of him. Fascinatingly, Walt's fate seemed to mirror Mickey's, with circumstances surrounding the development of the Disney shorts seeming to manifest in Walt's life as well. Thus when Donald, Pluto, and Goofy were added to the cast of regular characters in the Mickey Mouse shorts, Walt's social and personal life also expanded.

In an effort to avoid another mental breakdown like the one he'd experienced in 1931, he maintained an active lifestyle, trying out a variety of athletic pursuits. Eager to rub elbows with the Hollywood elite and frustrated with his golf game, Walt joined many actors, studio executives, and directors in regular polo games on the suggestion of friends Darryl Zanuck and Will Rogers. Walt recognised that his novice status in the game put him at a disadvantage to those who had been gathering on Sunday mornings to play at Will Rogers' ranch, so he recruited several members of the Disney Studio staff – including his brother Roy, Norm Ferguson, and Gunther Lessing – to learn the game and practise with him at the nearby DuBrock Riding Academy. He even went as far as having a polo cage erected on the studio lot so that he and his staff could swat balls instead of taking part in their routine softball games. The game quickly became one of Walt's favourite pursuits, which he would engage in for many years.

Walt practised his polo game as often as he could, but as this was difficult to do at his Franklin Hills home on Lyric Avenue, he and Lillian purchased five acres of land in the Los Feliz neighbourhood of Los Angeles, located at 4053 Woking Way. In addition to the larger yard, Walt co-designed his new twelve-room home with architect Frank Crowhurst. The estate featured a swimming pool, a gym room, and a screening room where he could watch the Dailies in the comfort of his own home. The house was designed in the Tudor and French Normandy styles, costing the Disneys $50,000 and constructed by carpenters who were out-of-work due to the Great Depression. Not only was the new home large enough for Walt and Lillian and any potential additions to their family, there was also enough room for a staff, including married couple Almice and Verda Buddhu, who served as butler and cook, respectively.

When Lillian discovered that she was pregnant in the summer of 1932, Walt encouraged the workers to expedite the house's construction in order to be ready for the new baby. Unfortunately, Lillian miscarried this baby, crushing Walt's dreams of fatherhood once again. A few months later in the spring of 1933, they learned that she was once again pregnant, but were slow to get their hopes up. After a few months without a miscarriage, they began preparations for the new member of their family. An additional member of the house staff was soon added: nurse Olive Smith would assist in preparations for the baby and would ultimately help Lillian raise the child.

Walt's excitement creeped into his interactions with his parents. Elias and Flora Disney were living in Portland, Oregon, but often visited Los Angeles to see Walt, Roy and their families. However, with the baby's impending birth, they found themselves with nowhere to stay in the Woking Way house. In a letter to his mother, Walt explained that "[t]he spare bedroom, where you and Dad stayed, is all fixed up like a nursery. We have a bassinet and baby things all over the place. On the dresser, bed, and everywhere else are all kinds of pink and blue 'tinies' that I don't know anything about. Really, it's quite a strange atmosphere to me – I can't conceive of it belonging to us. It seems all right for somebody else to have those things around, but not for us."

In spite of the surreal nature of Lillian's viable pregnancy, Walt doted on his firstborn even before their birth. He decided to purchase the baby a gift: a thoroughbred mare. Realising that his child wouldn't be able to make use of the horse until it was older, he figured he might as well take advantage of the horse in the meantime. "Don't fall over dead when I tell you I have six polo ponies now…I figured I would make use of [the mare] until the baby got old enough to use it. I will stable it and use it for polo until the youngster grows up and is able to take it over."

His plans for the horse, however, were soon eclipsed by one of the highlights of his life. While attending a ceremony hosted by *Parents* magazine where he was the guest of honour, a member of his staff interrupted the ceremony and took him aside. Without much explanation to the members of the press present, he grabbed his coat and rushed out of the room. The emcee of the event explained to those present that Walt's "wife is going to present him with another kind of award." It was on this day, 18 December 1933 that Diane Marie Disney was born. Walt couldn't be happier.

AN ILLUSION OF DEPTH

Walt Disney, Mickey Mouse, and the Silly Symphonies were beloved by America – and the world. After his wins with "Flowers and Trees" in 1933 and "Three Little Pigs" in 1934, Walt would go on to receive Academy Awards in the category Best Short Subject, Cartoon for "The Tortoise and the Hare" in 1935, "Three Orphan Kittens" in 1936, and "The Country Cousin" in 1937. Critics and the press alike lauded the Silly Symphonies in particular, with Florence Fisher Parry, a Pittsburgh-based journalist and art critic writing in the 25 August 1935 edition of *The Pittsburgh Press*: "When the immortal works of art are hung in the Last Great Salon, among them will be one of Walt Disney's Silly Symphonies… [who] offers even more to our little children than Frank Baum did to us."

Perhaps it was because Walt Disney and his artists pulled from such abundant source material that they were able to so successfully tell a variety of rich stories. In addition to taking a vacation to rest in the midst of a busy season of cartoon production and recover from treatment for a "defective thyroid", Walt escaped to Europe with Lillian, Roy and Edna to participate in various publicity events. Along the way, he nostalgically re-lived portions of his past, visiting his childhood friend Walt Pfeifer in Chicago, showed Lillian locations significant to the time he was stationed in France after the First World War, and even provided pieces of art that would decorate the side of an ambulance for the Royal Manchester Children's Hospital that were reminiscent of his own decorating of an American Red Cross ambulance. However, as the couples journeyed from England and Scotland, across France, through Germany, Austria and Switzerland before finishing their trip in Italy, Walt found himself fascinated and inspired by the stories, culture and architecture he witnessed and experienced.

In preparation for his trip, Walt hired Helen Josephine DeForce to serve as the studio librarian. On 1 July 1935, DeForce, who was officially a member of the Story Department, began to go through the piles of books used as inspiration – both literary and artistic – for the scores of Mickey Mouse and Silly Symphony shorts over the better part of the previous decade. Thus, when Walt and company returned from their European getaway in early August with more than three hundred books they had acquired during their travels, the studio's new librarian got to work. The books covered a wide range of topics, from guidebooks of British butterflies to zoological books about dinosaurs, from books of nursery rhymes and fairy tales to the plays of Shakespeare and popular novels including *Pinocchio* and *Alice's Adventures in Wonderland*, from books full of lithographs of European landscape vistas to books full of drawings of the creatures of European mythological creatures including fairies and Valkyrie. Some of Walt's favourite acquisitions, however, were those that featured illustrations of tiny people and small insects making their homes out of common forest flora, such as mushrooms, pumpkins, and tree trunks, which would eventually find themselves in future animated shorts.

The storymen and background artists loved these volumes, as they served as inspiration for scenery, characters, props, gags, and even plots of their films. Animators also found the library and its collection useful, with many of the books about animals proving helpful when it came to realistically portraying their nonhuman characters. In addition to its circulating resources, DeForce and her growing staff also provided an important service to the Story Department: as the plots and storyboards were being developed for particular shorts, the storymen and directors would often reach out to the library staff for help. A number of DeForce's assistants, including Mary Brown Salkind and Caroline Jackson, would dig into books relating to the shorts in development and provide summaries of the books, as well as notes or story ideas that could be pertinent to what the writers were looking for.

Desiring even more realism in his cartoons, Walt sought out a solution by establishing a Special Effects department at the studio. This department was initially staffed by only two artists, animators Cy Young and Ugo D'Orsi, with the goal of developing techniques to effectively animate previously hard-to-depict scenes. For instance, Young and D'Orsi would step out into a rainstorm to observe how a raindrop fell into a puddle on the street or watch the trail of a raindrop as it rolled down a windowpane. D'Orsi would then recreate what he saw

The first house owned by Walt and Lillian Disney was located at 2495 Lyric Avenue, with Roy and Edna owning a matching home right next door. (Andrew Kiste, 4 July 2023)

Now known as the Shakespeare Bridge, this bridge spanned the Sacatela Creek, opening East Hollywood's Franklin Hills for development. One of the first neighbourhoods developed was home to Walt and Lillian's home on Lyric Avenue. (Andrew Kiste, 4 July 2023)

Above left: While Walt Disney's first studio complex – located at 2719 Hyperion Avenue – no longer stands, this sign outside a modern supermarket marks the site's historical significance. (Andrew Kiste, 4 July 2023)

Above right: Pat Powers was a New York City film executive and distributor, with whom Walt signed a contract to use Powers' Cinephone to record a synchronised soundtrack for his early cartoons. Powers also helped facilitate the production of the soundtrack for "Steamboat Willie" with Carl Edouarde, as well as identify studios and theatres willing to show and distribute the shorts produced by the Walt Disney Studios. (Library of Congress)

After losing the rights to Oswald the Lucky Rabbit, Walt Disney and Ub Iwerks went back to the drawing board to create a new character. Mickey Mouse made his film debut in "Steamboat Willie" on 18 November 1928 at New York's Colony Theatre. (The Walt Disney Studios, 1928, Public Domain)

Composer Carl Stalling encouraged Walt to produce a series of shorts where 'the action is driven by the music,' which led to the development of the Silly Symphonies. The series' first short, "The Skeleton Dance," premiered on 22 August 1929. (22 Aug. 1929, Walt Disney Studios [Public Domain as of 1 January 2025])

In 1932, Technicolor signed a contract with the Walt Disney Studios, allowing the studio to have exclusive rights to produce animated shorts in its Process No. 4 for two years. This process involved shooting animation cels with a special camera–known as the Three-Color Camera–seen here. Disney's first animated short to use the Technicolor Process No. 4 was "Flowers and Trees," which won the studio an Academy Award for Best Short Subject, Cartoon in November 1932. (Wikimedia Commons)

Theatre-owner Sid Grauman opened his Chinese Theatre in 1922, which played host to some of Hollywood's most prominent films. Several Disney's films premiered at the Chinese Theatre, including "Flowers and Trees," Mary Poppins, and The Jungle Book. The Chinese Theatre's claim to fame was the celebrity handprint ceremony, which began in the theatre's forecourt in 1927. (Andrew Kiste, 14 July 2017)

Characteristic of America's great movie palaces of the 1920s and 1930s, Grauman's Chinese Theatre featured elaborate decoration, and was renown for being the first commercial movie theatre in America with air conditioning. Walt Disney and many of his respected artists often sat in the back row of this darkened theatre during his film premieres to gauge audience reactions. (Andrew Kiste, 7 July 2023)

With the advancement of animation in the 1930s, several film studios began the process of identifying methods to create the illusion of depth in their animated shorts. The Fleischer Studios developed the Setback camera, also known as the Stereoptical Process, which utilised three-dimensional background models with animation taking place in the foreground. (Wikimedia Commons)

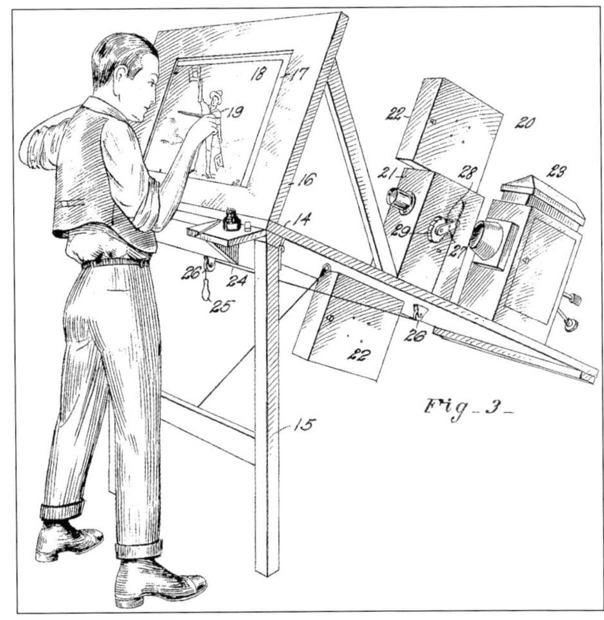

Animation studios often sought to create the 'illusion of life,' seeking to depict their subjects and movements in as lifelike as possible. Similar to a standard film camera, the Rotoscope allowed filmmakers to record the movements of a human actor, breaking the film strip into individual images. These images were then projected to allow for animators to trace each film still, making the animated figure appear to move realistically. (US Patent 1242674, 1915)

Left: Eighteen-year-old Adriana Caselotti was chosen by Walt Disney himself to provide the voice of Snow White after eavesdropping on a phone call between her father and Roy Scott, casting director of the Walt Disney Studios. (Wikimedia Commons)

Below: Located around the corner from Disney's studio lot on Hyperion Avenue, these cottages likely served as inspiration for the home of Grumpy, Dopey, and their brothers in Snow White and the Seven Dwarfs. (Andrew Kiste, 4 July 2023)

The Carthay Circle Theatre, located on San Vicente Boulevard of West Hollywood, played host to the 1937 premiere of Snow White and the Seven Dwarfs.

After her tragic and untimely death, Flora Disney was buried in the Great Mausoleum at Forest Lawn Cemetery of Glendale. She was later joined by her husband, Elias.

A map of Burbank taken in the 1950s. The Walt Disney Studios is located in the foreground at the intersection of Buena Vista Street and Riverside Drive. (Burbank Public Library, Burbank in Focus, 1950s)

Some buildings – such as this bungalow – were relocated from the studio on Hyperion Avenue to Burbank when the new studio was constructed. (Andrew Kiste, 6 July 2023)

With the construction of a new animation studio, Walt wanted to ensure that all buildings and features of his new campus were state-of-the-art. The new eight-wing Animation building, seen here, was designed to make the best use of natural light. (Andrew Kiste, 6 July 2023)

Special shutters were designed for the Animation building: an interior crank allowed artists the ability to open and close the exterior shutters based upon how much light they wanted to allow in or, in the case of north-facing offices, help guide the best amount of light into the rooms for work. (Andrew Kiste, 6 July 2023)

Above: Designer and architect Kem Weber worked closely with Walt to determine the layout and design of the new Burbank studio. Not only were Weber's buildings pleasant to look at, but they also were designed with the climate of southern California in mind: their lighter colour reflected the sunlight, partnering with the studio's new air conditioning system to keep the buildings cooler during the day. (Walt Disney Studios Casting Building, Historical American Buildings Survey No. CA-2639-C-7, Frank Scott Crowhurst, Library of Congress)

Opposite above: The new Burbank studio was not merely utilitarian, but spanned an entire campus, complete with soundstages, a cafeteria, a gymnasium, and abundant greenspace. Walt and Weber's design for the new studio also improved workflow in the animation process, logically organising the buildings based upon their role in the animation process. (Burbank Public Library, Burbank in Focus, 1950s)

Opposite below: Studio artists often worked long hours, especially when a deadline or film premiere approached, often arriving at work before dawn and staying until after sunset, as well as often working weekends. (Burbank Public Library, Burbank in Focus, 1950s)

Some of Disney's story artists brought Old World charm into the early films to give them a setting taking place in a distinct time and location. For example, Gustaf Tenggren was inspired by the Bavarian town of Rothenburg ob de Tauber for the village settings of Pinocchio. (Ludwig Mößler Rothenburg Weißer Turm Innenseite)

Famed conductor of the Philadelphia Orchestra, Leopold Stokowski partnered with Walt Disney to create Fantasia, which combined the majesty of orchestral music with the beauty of animation. (Bain News Service, 28 March 1918, George Grantham Bain Collection, Library of Congress)

Stokowski led the Philadelphia Orchestra in performing the full score of Fantasia (sans "The Sorcerer's Apprentice") for the official soundtrack recording at the Philadelphia Academy of Music, taking advantage of the auditorium's incredible acoustics. (Wikimedia Commons)

As a reward for their hard work completing Snow White and the Seven Dwarfs, Walt Disney held a company-wide "Field Day" at the Lake Norconian Club on 4 June 1938. Unfortunately, many on staff were frustrated that they were not paid a bonus instead. (Wikimedia Commons)

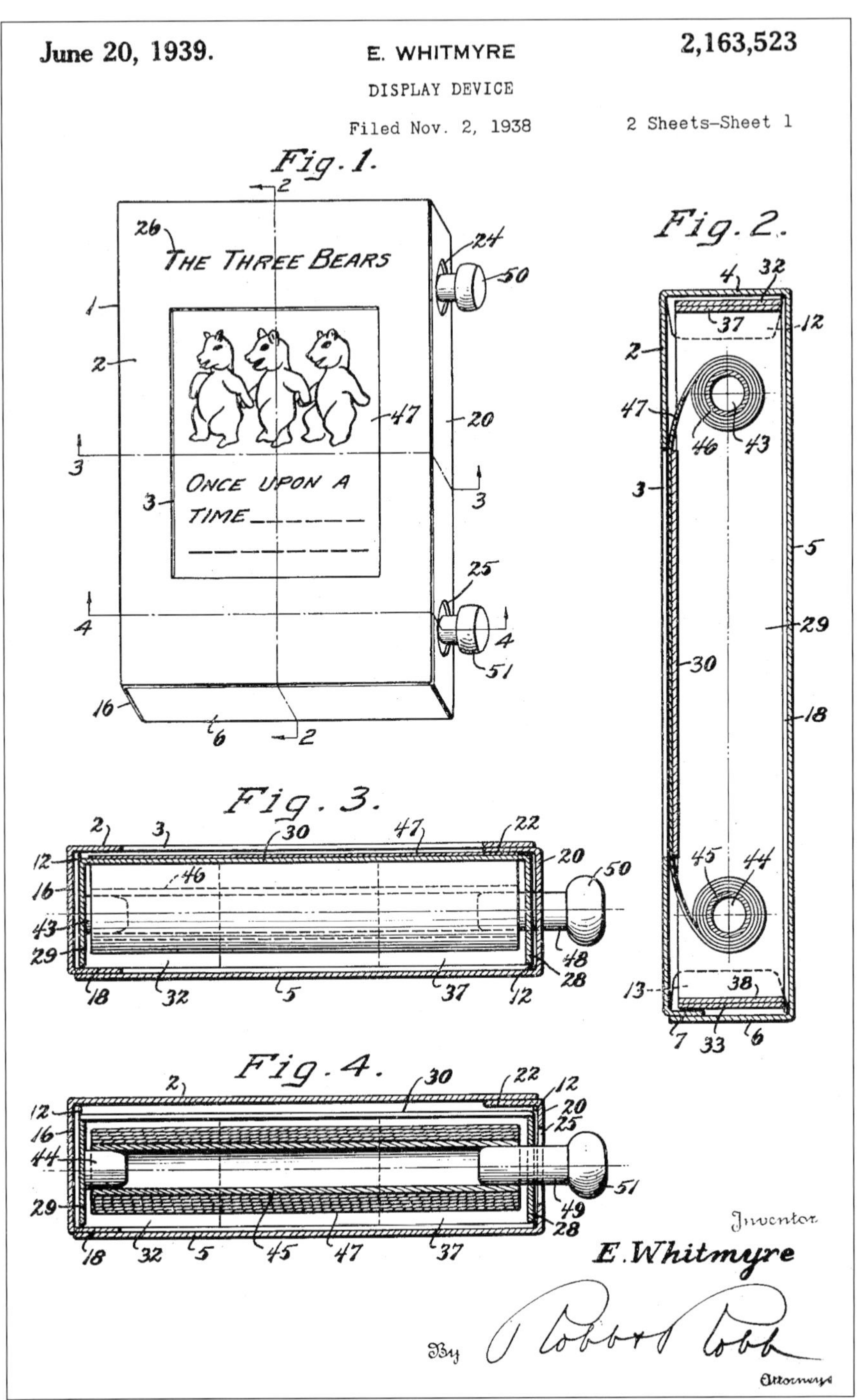

In the search for new ideas for feature films, the Disney Story department came across the story of Dumbo the Flying Elephant, which was presented to consumers using the revolutionary Roll-a-Book reader. (US Patent 2163523, E Whitmyre, 2 November 1938)

A meeting for frustrated artists was called by Art Babbitt to Los Angeles' Roosevelt Hotel on 22 May 1941. (Andrew Kiste, 7 July 2023)

An official vote was cast inside the Roosevelt Hotel on 26 May: 315 members of the Guild voted to strike, with four members in opposition. (Andrew Kiste, 7 July 2023)

Artists throughout California were hired to create insignia for different branches and divisions of the United States military during the Second World War. In total, the studio created approximately 500 separate insignia designs. (David Bransby, Office of War Information, June 1942)

To protect the important west coast factories that contributed to the war effort during the Second World War, film studio artists – including some from Disney – were contracted to develop camouflage patterns and techniques. Here, the Lockheed Plant in Burbank has been covered by a false town to hide it from enemy bombers. (San Diego Air and Space Museum, René Francillon Photo Archive)

by animating individual raindrops on each frame of celluloid using an oil-based paint. Other effects that they perfected for animation included realistic waterfalls and bubbling brooks, reflections in water, blazing fires, lightning, fog and mist.

While these advancements once again set Disney apart from its competition, Walt realised that his animated films still lacked something: depth. While portraying three-dimensional depth was difficult to do in a two-dimensional drawing, a handful of other animation studios had been working towards solving this problem. The issue lay in what was known as parallax, whereby features in the foreground of a shot would move faster than the background scenery. The animated films of the 1920s and 1930s either tended to have static backgrounds, or backgrounds that moved at the same speed as the foreground when the camera panned. By correcting the challenge of parallax, not only would the depth of field be portrayed in a more accurate manner, but an appropriate movement of characters, props, and backgrounds would be implemented while zooming in or out of a particular scene.

In 1933, Ub Iwerks created a new series of animated shorts called ComiColor Cartoons. However, to set these cartoons apart, Ub wanted to create a realistic depth of field in his films. After collecting various pieces of scrap metal including old Chevrolet parts, he retreated to the basement of Iwerks Studio with machinist LeRoy Richardson to engineer a solution. The result was the Horizontal Multiplane Camera: a series of glass panes – called platens – upon which the celluloid drawings were held in place by 2x4 wooden studs, placed horizontally one behind the next. While the last mounted platen, which held the background, was stationary, the platens closer to the camera could move forward or backward independently of one another while a camera mounted on a wheeled dolly and placed upon a metal track could be incrementally moved forward or backward, simulating the desired depth and corresponding parallax. While Ub produced a handful of cartoons using this new multiplane camera, these films were not as popular as his previous Flip the Frog series, and he quickly lost MGM as his distributor. Shortly thereafter, the Iwerks Studio shuttered regular production of animated shorts, only producing films on a freelance basis.

Fleischer Studios also created its own process to simulate depth of field in its animated cartoons. A new method was developed, known as Setback or Stereotipical Process, by which a physical, three-dimensional model was built and used as a background. Like Ub Iwerks' horizontal multiplane system, an upright platen holding a cel with a single frame of animation stood in front of the model. The camera could be moved toward or away from the platen to create the illusion of zooming in or out, while the model, which was mounted on a turntable, could be rotated incrementally while photographing the cels to follow a character as he moved or pan across the scene, creating the parallax with a physical background.

This physical model could be used in different ways: camera angles could be modified to take advantage of the forced perspective of the model to create the illusion that the audience and its characters were dwarfed to their surroundings, and light could be altered to differentiate between time of day and year. Characters were even able to "interact" with parts of the model, such as in "Popeye the Sailor Meets Sinbad the Sailor" from 1936 when Popeye seemed to climb a flight of physical stairs or when his rival Bluto puts his hands into a physical treasure chest only to pull out hand-drawn gems. Unfortunately, the Fleischer's new camera setup had a number of problems which plagued it, such as a difficulty with camera focus on the physical elements and lighting challenges which resulted in glare and inopportune shadows.

Shortly after these depth of field processes emerged at Iwerks and Fleischer Studios, the Walt Disney Studios began to develop its own system. Studio technician Bill Garity was charged with developing a multiplane camera to simulate the illusion of depth, which was completed in 1937 and cost $70,000. The Disney multiplane camera was similar to Ub's, using a frame constructed using 2x4 beams. However, one notable difference between the two was that while the Iwerks model was a horizontal system, Disney's development was a vertical multiplane camera, which allowed for a more realistic casting of shadows and an easier control over lighting than its predecessor. Once Garity's initial model had been perfected, two identical models were constructed, allowing for work to be photographed on three multiplane cameras at the same time if necessary. Of course tweaks and improvements were occasionally made to Garity's creation: for example, the bright lights, lenses and mirrors used to accurately photograph the cels caused the paint to become tacky, leading Garity and his team to develop a cooling system. Another development was a special tool which would blow a brief puff of air to clear the platen of any dust which would settle and obscure the cel before a photograph was taken.

Disney's vertical multiplane camera also allowed for a more believable representation of depth in animation by separating layers of drawings in their own individual platens. These platens could be moved closer to each other or further apart depending on the depth desired in a particular shot. For instance, a character might be walking through a forest: he might be walking between trees and in front of a house in the distance when a bird swoops by, obscuring his torso as it passes. Each of these elements – the trees, the house, the character, the bird, and any other items such as grass or flowers – were individual drawings on their own cels and placed at various intervals in the layers of the multiplane camera. After photographing the cel setup, they would be swapped out for the next in the sequence to create movement of the different elements. To simulate the tracking or panning of the background, which was painted on an opaque surface larger than the individual cels, the image would be moved incrementally to match the progression of the strolling character.

In practice, while the multiplane camera allowed for a greater illusion of depth and perspective, it consumed an immense amount of manpower and time to operate. For example, most of Disney's animated shorts were photographed by one or two camera operators, such as Mike Marcus who was the sole cameraman for "Steamboat Willie". The multiplane camera, however, utilised between four and eight camera operators who worked together to place each individual cel onto its respective platen, move the foreground and background layers to simulate motion, ensure the lighting was right, and maintain environmental conditions so they were consistent during the photography process. The pace of work using the multiplane camera also slowed considerably: while 1200 individual cels, equivalent to fifty feet of film, could be photographed daily on a conventional camera, the amount of transition time between photographs on the multiplane only allowed for 240 images, or ten feet of film, per day.

With his new camera system complete, Walt wanted a project to test out what the multiplane camera was capable of. After looking over some of the European-inspired sketches of story and background artist Gustaf Tenggren, Walt decided to produce a Silly Symphony which would showcase the depth of field offered by the multiplane camera and the special effects created by Cy Young and Ugo D'Orsi. As someone born and professionally trained in Sweden, Tenggren was identified by Walt to be the best one to give this new short the old-world feel that he desired, requesting that he paint watercolour backgrounds to inspire other artists producing the short. Artists including Sam Armstrong, helped develop the layouts for the various elements – including background paintings based on Tenggren's concepts – for the short to determine how to best utilise the multiplane camera in the short. To assist the layout artists, animators, and camera technicians visualise the cinematography, storyman and sketch artist Ferdinand Horvath constructed a large model of the mill to study. "The Old Mill" would be a short centred around the natural wildlife that calls an abandoned windmill home, hoping to survive the violent pounding of rain and wind arising from a passing storm.

Disney's team of directors, layout men, animators, background artists, camera operators, and technicians made masterful use of the multiplane camera in this production. From the first opening shot, audiences see the crumbling and leaning mill with its tattered canvas sails unfocused in the distance. A silky spider web, which glistens in the fading light of dusk due to the movement of a spider, stretches between a pair of plants in the foreground. As the camera begins to zoom in, the spiderweb seems to move toward the viewer before disappearing while the focus becomes the windmill itself. The next successive shots show a closer, more detailed view of the mill as ducks and tall blades of grass pass by in the foreground. Later in the short, a nighttime view of the mill is shown with the out-of-focus lights of fireflies dancing amongst the marshy cattails situated between the viewer and the solitary structure, the moon shining in the distance. As a storm rolls in, clouds begin to obstruct the moon. The camera zooms in to draw focus to the rolling clouds and the sails of the mill blowing in the wind, but because of the illusion provided by the multiplane camera, the moon off in the distance not only remains rooted in place, but also does not change size. As the storm strengthens, torrential rain begins to fall, making the mill in the distance difficult to see, while the occasional dead leaf flies by, carried on the invisible wind. Lightning flashes from behind clouds, with spans of the bolts visible in the parts of the sky not obstructed by the dark storm clouds. At the end of the short, as the storm subsides, a mist arises around the mill, and as the camera withdraws, the spiderweb once again appears between its two plants. As the web comes into focus, the dilapidated structure in the distance goes out of focus.

When considering how Disney's multiplane camera works, one can watch "The Old Mill" through a new set of eyes. The background, which featured the moon hanging in the night sky and some of the landscape in the distance, was a watercolour painting that did not change. The windmill was a separate drawing, suspended on a platen that could move closer or further from the camera to create the illusion of zooming in or out. Another layer of drawings allowed for the movement of mist, fireflies, animals, the blowing leaves, and rainfall to appear in front of the mill, closer to the camera, while the cel featuring spiderweb suspended between the two plants were closest to the camera. Thus, when the film called for a zoom, the layers of platens could be moved closer or further from the camera in small increments between photographing the cels, helping to create the depth of field and parallax. Even the Special Effects department found new ways to animate, using "The Old Mill" as their proving ground: small light bulbs were lit and photographed as part of the animation to create the illusion of bright, illuminating fireflies.

As production came to a close on the experimental "The Old Mill", trouble was brewing with the existing distributor that partnered with the Walt Disney Studios. As the agreed-upon contractual period came to a close in late 1935, Walt was unsure whether he wanted to renew his contract with United Artists. The distributor was pressuring Walt to give them exclusive rights to broadcast shorts on a fledgling technological innovation: the television. Walt had become almost immediately fascinated with the new technology and its implications for entertainment and thus, didn't want to sign away an opportunity to take advantage of exposing his films to a wider audience in the future, refusing UA the rights. He also complained to Roy that they were keeping too large a percentage from foreign markets.

Instead, distributor RKO Radio Pictures and Walt were courting each other. Walt recognised that RKO was one of the larger and more successful film distribution companies in Hollywood, and could afford to invest more in current and future Disney projects, as well as sell the animated shorts to more theatres than its predecessor. The studio had been using the RCA recording process to record the soundtracks for their recent shorts, and with RKO owned by RCA, it made sense that Disney and the distributor work together on a deeper level. Another aspect of the pending contract with the new distributor was the fact that while the Walt Disney Studios were expected to deliver eighteen films in the first year, they were given more freedom to determine how many Mickey Mouse and Silly Symphonies shorts made up the required number. The benefits were too good to be true, and RKO Radio Pictures and the Walt Disney Studios signed a contract on 2 March 1936. Newspapers, magazines, and trade journals praised the deal, with *Film Daily Cavalcade* calling it "one of the biggest deals in motion picture history." Disney continued to release their shorts through United Artists through the end of 1936, with "The Old Mill" as the first film delivered to RKO in 1937.

This animated short, which was the most expensive produced by the Walt Disney Studios to-date, premiered on 5 November 1937, with a week-long run at Los Angeles' 4 Star Theatre near the end of the month before playing for two weeks at New York City's Radio City Music Hall, where RKO had a history of hosting their east coast premieres and where every remaining Silly Symphony produced under contract with RKO would premiere until the end of the series in 1938. "The Old Mill" was seen as a significant contribution to the film industry, not only securing an Academy Award for Best Short Subject, Cartoon, but also winning Walt a special award for the scientific and technical innovation of the multiplane camera and its successful use in his award-winning animated short.

Walt Disney and his studio had been the undisputed winner of the animated shorts Oscars for six years. But his success with animated shorts spanned the better part of a decade, longer if one counted the years he produced the Oswald cartoons. Producing shorts had become easy, and his team had only perfected the medium of animation through their numerous innovations including synchronised sound, the successful use of colour, realistic anatomy and movements, personality animation, and effectively portraying a depth of field. There didn't seem to be a challenge in animating for the Walt Disney Studios any more.

Walt wanted a challenge. It was time to combine everything they had learned over the past ten years and do something new. Something which would change animation – and Hollywood – forever.

PART 3

WE'RE GOING TO MAKE A FEATURE 1934–1941

FAIREST OF THEM ALL

As the workday came to a close on Tuesday 30 October 1934, Walt circulated around the studio, making stops at the desks of approximately fifty of his most talented artists. He gave each of them fifty cents, instructing them to grab some dinner at a nearby restaurant and return back to the studio by 8pm.

As requested, the artists arrived back at the studio after dinner, making their way in small groups to the soundstage. Their eyes didn't require much adjusting from the dusk of the California sky: the group stumbled over rows of chairs organised in a circle to find a seat, the room pitch black with the only light coming from a single spotlight pointing at the empty space in the centre of the circle of chairs.

A few minutes after the expected curfew, Walt made his way into the circle. Because a large-group meeting like this taking place after hours was so unprecedented, those in the audience became silent. Slowly looking around at his employees, Walt began to speak in a serious manner.

"We have had great success with our shorts. But with the advent of the double-feature bill in theatres, animated shorts are becoming obsolete. Shorts like ours don't draw audiences to the theatres anymore, and the theatres need money because times are hard. If we continue doing business like we are, we will soon be out of business. Features make more money than shorts, and as of now, we can't compete with live action studios for slots on theatre bills: features will win out every time. As a result, I intend to release an animated feature for a worldwide audience."

The room was silent. The animators weren't sure that they had heard correctly. But Walt didn't give them a chance to process what they heard, because he began to do what he did best: entertain. A shift happened with his body language, as he seemed to instantly change from the professional demeanour of a Hollywood executive to more relaxed, the friendly everyman that Walt was around his friends and employees.

"I'm going to tell you a story," he began, gazing as though through the fabric of time and into the past. A small smile spread across his face. "This story has been with me all my life. From my earliest days as a farm boy in Marceline, my Grandma Disney would take a battered copy of *Grimm's Fairy Tales* off the mantel, and read from it tales of fancy, adventure, and tragedy to me, Roy, and our sister Ruth. It was the best time of day for me, and the stories and characters in them seemed quite as real as my schoolmates and our games. One of my favourites, the one story which would hold me spellbound, was 'Snow White,' a fair maiden who escapes from her jealous stepmother and is cared for by seven little men, dwarfs if you will.

"Fate had me in her grips, and it seemed that she wasn't finished with me and that girl with skin like newly fallen snow and lips red as a rose. As a young man in Kansas City, my father owned a paper route, and he expected Roy and I to deliver the papers. The city hosted an event for all of the paper boys where we were invited to attend a showing of *Snow White* with Marguerite Clark as the princess. There were hundreds of us in that room, so many that they had the film showing on four screens at once so all of us could see. We were a rough bunch of boys, and everyone was yelling, climbing over the chairs, and a few fights even broke out. But I was unaware of what was happening around me: I couldn't take my eyes off the screen. I laughed at the little men as they entertained the girl, was terrified when the witch turned into a hag, cried when Snow White bit into the apple, and cheered when she was revived by the prince's kiss. When I began to think about producing an animated feature, there was no doubt in my mind what story to choose."

Over the next three hours, Walt stood in the midst of his artists and began to tell them the story he wanted to portray on-screen. It was a one-man show, with Walt simultaneously narrating the story and acting out each individual character, taking on the personality, movements, and voices of each to fully convey his vision for this new, grand story. Walt so effectively and completely changed his persona when transitioning from character to character that it was described as if he were changing entire costumes to more successfully become the evil Queen, the Hag, Snow White, and the dwarfs. The animation staff were even more dumbfounded when Walt began to suggest the type of music and song topics and placement for the film, demonstrating to them how much thought he had actually put into this film as the studio's next major project. The artists were so enchanted by the performance that even after Walt's presentation was finished, many milled about the soundstage for nearly another hour, while the air buzzed with excitement. Even though it was close to midnight, they couldn't wait until they would be back at their desks and pre-production could begin.

This wasn't the first time that Walt had thought about a full-length animated feature. He had been considering the idea of producing an animated feature as early as 1931, planning to echo the start of his career in animation by making a full-length version of *Alice in Wonderland*. Unfortunately, shortly after conceiving of the idea, Commonwealth Pictures Corporation released its own version, leading Walt to shelve the idea. A number of other versions released over the next few years, including one starring WC Fields, Gary Cooper, and Cary Grant, led Walt to determine that Hollywood was already saturated with stories by Lewis Carroll, so he began to look at other ideas.

Another consideration for an animated feature was one based upon Washington Irving's "Rip Van Winkle". Unfortunately, Paramount Pictures owned the rights to the short story, preventing Disney from being able to produce its own film based upon the American classic. A third idea was based on Victor Herbert's operetta *Babes in Toyland*, but similar to "Rip Van Winkle", RKO owned the rights to the stage performance, opting to make its own version with Stan Laurel and Oliver Hardy rather than relinquish the opportunity to a competing studio. Finally, upon considering stories that had a significant place in his own childhood, Walt decided upon a feature-length treatment of "Snow White", especially after screening the 1933 Fleischer short by the same name and starring Betty Boop, determining that his studio could produce a better version of the story. He also recognised that the story of Snow White and her friends the dwarfs was known around the world, with nearly every culture possessing its own version of the tale. To help flesh out his ideas for the film, he wrote the initial treatment of the film himself, likely completing it sometime around 9 August 1934.

Shortly after his performance to the staff on the studio soundstage, the news broke that Walt Disney was going to attempt to create a feature-length cartoon. Hollywood was unsure of this choice, with many mocking the respected studio. Some experts believed that sitting through a ninety-minute animated film, especially one in Technicolor, would be detrimental to one's health. There was a general assumption by many in the film community and critical press that the public wouldn't take something of the sort seriously. Perhaps more hurtful was the rumblings of various studio executives and producers, many of whom had rubbed elbows with Walt and Roy; they not only made the assessment that this project would be the studio's undoing, but even publicly called it "Disney's Folly".

To combat many of these assumptions, Walt knew that he needed to prove each of these preconceived judgments wrong. To successfully produce a full-length animated motion picture, the Walt Disney Studios would need to pull out all the stops, implement everything that they had learned as an artistic team and utilise every innovation they had developed. While the Silly Symphonies had used vibrant colours to help drive the shorts' narratives, this new film would need to tone down the colours and expand the tones and shades to create a more realistic depiction of characters and environment, as well as make the long exposure easier on the eyes. The animators would need to concentrate on portraying the human form and movement accurately for the more dramatic characters, such as Snow White, her step-mother the Queen, the Prince, and the Huntsman, but caricature those who were meant to be more lighthearted, such as the dwarfs and the Old Hag. This also meant that the movement of objects and the laws of physics needed to be accurately adhered to, such as in the way clothing hung on and moved with a character, birds flew, light and shadows danced, and in how water flowed and dust settled.

As Walt's newest pet project, he assumed full control over production, installing the artists chosen for developing the film, its story, and its characters in a room next door to his office. Because success carried so much weight, he chose what artists would play an integral role in developing the look and feel of the film. He also selected some of his best artists and storymen to direct the film, with Wilfred Jackson and Ben Sharpsteen among sequence directors and Dave Hand serving as Supervising Director.

Early on, inspirational sketch artist Albert Hurter was made supervisor of keying the art style for the feature, primarily due to his experience as an artist and the fact that he spent his first three decades of life living in Switzerland and Germany, which inspired the style and details of much of his art. To help place the narrative of *Snow White and the Seven Dwarfs* in a specific time and place, Hurter began by designing interior and exterior architecture, furniture, and fixtures of the dwarfs cottage. While they never overtly identified where in Europe the story took place, the landscape and design had a distinctly Old World, German influence with Bavarian undertones. All of the furniture and fixtures appeared to be handcarved, with animal motifs and, in some cases, grotesque human features.

A handful of houses around the corner from the studio likely played a part in inspiring the architectural styles used in the film. These homes were designed by architect Ben Sherwood, who specialised in the Storybook/Provincial Revivalism Architecture style throughout Los Angeles in the 1920s and 1930s. Sherwood's storybook cottages were completed in 1931 and featured exposed exterior beams, high-pitched roofs made of uneven wooden shingles, and in some places, purposely exposed masonry showing through holes in the exterior whitewashed clay stucco walls. Tall, angled chimneys terminated in wood-burning fireplaces, completing the cosy cottage feel, and giving passersby – or artists drawing inspirational sketches – the feeling that a pre-Renaissance European labourer, or perhaps a number of dwarfs, could call them home.

Walt joined a team of directors, as well as a number of members of the Story Department to develop the plot of *Snow White*, using his performance on 30 October as a starting point. As a new member of the Story Research Department, Dorothy Ann Blank was hired to read through source material in the studio library and condense the stories into major plot points, providing input as to how the stories could be adapted into an animated film. For *Snow White* in particular, Blank provided suggestions for lines of dialogue, descriptions of the different characters in the Grimm tale as well as ideas for characters not original to the source material, and even thoughts about sequences and scenes that would help drive the story forward.

One of the suggestions made by the team was how tied to the original plot and details of the Grimm fairy tale Disney's version would be. Decisions were made to cut details and plot points from the original story to ensure that the film's narrative did not bore audiences. For example, in the original Grimm tale, the Queen attempts to kill Snow White three times, using a comb, bodice, and apple respectively. However, finding these attempts too repetitive, Disney made the decision that Snow White would succumb to the first murder attempt, a poisoned apple.

Consideration was also given to the idea of the film being narrated by an unseen voice, telling the story in rhyme. But this idea was quickly thrown out and instead it was decided that it would take place inside a storybook and audiences would watch as the story came to life before their eyes. Walt also wanted to play off the successes of the Silly Symphonies by bringing music into the film.

Musical films, such as those directed by Busby Berkeley, were very popular in the 1930s. These movies often featured big show-stopping numbers complete with dozens of choreographed dancers, often performing in a variety of locations for novelty purposes, including on theatre stages, honeymoon hotels, mountain forests, and swimming pools. But Walt noticed that these musical numbers were solely used for entertainment purposes and to add length to a film: they did very little to advance or support the story at the centre of film, with characters spontaneously breaking out in song for seemingly no reason.

Walt was more interested in intertwining story and song, with the latter helping to tell the overarching story with character dialogue seeming to naturally lead into song. This led him and his story team to be more discriminating with songs: if a song didn't support the story or seemed to hold the story back as deadweight, it was cut from the final film. With the music being such an important part of the film and its story, Walt needed a strong musical team to bring the story to life. Paul Smith and Leigh Harline were brought on to compose the score, while Frank Churchill (of "Who's Afraid of the Big Bad Wolf" fame) and Larry Morey wrote the songs. The songs written by Churchill and Morey spanned a variety of genres, from the dreamy, lovestruck "I'm Wishing/One Song" to the lighthearted "Bluddle-Uddle-Um-Dum" and "The Silly Song".

With the music and accompanying songs planned and the main plot being hashed out by the Story Department and production team, it was time to determine how the characters would look. Walt turned to many of his experienced artists, including the inspirational sketch artists and those in the Story Department to design the protagonists, antagonists, and supporting cast.

Albert Hurter was joined by storyman Joe Grant, and together they provided preliminary designs for many of the film's characters, including Snow White, the Prince, and the Queen. With Grant's background in caricature for newspapers, inspiration for the lead characters was taken from popular celebrities of the day. For example, Snow White was inspired by actress Janet Gaynor and was originally depicted with blond hair rather than the black bob she ultimately ended up with. Meanwhile, the dashing Prince, who was meant to embody debonair heroism, was influenced by the personality and roles of Douglas Fairbanks.

Walt wanted *Snow White and the Seven Dwarfs* to inspire true emotion in the audience, eliciting the full spectrum of emotion that was a trademark of the live-action feature, including slapstick comedy, passionate romance, anxiety-inducing suspense, and tearjerking tragedy. As a result, the primary antagonist of this animated film – the Queen – had to embody some of popular culture's most wicked and menacing villains rather than real-life actresses. Thus, when developing the personality of the Queen, Walt and his team determined that she be a mix of the manipulative and mad tyrant Lady Macbeth and the crafty, bloodthirsty Big Bad Wolf from Disney's "Three Little Pigs". To fool Snow White, the Queen would transform into an old hag, which hearkened back to the witches in *Macbeth* and had design elements from the drawings by German illustrator Hermann Vogel, who did art for some of the Grimm fairy tales in the late 1800s, including "Snow White".

While the dwarfs were originally depicted as "earthy and warty" to fit in with their natural surroundings, including their wilderness home and subterranean diamond mine, Lillian Disney was less than impressed, and their designs became more jovial and elderly as seen in the final film. Much like the protagonists of "Three Little Pigs", the seven dwarfs were characters who would all look relatively similar. To help audiences differentiate between them, Walt decided to give them distinct personalities with names that were apt descriptors. He knew that while the seven dwarfs were meant to be supporting characters, they would steal the show. In fact, his ideas for the dwarfs predated the first official treatment for the film, with Walt brainstorming some of the names and corresponding personalities prior to his 30 October performance. In one of his earliest outlines, Walt listed fifty potential names for the dwarfs, including "Weepy", "Dirty", "Hungry", "Flabby", and "Biggy-Wiggy". After going through several lists with the directors, the list of names was honed down to Doc, Happy, Sleepy, Sneezy, Bashful, Grumpy and Dopey.

This strong focus on each dwarf's distinctive personality required their movements, behaviours, and actions not only represented realistically but also exaggerated to bring comedic effect. True to form, the team of storymen, directors, and supervising animators used every tool and trick they had learned over the previous several years to bring the dwarfs to life. Shamus Culhane, a recent hire at the Walt Disney Studios and supervised by Ben Sharpsteen, was given the opportunity to animate the "Heigh Ho" sequence, when the dwarfs left their diamond mine and journeyed back to their cottage in the woods. Making sure to keep each dwarf's unique personality in mind while animating, Culhane spent six months painstakingly sketching the characters, assigning each of them a distinctive walk to make them more believable characters. He was particularly proud of his work on Dopey, who skipped several times in the sequence to try to get in step with his companions.

Early on, it was recognised that height played a part in how an individual walked and moved. Vaudeville performers with dwarfism were brought into the studio for observation. The artists watched how they walked, held themselves, and interacted with each other and with everyday objects to ensure they were accurately portrayed. Work was also done to give the dwarfs aged, flabby jowls that responded to real-world physics in an animated world, as well as accurate texture to cloth and hair.

In developing the characters of the dwarfs, inspiration was also taken from real-life individuals. In his early outline, Walt brainstormed actors who could provide voices for specific characters and whose mannerisms could be copied. For example, he suggested that Sleepy was inspired by and could be voiced by Sterling Holloway, a popular actor who would later go on to provide voices for characters including Mr. Stork from *Dumbo*, Kaa from *The Jungle Book*, and Winnie-the-Pooh. Popular radio personalities, characters, and gags were also chosen to depict the dwarfs, such as Buelow as Bashful, while Doc's rushed misappropriations and verbal stumblings were a popular radio trope.

To do this effectively, Walt assigned some of his best animators to bring the dwarfs to life, and some even provided lectures to the in-betweeners and cleanup artists. For example, Bill Tytla, who had been assigned to animate Grumpy, highlighted the importance of the accurate depiction of draped clothing and facial expression in a lecture given on 10 December 1936. He explained that when the realistic movement of a character's hands were paired with dialogue, it provided a more accurate representation of a monologue or interaction between two characters.

The artists responsible for animating Snow White's animal friends continued making observations of animal movement and behaviour, as well as studying books and diagrams of animal anatomy. Lectures were given by veteran artists to train those with less experience, and weekly trips were taken to a local zoo, where the animators would sit in front of the cages to sketch the inhabitants. A variety of creatures were also kept at the studio for reference, including ten parakeets who were kept in a cage, crowding the workspace of animators Milt Kahl, Milt Schaffer, and Eric Larson. A patio on the studio lot was enclosed and served as a makeshift menagerie for rabbits, squirrels, a turtle and a raccoon, all of which found their way into the forest scenes of *Snow White.*

Animals and individuals with dwarfism weren't the only live models used by the animators to help provide realism to the film's characters. These models were used primarily to provide visual reference for posture, motions, and movement. In watching how an individual twirls while dancing, walks angrily, or runs in fright, the artists were better able to bring life to their animated characters. Dorothy Ann Blank, a member of the studio's Story Department, provided a visual reference for the Queen, while Marjorie Belcher, who performed in ballets throughout Los Angeles, was the model for Snow White. Belcher, in particular, was asked to perform strange actions and dress in some odd outfits for the animators. In one instance, she was observed pushing through strands of rope hanging from a clothes-line to simulate Snow White pushing through hanging vines as she flees through the forest. In another assignment, she danced with a male partner, who was draped in a baggy overcoat as a reference for Snow White dancing with Dopey perched on Sneezy's shoulders in "The Silly Song".

Blank, Belcher, and the other live models weren't always available whenever the animators required reference for a particular movement or to study the accurate movement of cloth or hair. Instead, the studio began using the process of rotoscoping, or tracing still images of live-action film onto sketch paper or celluloid, to assist in the completion of the lifelike movements of a character or the realistic motion of hair and fabric.

Rotoscoping was an animation process that was nearly as old as the craft itself. Early versions of rotoscoping, known as chronophotography, were implemented by animation pioneer Eadweard Muybridge in the late nineteenth century, when he traced his famous *Horse in Motion* photographs onto metal discs. A few decades later, Max Fleischer improved upon the rotoscoping process by using it extensively in his *Out of the Inkwell* series, owning the exclusive rights to implement its use until 1934. Fleischer Studios co-owner, Dave Fleischer, was filmed dressed in a clown costume, dancing, running around, and interacting with various props. After the live-action reference film was complete, artists would project individual stills of Fleischer and trace them, providing unsettlingly lifelike movements for their series' main character, Koko the Clown. While not used as a time-saving technique, the Fleischers used rotoscoping to provide accurate and lifelike movement for all parts of a character's body, rather than trying to animate several different parts (i.e. the arms, legs, head, and face) freehanded and all at once.

Walt and many of his veteran animators considered the process "cheating", and instead chose to tape the live-action movements and behaviour of the character models for drawing reference later. Of particular help was the function of being able to examine the reference images frame-by-frame to see how difficult-to-animate objects moved, such as the folds of a woman's dress as she ran or the flowing of individual hairs as they blew in the wind. In some instances, artists would advance the frame forward and backward to see how an object moved, much in the same way that they rolled their individual sketches back and forth to ensure animated movements were correctly drawn. In some cases, individual still frames could even be blown up so that minute details could be examined more closely, like the ruffle of individual bird feathers or the way light reflected off a metal crown.

The rotoscoping process was an expensive undertaking for the Walt Disney Studios, who had already borrowed so much money from the Bank of America. Introducing any new filmmaking technology could be pricey, but rotoscoping required capital – both in terms of finances and equipment – to function well. Additional cameras for the filming of live-action reference were required, as well as the projectors and moviolas needed to reference the footage. Money was also needed to pay the additional camera operators, to pay for the film developing process, and to pay the models themselves. The bank, who was as wary as the rest of Hollywood about Walt's groundbreaking undertaking of an animated feature, agreed to finance a loan for the studio's rotoscoping process with Walt signing the studio over as collateral, as well as taking out second mortgages on the homes of both Roy and Walt.

Some artists, however, were so gifted at their craft, that they successfully completed their work without the assistance of rotoscope. Grim Natwick, who had been hired at Disney as an animator in 1934, was often given many of the female characters in the Silly Symphonies. As a result of his excellence in shorts like "The Cookie Carnival" and "Broken Toys", Walt assigned him the responsibility to be the lead animator for Snow White. The realism of the princess's movements, gestures, and mannerisms won Natwick rare praise from Walt, who was especially impressed with the minute movements of her fingers and hands, especially while she was talking. In one instance, while screening the Dailies, Walt was blown away by the accurately flowing swirls of Snow White's dress as she ran down the stairs. Standing up, he pointed the movement out to his artists, demanding that they use the rotoscope as well as the artist who had done the work on the dress. Natwick sat nearby, a smirk on his face: he had blatantly refused to use the live-action reference material of Marjorie Belcher in her flowing dress.

To bring these animated drawings to life and further encourage audience buy-in, it was crucial that fitting voices were found for the respective characters. Pinto Colvig, who had been on the Disney payroll as Goofy since 1932 and had also voiced some additional characters in Silly Symphonies including Practical Pig in "Three Little Pigs" and the main character in "The Grasshopper and the Ants", was brought on as Grumpy. Billy Gilbert, a radio performer known for his loud, dramatic sneezes, auditioned for and received the part of Sneezy after reading a piece about the dwarfs in *Variety*. Stage performer and film actress Lucille La Verne was given the part of the Queen and her alter-ego, the Old Hag, because of her experience playing the parts of old crones and stern mother-figures in many of her earlier films.

Perhaps most important to Walt was finding the correct actress for the film's heroine: someone who was innocent and virginal, sweet and joyful, who could not only deliver lines but also transition quickly into song. While it was hoped that the actress who voiced the princess had experience, Snow White was meant to be a young teenager, which meant that the performer also needed a voice that sounded like an adolescent girl.

Walt had a very specific vision for his film, and as a result wanted to be involved in the audition process to find the correct voice for Snow White. However, he knew that his presence in such an audition could be intimidating. A special intercom was wired with a hidden microphone placed in the audition room so that Walt could listen in from his office. Not only would this help the auditioning girls be more confident, but Walt could also be unbiased and not take the girls' looks or names into consideration.

Over the next several days, dozens of individuals auditioned for the role of Snow White, but Walt was unimpressed with all of them. Even celebrities auditioned for the part, including child actress Deanna Durbin, who had toured southern California as a pre-adolescent, singing in various venues and would go on to star in a number of short- and feature-length films in the 1930s. However, when Walt heard her fourteen-year-old voice through the speaker in his office, he judged it to be "too mature", guessing she was in her twenties or thirties. Instead, he wanted someone who had a soprano voice, bringing credibility to the idea that his princess was young and innocent.

Walt and his team began to feel discouraged and frustrated by the lack of success in finding Snow White's voice. Roy Scott, the studio's casting director, phoned a local vocal coach, Guido Caselotti, asking if any of the girls he worked with might be a good fit for the part. Caselotti's daughter, eighteen-year-old Adriana, had been quietly listening on the line in another room.

"What we're looking for is a fourteen-year-old girl who can speak like a child, but can sing in high notes," Scott explained to the singing teacher.

"Papa, what about me?" Adriana asked her father on the line, interrupting the conversation. She began to sing, trilling her voice in a high register.

"Oh, for heaven's sake. Get off the phone, Adriana. I'm speaking to someone about business," her father scolded.

"I know you are," she pleaded. "Please let me try out. Maybe I can get the part!"

Scott agreed. "Bring her down, Guido. You never can tell. Even if we don't have her do the lead, she might be able to do some other little part."

Shortly thereafter, Guido took Adriana to the Walt Disney Studio for her audition with Roy Scott and Frank Churchill. The two men reiterated the type of girl that they were looking for to fill the role of Snow White, highlighting that she should be no older than fourteen with the voice of a young girl and the skill of singing in higher registers. When they asked the auditionee for information about herself, Adriana fudged her age as seventeen, hoping that her soprano voice and singing talents would convince the casting and music director of her qualifications, regardless of the fact that she was nearly nineteen.

Churchill handed the girl a script with the lyrics of her auditioning song, "Someday My Prince Will Come", which defined the pining love that the princess had for the mysterious and handsome prince. In many ways, it would be this song which would define the overarching plot of the film and character of Snow White herself.

Churchill explained that he would play the musical accompaniment on the piano a few times so she could get the tune of the song before singing along. As he turned and walked away from Adriana, however, he was stopped in his tracks when she began to sing without the musical accompaniment, demonstrating her ability to sight-read the music.

Spinning on his heel, he looked in surprise at the girl before turning toward Scott. "My God!" he exclaimed. "She can sing *and* read music!"

Frank Churchill and Roy Scott weren't the only ones impressed by Adriana Caselotti's performance. With his special intercom system connecting the music room to his office, Walt heard the whole thing. Churchill practically sprinted to his boss's office to find out what he thought. As he passed through the door, Walt, who was sitting at his desk looked up at the music director and simply said, "That's our girl. That's our Snow White."

However, Walt Disney, who was never satisfied to settle for anything, continued to audition several more girls for the part of his inaugural princess. Before long, nearly 150 girls had auditioned for the part. After a year of additional auditions, Walt, Scott, and Churchill decided that Adriana Caselotti was perfect after all. They called her back to the studio and signed a contract with her, setting her start date for recording the songs and lines for the film. All of Adriana's voice work was recorded and finalised in a mere forty-eight days, for which she was paid $970 before being thanked and dismissed from work at the studio. In such a short period of time, she had been forever immortalised as the first princess in a long line of Disney royalty, the voice of the character who would change animation forever.

Walt Disney and his directorial team recognised that to create a feature film made up of animated drawings, filmmaking technology needed to improve in order to prove it was grander than simply a ninety-minute short. Walt expected a lifelike depiction of realism that showed landscapes, building interiors, animals, characters, the flora and fauna, and an adherence to the laws of physics and movement through space. While Bill Garity and his team were in the process of developing Disney's multiplane camera, the process had still not been perfected: experimentation was still being conducted by animators working on "The Old Mill", which would be released to theatres seven weeks before the premiere of *Snow White and the Seven Dwarfs*. As a result, it was used in a limited capacity for the film, such as when Snow White collapses in fear after running through the forest and when she discovers the dwarfs' cottage.

More importantly to the production of *Snow White* was the level of detail required to help the audience in their suspension of disbelief. This was a challenge, however, because a frame drawn, inked, and painted on a piece of celluloid measuring 10 by 12 ½ inches could only feature so much detail. Also, the smaller an object was in each drawing, the less detailed it would become. Altogether, this lack of detail and visual sharpness would prevent Walt's animated feature from feeling like the animated version of a live-action film.

To solve this problem, larger paper – and thus larger cels – were used to give the artists more space to draw and thus have an easier time drawing wide shots of the action or adding minute details, such as the folds in Snow White's dress, the texture of the Prince's hair, the wrinkles on the faces of the dwarfs, the feathers and stripes on the forest's quails and raccoons, or the arthritic fingers of the Old Hag. This new animation field measured 12 ½ by 15 ½ inches and was known technically as a "six-and-a-half field", increasing the size of the cels – and thus the animation field – by twenty per cent.

With the increased size of drawing space, modifications had to be made to the existing artist workspace, resulting in the construction of larger lightboxes and animation boards for the animators to draw on. The existing cameras and accompanying platens were initially built to accommodate the original sized cels of 10 by 12 ½ inches, but with the larger drawings, they needed to be modified to handle six-and-a-half field images. In some cases, such as in close-up shots, the larger drawings needed to be photographed and then shrunk down and printed to reduce the size of the paintings before being photographed for the film.

In addition to improving the technical aspects of filmmaking to provide greater detail, the artists also ran into some unique challenges in trying to authentically recreate details like the flickering of a candle, the ripple of water, or the movement of individual strands of hair that were otherwise taken for granted in the real world.

Cy Young and Ugo D'Orsi were also asked to develop a number of special effects for *Snow White and the Seven Dwarfs* to help provide as much realism to the animated feature as possible. With many of the scenes taking place in the forest, it made sense that the scenery include ponds, rivers, and streams. However, animating the realistic flow of water had always been a challenge to animators. Utilising practical effects, Young and D'Orsi took a piece of tin, polished it, and then pressed ripples into its surface to simulate the current of the water. The shiny metal also allowed for the reflection of the animation, helping to bring "life" to the water and realism to the scene.

At times, the animators, Special Effects department, and the camera department worked together to provide incredible work. In the sequence where Snow White sings "With a Smile and a Song", a young stag stands on the banks of a pond chewing on some grass. While the animation team provided the drawings and movement of the stag and the birds perching in his antlers, the photography department effectively utilised the multiplane camera, inserting trees and fallen logs in the foreground and a darkened forest behind Snow White's animal friend. The polished, rippled tin lay between the deer and the viewer, slowly moving to simulate the meandering current and small waves moving toward the shore while an inverted image of the animation is reflected below.

The Ink-and-Paint department also provided their expertise with providing realism to the human characters of the film. To make Snow White and the Queen more accurate representations of beauty standards of the time, the girls of Ink-and-Paint wanted to ensure that the expectations of their femininity translated well on-screen. The challenge in particular was depicting Snow White with girlish beauty that not only made her appealing and a beautiful role model to young teenage girls of the 1930s, but to still portray her as innocent and pure.

Early in 1937, research began to be conducted to determine what transparent stains or dyes could be used to create the blood-red lips that Snow White was known for, as well as a warm, rosy appearance of life over her pale skin. A pink-tinted stain was selected, and those artists assigned to the princess began to apply the colour to the front of the cel – which was typically the unpainted side – using cotton. Soon, to make the process easier, a special tool was developed and patented to do the same thing. So lifelike and realistic was the work by the Ink-and-Paint department on her blushing cheeks and rosy complexion that rumours began to circulate that the paint girls were applying their own makeup – particularly lipstick and blush – on the cels to give Snow White the required look. Loving the free publicity, the studio embraced this speculation and began to use it in their own publicity materials for the film.

As work ramped up on the film, which was due to premiere in late 1937, the studio needed a large staff to animate, cleanup, ink, and paint, as well as the support staff – such as storymen, camera operators, technicians, and even custodians and kitchen staff – to support such an effort. While studio staff numbered a little over one hundred when production on *Snow White* first began in 1934, by the time the film was complete in December 1937, 650 artists were on the payroll, with many of them working overtime – including on Saturdays and Sundays without pay – to ensure the film was completed on-time. In some cases, artists even brought bedrolls or cots into their offices so they could work through the night, taking short naps during breaks.

Even the Ink-and-Paint girls began to pull long shifts to ensure that work was completed in time for the December premiere. The studio began to mandate that employees work from 7-10 pm on Tuesday, Wednesday, and Thursday evenings. Many employees would stop working around 5 pm before grabbing dinner and returning to the studio for their remaining three hours. Not ready to go home after completing their work at 10 pm, many would head to the Tam O'Shanter, a local pub, to enjoy a few drinks and gossip. When some of the work seemed too much, contracts were signed with other animation studios, including Harman-Ising, to ink-and-paint cels to ensure the film was completed in time. Some of the most dedicated girls even slept overnight in the studio's women's lounge in case corrections were needed: the photography department was working through the night and would alert Ink-and-Paint if colours on the cels were not consistent or if the platen of the camera smeared the paint.

Work on *Snow White and the Seven Dwarfs* was completed in the eleventh hour. Approximately 362,000 cels had made it into the final film, with each individual drawing done by an animator and then traced on a cel and painted before being photographed. Thousands more sketches and cels were completed, but most of them did not make it into the final film because Walt believed they did not advance the overall plot. The total amount of paper used in sketching the film would have measured 500 miles if stacked side-by-side. The 750 studio employees assigned to the project spent nearly 44,000 hours of work on the film during the three years of production.

The film itself cost $1,488,423, which was nearly six times more than the initial budget of $250,000. Every time Walt and Roy requested that the loaning institution increase the film's budget, Bank of America became more and more indignant. Finally, Joseph Rosenberg, an executive for the bank who dealt with providing loans to Hollywood's movie studios, resisted Disney's request for additional funds. Roy, who had experience dealing with bankers because of his role at the studio as well as previous experience working at a bank in Kansas City, suggested that Walt show Rosenberg part of the film. Walt, who was very proprietary about his work, refused, because the film wasn't finished. Roy then asked his brother to show the bank a combination of completed animation and unfinished pencil sketches. Walt relented, understanding that the future of his film was at stake.

One afternoon soon after, Walt hosted Rosenberg in the studio's small projection room and showed him a rough cut of the film. Walt, embarrassed by the unfinished nature of the animation and the film's soundtrack, closely watched for the banker's reaction: but his features gave nothing away. Walt, who was usually prepared for anything, felt incredibly anxious. When the screening finished, Walt personally walked the investor, who made small talk, to his car. As Rosenberg got into his car, he finished their time together with pleasantries and closed the door. Walt's heart sank as he turned to walk back to his office – only to hear the car door opening again behind him before Rosenberg's voice called him back. Walt looked around expectantly.

"Mr. Disney, that thing is going to make you a hatful of money." Closing his door, Rosenberg settled himself in his car and drove away.

As the premiere drew closer, the Walt Disney Studios began to provide an increasing amount of official publicity for the film. To create interest for the film, the studio produced several supplemental materials and consumer goods. Walt recognised the talents of many in his accomplished staff, giving them specific tasks to assist in the publicity. For example, sketch artist Ferdinand Horvath illustrated a Snow White children's book and comic strip, while Gustaf Tenggren was asked to design the film's official movie poster. Members of the artist team were even assigned the roles of designing and illustrating displays for department store windows during the 1937 Christmas season, as well as licensed products including children's tea sets, paper dolls, board games, and more.

With *Snow White and the Seven Dwarfs* being such a groundbreaking effort, several articles in newspapers and magazines were focused on its producer, studio executive Walt Disney. While many Americans were very familiar with Mickey Mouse and some of the Silly Symphonies and likely knew the Disney name, few of them were very aware of the studio's founder. These articles sought to change all that, conducting "exclusive" interviews with Walt and Lillian, conducting personality pieces, and even writing about their marriage and home life.

Walt Disney quickly became such a notable person, that it was even decided by the studio to include him in the film's trailers: after an unseen narrator explained the premise of *Snow White* while cels and still images were shown, with descriptions given for Snow White and the dwarfs. The narrator then suggests that "Walt Disney tell you about them himself," with the camera coming to rest on Walt sitting at his desk in a tweed sport coat, the collar of his cream dress shirt thrown open to reveal a grey scarf around his neck. Four inch tall painted maquette figurines of the dwarfs sat in front of Walt, as he described their personalities, touching each maquette in turn. The thirty-five year old movie executive was quite nervous in front of the camera, there's a slight tremor of nervousness in his hands as he lifted the figures, and a very serious demeanour in his presentation, very different to the kindly "Uncle Walt" persona that he would portray later in his career on the studio's television programmes.

Not all of the advance publicity for *Snow White and the Seven Dwarfs* was positive, and much of it had malicious intent. For example, when many journalists disparaged Walt's efforts, Gilbert Seldes of *Esquire* came to his defence. To silence detractors, Seldes suggested that he wanted to prove whether or not ninety minutes of animation was doable for a person. To test his curiosity, Seldes scheduled and sat through a series of ten consecutive Disney shorts in September 1937. The results of the experiment were favourable: "I should say that you can, with excitement unabated, look at these pictures for about an hour and a half which is longer than the average feature picture", Seldes wrote. Regarding the assertion that a feature animated film would have detrimental effects on the human body, the journalist explained that "[t]here are moments of extreme physical exhaustion if you abandon yourself to laughter." He finished explaining his anticipation for *Snow White and the Seven Dwarfs* by arguing that "the Disney technique is quite subtle; there are moments of surprise and moments of pure physical beauty spaced in between the great climaxes of hilarity."

Shortly before the official film premiere of *Snow White and the Seven Dwarfs* which was to take place on 21 December, the studio scheduled a secret screening premiere at Los Angeles' Fox Pomona Theater. Attendees entered the theatre under the assumption that they had purchased tickets for a different film, but were soon silenced by the hand-drawn majesty of Disney's newest film. Studio stenographers were scattered throughout the audience with timers, taking notes on the emotional response of those sitting around them. Initial reactions were positive, while Walt, ever the perfectionist, was embarrassed by some of the animation. While most of his complaints would go unresolved due to the short span of time before the film's official premiere, a few weeks allowed for the opportunity to make some minor fixes and reshoots of the offending cels.

Snow White and the Seven Dwarfs had its premiere at one of Los Angeles' top film premiere venues, the Carthay Circle Theatre, on the evening of Tuesday 21 December 1937. Crowds lined up along San Vicente Boulevard to catch a glimpse at the celebrities due to attend the show, as well as take in the impressive sights and entertainment the Walt Disney Studios had lined up for this red letter evening. The theatre's tall, octagonal, whitewashed belltower was lit with spotlights, drawing the eyes of Hollywood on the festivities. A few steps away from the theatre's entrance sat a small recreation of the dwarfs' cottage with a working water wheel, large enough to be a child's playhouse. Costumed characters, such as the dwarfs, as well as Mickey Mouse, Minnie Mouse, and Donald Duck, milled around the crowds, posing for photographs. A gallery of background art and cels used in the film were also on display for attendees to enjoy.

While top celebrities and film stars were often invited to major film premieres, most of Hollywood showed out for Walt's landmark film.

Marlene Dietrich, Carole Lombard, Cary Grant, Ginger Rogers, Shirley Temple, and others filled the rows of the auditorium to witness Walt's accomplishment. Even one of Walt's film heroes, silent film star and co-founder of United Artists, Charlie Chaplin, was in attendance. Everyone was smiling for the public, but once past the gauntlet of photographers, the countenances of the many movie stars, directors, and studio executives changed: they were prepared to judge the film they were about to see and witness the downfall of the thus-far great Walt Disney Studios.

Employees of the Walt Disney Studios, particularly the film's lead animators and directorial team, were also invited to the premiere, with reserved seats at the rear of the theatre. They had been invited not only for pleasure – as a celebratory thank you for all their hard work on the film – but also for work purposes: much like the studio stenographers attending the secret showing at the Pomona, attendees from the studio were expected to pay attention to and take note of audience reactions so that future projects could be improved upon.

While many of the individuals who had exerted great influence on the production of *Snow White and the Seven Dwarfs* had received invitations and were in attendance at the premiere, the two individuals who were perhaps most important in bringing the film's characters to life had been overlooked on the guest list. Adriana Caselotti and Harry Stockwell, who had provided the voice of the Prince, did not receive invitations. Stockwell reached out to his co-star, suggesting that they attend the premiere, even though they had not received a ticket from the studio nor acquired one through advance sales. Stockwell went on to explain that as influential as they had been to the film, they didn't need tickets: he planned to simply walk into the Carthay, find a seat, and enjoy the film.

On the evening of the premiere, the pair executed their plan. As they walked up to the theatre, the girl at the door asked for their tickets. Emboldened by the courageous plan of Harry Stockwell, Adriana straightened her posture, looked the ticket girl in the eye, and confidently told her "I am Snow White and this is Prince Charming!"

The theatre employee, taking her job seriously, scoffed. "I don't care if you're the Witch. You're not getting in without tickets." Caselotti and Stockwell stepped off to the side to allow those behind them to enter the theatre. Suddenly, the ticket taker looked away from her post, distracted for the moment. The two voice actors looked at each other, smiled, and quickly snuck past the girl and into the theatre. The theatre employee saw the quick movement out of the corner of her eye and, turning, saw the two young people scampering past her station. She yelled for them to stop, abandoning her post to give chase, unfortunately losing the laughing couple as they climbed the stairs to the balcony, disappearing into the dimly lit theatre.

As audience members filed into the theatre, ushers handed them a program, which for the first time identified a Disney film as the headliner. It was also the first time that a Disney film was accompanied by supporting shorts rather than the work of the studio serving as an accompaniment to a feature film. The evening began with the latest instalment of RKO's newsreel, "The March of Time", with features on a loophole in Britain's gambling laws, the frustrations of Alaskan fishermen about Japanese competition, and a highlight of recent research findings on cardiac health. Next came a live-action short film, MGM's "A Friend Indeed", featuring Sparky, a German Shepherd dog who was trained to assist his blind owner, a country doctor, as he made his medical rounds.

With the first title cards flashing across the screen, Walt Disney's dream for a feature-length animated film were realised. Recognising that it was impossible to give on-screen credit to the more than seven hundred staff who worked on the film, Walt included a short message as part of the film's introduction, giving his "sincere appreciation to the members of my staff whose loyalty and creative endeavor made possible this production." This was the only recognition that some of the artists would ever receive for a Disney animated film – especially the women who worked so hard as part of the Ink-and-Paint Department.

Beginning with live-action opening of a gilded storybook and the title cards which provided the film's exposition, the audience immediately suspended their disbelief and found themselves sucked into the animated world of a jealous queen, a princess on the run, a gallant prince, and seven bumbling and hilarious dwarfs. Throughout the film, Walt and his staff saw the audience – who had been scornful and refused to take an animated feature seriously – laughing continuously. While audiences typically applauded at the end of a major motion picture premiere, this audience was applauding after individual *sequences*. Many in the audience were even brought to tears at the death of Snow White and the grieving of the dwarfs, forgetting that the story was a mere collection of drawings. As the film came to a close, with Snow White and Prince Charming standing on the hill as the camera zoomed in toward the castle in the clouds, the audience cheered. The screen faded to black, returning to the opening storybook, the last page reading "...and they lived happily ever after." A chorus of voices singing the final lyrics of "Someday My Prince Will Come" swelled, accompanied by booming timpanis as the book closed and the screen faded to black.

The crowd immediately stood to their feet, giving *Snow White and the Seven Dwarfs*, this film which had been so prematurely disparaged by many in attendance, a lengthy standing ovation. After several minutes of clapping, cheering, and celebrities gushing in awe about the storytelling and artistry of the film, the Carthay Circle Theatre slowly began to clear out. Those gathered outside the theatre were shocked to find many of the attendees leaving with large, dark sunglasses covering their eyes: it was late at night and the December sky was dark. Most of these curious onlookers didn't realise that this was intended to hide the red, swollen eyes and runny makeup from the tears shed over the princess's near-demise.

A few hours later, with the publishing of the morning newspapers, the reviews of "Walt's Folly" -both positive and negative – began pouring in. The local newspaper, *The Los Angeles Times,* described *Snow White* as "revolutionary…true poetry…a great screen contribution." The Carthay Circle Theatre also ran an advertisement on 22 December, featuring Grumpy, Doc, Happy, and Sleepy talking to one another, with one asking "Did you see all those people last night?" The ad went on to encourage readers to call York 7144 to make their reservations and purchase tickets to see the film during Christmas week.

Punch was disappointed, stating that Disney's *Snow White* had bastardised the original Grimm story. *Variety* perfectly summed up the emotional response of the premiere's audience, when it explained that "[s]o perfect is the illusion, so tender the romance and fantasy, so emotional are certain portions when the acting of the characters strikes a depth comparable to the sincerity of human players, that the film approaches real greatness."

Reviews were also reported over the next several months, as the general public had the chance to see the film. After an unprecedented five-week run at Radio City Music Hall, the *New York Herald Tribune* described the studio's first feature that the studio's first feature "belongs with the few great masterpieces of the screen…[it is] one of those rare works of inspired artistry that weaves irresistible spell around the beholder…

[*Snow White and the Seven Dwarfs*] offers one a memorable and deeply enriching experience." *Time* gave high praise, saying that *Snow White* was "as exciting as a western, as funny as a haywire comedy, as sad as a symphony", a line that would be used in a trailer for the film as it traversed the nation. The *Lincoln Heights Bulletin-News* of Los Angeles wrote that "Hollywood says that Disney went considerably beyond the goal of simply filming a popular, sure-fire story. It is generally conceded that the Disney studios worked overtime to embellish "Snow White" with every conceivable photographic effect." Art critic Jean Charlot, described Disney's newest characters as something beautiful, comparing Doc to Raphael's Virgin.

Even the peers of Walt Disney – studio executives and producers alike – had praise for the studio's masterpiece. In an article about Walt featured in *Time*, Warner Bro. producer Leon Schlesinger commented that most animation executives were "businessmen…[but] Walt Disney's an artist. With us, the idea with shorts is to hit 'em and run. Disney is more of a Rembrandt." Some were jealous of their rival's success. Max Fleischer argued that Walt's film was "too artsy", focusing more on the spectacle rather than the comedy and narrative that made animation so popular. Leon Schlesinger, who produced Looney Tunes and Merrie Melodies for the Warner Brothers, disagreed with Fleischer, also describing Disney as "a Rembrandt."

The Academy of Motion Pictures Arts and Sciences agreed with those who praised Walt Disney's *Snow White and the Seven Dwarfs.* The 10th Academy Awards Ceremony took place at Los Angeles' Biltmore Hotel on the evening of 10 March 1938. Unfortunately, no category then existed for a feature-length animated film in the lineup for the Academy Awards, so *Snow White* was up against the highest grossing films of 1937 which were nominated for Outstanding Production (now known as Best Picture), including *Captains Courageous, The Good Earth, A Star is Born,* and *The Life of Emile Zola,* which won the award. The Walt Disney Studio did receive recognition at the 1938 Academy Awards, however: *Snow White and the Seven Dwarfs* was a nominee for Best Music (Scoring), losing to *One Hundred Men and a Girl*, and the studio's Silly Symphony "The Old Mill" won the award for Best Short Subject, Cartoon.

While Walt likely walked away from the 10th Academy Awards disappointed that he had gone unrecognised by his peers for this groundbreaking accomplishment, these disappointments were dashed the following year at the 11th Academy Awards of 23 February 1939, which also took place at the Biltmore Hotel. In addition to four of the five nominees for Best Short Subject, Cartoon coming from the Walt Disney Studios (with "Ferdinand the Bull" chosen as the winner), Walt was called on stage to receive a Special Award.

Awaiting him was child star, Shirley Temple, standing next to a table upon which was an award veiled by a dark cloth. Trying to seem joyful at the honour of the award while feeling uncomfortable about his recognition before his peers, Walt plastered a smile on his face and put his hands on his hips. Temple encouraged him not to be nervous, and explained that "the boys and girls in the whole world are going to be very happy when they find out that the daddy of Snow White and the seven dwarfs, Ferdinand, Mickey Mouse and all the others is going to get this beautiful statue." As the child star presented her short monologue, Walt realised that her presentation and speech was saying that his peers in the Academy believed that the Mickey Mouse and Silly Symphony shorts and *Snow White and the Seven Dwarfs* were made solely for children.

As Temple pulled the velvet cloth off the award, she gasped, asking Walt, "Isn't it bright and shiny?" Designed by Academy president Frank Capra, the award was a full-sized Oscar statuette standing tall on a cylindrical wooden pedestal, while seven miniature Oscars stood in a line on descending steps. The award recognised that *Snow White and the Seven Dwarfs* was "a significant screen innovation which has charmed millions and pioneered a great new entertainment field for the motion picture cartoon."

Mustering all the enthusiasm he could, Walt responded with "Oh, beautiful!"

"Aren't you proud of it, Mr. Disney?"

Walt chuckled. "Well, I'm so proud I think I'll bust." Not wanting to discourage the young performer who seemed legitimately excited for the producer, and feeling truly honoured for the recognition nonetheless, he went on to say that "I think that Mickey Mouse and Ferdinand and Snow White and all the dwarfs are going to be very proud that *you* presented it."

"I'm glad," Shirley blushed.

Snow White and the Seven Dwarfs did indeed have a significant impact upon the animated film industry, as well as American and global culture in general. While the final budget for the film was approximately $1.5 million, the film made between $8 million and $8.5 million in box office sales worldwide, making $2 million in the United Kingdom alone. America continued to celebrate the characters of Walt's first film, which had quickly become a part of national culture. Kay Kamen secured additional licensing deals for *Snow White*-themed merchandise, including "Snow White Make-up" designed by cosmetics entrepreneur Helena Rubeinstein, and the licensing of the dwarfs in an advertisement for Boston and New York's gentlemen's clothier, the Rogers Peet Company. Marjorie Belcher, who had served as the live-action model for Snow White, was dressed up as the princess and made several tour stops for public events, including participating in the Tournament of Roses Parade on 1 January 1938. Belcher, in full costume, sat on a Disney-sponsored parade float depicting the dwarfs' forest cottage and larger-than-life mushrooms, while actors dressed as the dwarfs waved at the crowds from the front and sides of the float.

The film also had a huge international impact and was dubbed into ten different languages, including French, Spanish, Italian, German and Scandinavian. In addition to recording new soundtracks, alterations were made to the film itself, with new names given to some of the dwarfs to accurately translate into the new languages, as well as additional art to replace the American version. For example, the dwarfs' Italian names were redrawn onto their beds in the scene where Snow White explores their cottage. In some cases, even background art was altered to be more appropriate to the regional differences.

Snow White and the Seven Dwarfs was not just an achievement in the motion picture industry: it was also recognised as an artistic achievement. The Courvoisier Art Gallery of San Francisco signed a contract with the Walt Disney Studios to display and ultimately sell work from *Snow White and the Seven Dwarfs*, as well as a stipulation to sell work from later Disney films as well. Approximately 7,000 cels were chosen for sale. The success of Courvoisier's contract led to travelling shows of Disney cels and background paintings from *Snow White and the Seven Dwarfs,* which would find their way onto the walls of galleries around the nation.

Walt Disney and his studio had done it again. Despite the preconceived judgement and assessments of the critical experts and royalty of Hollywood, *Snow White and the Seven Dwarfs* was anything *but* a folly.

BURBANK

Snow White and the Seven Dwarfs brought incredible success to the Walt Disney Studios. The profit gained from ticket sales over the following year after its premiere at the Carthay Circle allowed Walt to pay off the debts owed to Bank of America, as well as put a few million dollars into the bank as a cushion.

Walt and Roy decided that one of the first ways they would spend their new-found wealth was to honour their parents, Elias and Flora Disney, who had been living in Portland, Oregon with their older brother Herbert. They encouraged their parents to pack up and move the nearly 1600 kilometres to California, citing the better weather for health purposes and the opportunity to spend more time with their young grandchildren, including Sharon Mae Disney who had been adopted by Walt and Lillian shortly after her birth in 1936. The brothers used some of the money they earned from the success of *Snow White* to hire a contractor to construct a new home for their parents, located at 4605 Placedia Avenue in North Hollywood. A few weeks after Elias and Flora moved into their new home, Flora complained that the furnace in their home was not working correctly. Wanting to take care of his beloved mother, Walt asked some of the studio repairmen to go and look at the furnace, and two separate trips were made with no success. When she was asked by her daughter Ruth, who was still living in Portland with Herb, how she liked their new home, Flora gushed. She called the new home gifted to her and Elias as "wonderful", raved about the beautiful California weather and was clearly ecstatic about being close to Roy and Walt once again. Her only complaint was the furnace, which no one could seem to fix, and the resulting gaseous fumes which were occasionally perceptible.

Walt loved having his parents nearby, especially his mother: he had always been close to Flora, and the two had enjoyed a special relationship when he was a boy. When Elias had become frustrated, targeting his ire on his youngest son, Flora had always come to his rescue and diffused her husband's anger. Thus, it was incredibly special for Walt when he, Roy, and their families got to enjoy Thanksgiving 1938 with Flora and Elias, likely for the first time since they had all been together in Chicago in the early 1920s. The day was full of delicious food and joyous laughter. The film producer particularly loved seeing his parents lovingly doting on his children. As the family members parted at the end of the day, Walt wished that their time together didn't have to end.

On the following Saturday, 26 November 1938, less than forty-eight hours later, these wonderful emotions were shattered by a phone call. While performing her daily chores, Flora had taken a break and excused herself to the bathroom. After several minutes, Elias realised that she had not returned and went to check on his wife. After several attempts to elicit a response by knocking on the bathroom door, Elias let himself in and found Flora unconscious on the tile floor. Collapsing to the floor to render help, he immediately found himself dizzy and weak and called out for help for both himself and his wife. The housekeeper who had been hired to assist the couple, Alma Smith, ran to the doorway, and quickly became dizzy and nauseated herself. She stumbled out of the house, yelling for help from anyone nearby. A neighbour heard Smith's cries and joined her in the home. Together the pair dragged Elias and Flora out of the house and into the fresh air of the yard before calling for medical help, and phoning Roy and Walt to inform them of the situation. The clean air revived Elias slightly, but Flora did not regain consciousness: she succumbed to carbon monoxide poisoning as a result of the still unrepaired furnace. She was interred within the Great Mausoleum at the nearby Forest Lawn Cemetery in Glendale.

Walt was inconsolable at the loss of his dear mother. He blamed himself: he was the one who had suggested that Elias and Flora move from Portland to Los Angeles, had built the home for them, and had asked the repairmen under the company's employ to inspect the furnace rather than a professional. Elias was also immediately changed by the loss of a wife who had been his helpmate, seemingly completing him by complementing everything that he wasn't and ensuring he was always taken care of. Elias had always been the sternly moral backbone of the pair and had been a hard worker and provider, while Flora had been the homemaker and softer, more rational member of the couple who served as an intermediary between Elias and his children. The vacuum caused by Flora's death immediately dulled the sharpness of Elias' perceived self-sufficiency and also his harshness, leading him to rely upon his sons for emotional and tangible support, ultimately leading to a closer relationship between them for the first time. Roy in particular took it upon himself to support his father and younger brother, assuring them both that Flora's death was no one's fault, but rather a tragic accident.

To distract himself, Walt began pouring himself into his latest project: growing the studio. The grand surplus of finances from *Snow White and the Seven Dwarfs* encouraged Walt to dream about what could come next. As the premiere approached for the film, the studio announced that a new feature would be released every year, with production soon beginning on its next feature film, one based upon Carlo Collodi's tale of a little wooden puppet. Both the fanfare of the public and the accolades of the press had convinced Walt that true money was in animated features, and development began on a few potential stories, including *Pinocchio* and *Bambi.*

But space had become tight at Walt Disney's Hyperion studio. The staff had outgrown the buildings on the studio lot, with work spilling over the two-metre-tall walls and out of the front gate: sketching was being done across the street from the studio, while some artists worked at leased bungalows located in the shadows of John Marshall High School, perched atop a nearby hill a half mile from the studio. They would need more space to accommodate the unique needs of the Disney staff, as well as ensure there was an abundance of space for the growing number of employees needed to work on multiple features, in addition to the Mickey Mouse and Silly Symphonies shorts.

Initially, an idea was floated that the studio should simply acquire land across Hyperion Avenue from the existing lot, since a handful of structures there were already being used in animation production. To ensure the safety of the artists and employees, a tunnel would be built beneath the road, connecting the two halves of the studio. However, Walt wanted something more up-to-date and uniform, as several structures had been added to the original building at the studio – which was now decades old – and many others had been moved from offsite to accommodate new or expanded departments. Looking ahead, it was also decided that more space was necessary, and that the Hyperion studio was not designed with animation in mind, often resulting in creative solutions to allow for the prevalence of natural lighting, preservation of film stock, and the mixing and curing of celluloid paints.

The brothers began searching greater Los Angeles to find a suitable location for the Walt Disney Studios to call home. A fifty-one acre piece of land was identified along Buena Vista Street and between Alameda and Riverside Drive in the Los Angeles suburb of Burbank, which had once been owned by the Burbank Department of Water and Power before being converted into a polo pitch. On 31 August 1938, the studio placed a deposit of $10,000 on the land, which had a total cost of $100,000.

Vacant land was not useful to Walt Disney unless a studio was built upon it. A vision of what he desired with dozens of ideas, including architectural style and how to streamline production, filled his mind, but Walt was not equipped to design the layout of a new studio lot or draw the blueprints and elevations of individual buildings. He needed someone who could take all of his ideas, as well as the practical needs of an animation studio, and create a campus which left opportunities for future growth, preventing the potential unplanned additions and expansion that had happened at the Hyperion studio.

With the growth of his production schedule in the early 1930s, Walt had utilised many of the management and production habits of early twentieth century industrialists like Henry Ford, namely scientific management and the assembly line system. The studio had been organised into various departments with experts focusing their efforts on their particular field such as inking and painting cels, animating, sound production, photography, and editing. He also ensured a proper workflow, with a specific order to the filmmaking process: the story team would draft an initial treatment, with some members drawing conceptual art. These treatments and concepts would then be passed on to the directors, who would hone the story and determine the specific art design for the film, giving instructions and assigning sequences to lead animators. The lead animators would animate the major frames, with inbetweeners and cleanup artists doing the rest of the work. When that was done, the sketches would be sent to the Ink-and-Paint girls, who would trace the drawings on cels and fill them in with coloured paint, before being sent to photography to capture the stills to bring the drawings to life. Unfortunately, with the seemingly random growth of the studio and its lot, departments were put up wherever there was space, or in some cases housed off-site, with the workflow often criss-crossing the lot. This wasted a lot of time and, in an industry where time is money, held up the process of animated film production. Thus, with the designing and construction of a new lot for the Walt Disney Studios, Walt hoped to remedy this problem.

Walt wanted his studio to be uniform in architectural design, looking to the popular architectural styles of the day. He was particularly interested in Streamline Moderne, which was a popular style of the 1930s, reminiscent of ocean liners and trains: sleek, curved rather than straight surfaces, stripes to simulate motion, and a prevalence of steel railings such as those on the decks of ships. He also wanted the studio furniture to be custom to the studio and, while still being functional pieces for the specific needs of the animators, also fit into the larger story being told by the design of the new studio.

The perfect candidate was Karl Emanuel Martin Weber, who went by his nickname "Kem," a combination of his initials. Weber, a German immigrant who had dabbled in architecture at San Francisco's Panama-Pacific Exposition of 1915 before working as a furniture draughtsman at Los Angeles' Barker Bros., was a believer that buildings and their accompanying furnishings should be "good to look at, practical, and affordable", and believed that the best spaces had uniform design in their exterior and interior designs and accompanying furniture and fixtures, a concept known as "Holistic Design." He had also contributed to the film industry, designing sets for films on the studio lot of the Paramount-Publix Corporation.

Walt was sold. He quickly hired Weber as the supervising chief designer for the new Burbank studio. Of course, just like every other major project undertaken by the Walt Disney Studios, Walt himself was very involved, often providing the designer with his own ideas and, at times, advising that Weber change drawings if a feature didn't meet his hopes or vision.

To be most effective, the new studio lot would need to support an effective workflow through the logical placement of buildings to best support the animation and filmmaking process. Small models of each building were produced, allowing the executives to move them around, study, then discuss which layout was best.

Walt often brought his top artists into meetings with Weber and his team so they could provide input on what they believed would work best. One discussion revolved around the transport of sketched frames from the animation building to the Ink-and-Paint department where they would be traced and coloured onto the cels. What would happen, it was suggested, if southern California experienced a rare rainstorm? All of the drawings on thin sketch paper would be ruined, wasting valuable time and money. The solution was a tunnel which ran below B Street, better known by studio employees as Minnie Avenue, which would allow for the quick, cool, and dry transfer of materials between the two buildings. From there, the completed cels could be easily transported to the Camera department for photography and the Cutting department for the editing of film which were organised sequentially in the same block of buildings.

One brilliant design idea that Walt suggested regarded the Animation building. Walt Disney had firsthand experience as an animator beginning in the early 1920s before handing production over to more talented artists – like Ub Iwerks – while he took over the creative, management, and production duties of his films. As a result, in designing a new studio, he insisted that the three-story Animation building be oriented north-south to allow for as much natural light as possible to aid the drawing process. To ensure as many artists were able to take advantage of the sunlight as possible, he insisted that the building be shaped like a double-H, with a total of eight wings with artist offices looking into narrow courtyards. Unfortunately, the north-facing offices rarely, if ever, received direct sunlight. Instead, specially-designed horizontal shutters were designed for the windows, controlled by an interior crank so office occupants could control how much light entered the office or – in the case of the north-facing artists – angle them to guide light into the office.

The Animation building was also organised as a makeshift social ladder. On the bottom floor of the building were the animators, closest to the tunnel to the Ink-and-Paint building. On the second floor were offices of the directors, who had easy access to the animators on the floor below for instructional and supervisory duties. On the top floor was the Story Department, with Walt's office complex, known as Suite 3H, on the northeast corner of the building where he could easily pop into story meetings and provide his input and direction on upcoming films and shorts.

Walt also recognised the importance of including a number of unique amenities to reward his star employees and keep up morale. The design of the studio allowed for an abundance of green space and athletic fields, reinforcing the joyful camaraderie and friendly competitiveness that had existed at the studio on Hyperion. A gymnasium with equipment was also provided for employees to let off steam after a long day of work. An excellent restaurant called the Coral Room was near the front of the studio lot, and even provided room service-style delivery of snacks, beverages, and meals to those who were unable to step away from their desk due to pressing deadlines or personal motivation. Recognising the limited space available for screening the Dailies at his current studio, Walt made sure this new lot included a larger theatre, which could hold an audience of 419 individuals.

One notable feature of the Burbank Studio was the inclusion of a central heating and air conditioning system, which operated in a plant occupying its own building. Co-planned by Walt, Bill Garity, and a handful of technicians from General Electric, this new cooling system posed a handful of challenges: not only would this revolutionary system need to create a comfortable working environment for studio personnel, but it would also need to be quiet enough in spaces like the dialogue and music recording studios. This new system would also need to ensure air purity through the collection of dust, ensuring that artist sketches, the Ink-and-Paint lab, finished cels, and the Camera department would not be "polluted," as dust was considered a perennial enemy of the film industry. Throughout the process of design and implementation, an informal slogan was created to remind all involved how important it was that the system "Keep it clean!"

While the heating system was powered by two 190 HP gas boilers, the air-cooling system utilised a process whereby air was drawn through vents and passed over cooled metal coils. This system sent cooled air to one of 158 zones across the twenty-three interior acres, automatically controlled by a series of sensors. Disney's powerful air conditioning helped reduce moisture inside the buildings to prevent the saturating of sketch paper and help the ink and paint on animation cels dry quicker. An interesting feature in the Animation building was a specially-designed fixture that served as both a ceiling light and Volocitrel air distribution unit, while special baseboards with small air ducts embedded in its louvred base were installed that served as exhaust for the system to ensure adequate circulation. In addition to the central air conditioning, additional air conditioning units were installed in some buildings, including the orchestra stage, theatre, dialogue stage, live action stage, and Coral Room. These locations were often used by studio personnel after working hours or on weekends; individual a/c units offered the opportunity to enjoy cooled air even when the central plant was not being operated.

In order to power the heavy-duty air conditioning and heating systems, the studio was also fixed with a unique electrical system, making the Walt Disney Studios, according to a 1940 article in the trade journal *Electrical West*, one that "employ[ed] electricity in more ways and newer ones than most any other theatrical enterprise" in Hollywood. Not only did this electrical network power the high-capacity heating and cooling processes, but it was also used in the technical production of films. The Camera department required a stable flow of electricity for its 70 kilowatt lamps in order to ensure consistent lumens and colour. Any sort of surge or sag of electricity could change the lights' colour temperature, leading to inconsistent photography, which would result in jumpy animation.

In addition to designing the studio lot, Walt tapped Kem Weber's experience designing furniture and fixtures to bring a cohesive style to the new Walt Disney Studios. The furniture used at the Hyperion studio was often hodgepodge: new desks, chairs, and tables were found throughout southern California and purchased for the studio as additional artists were hired. With an opportunity to start fresh, it only made sense to replace existing furniture with something personalised to the type of work done at the Walt Disney Studios that also matched the overall style of the complex as a whole.

Weber was asked to design furniture and workspaces for several different positions at the studio, all of which was built for the specific needs of each artistic role. For instance, a director's desk was designed with a desktop large enough to allow the film directors to spread out layout and barsheets. Desks for the artists of the Story Department were given smooth drawing surfaces and allowed for artists to draw with or without a backlight. Because much of their time was spent at their desks drawing concepts for characters or the settings of a particular sequence, a stainless steel bar was mounted to the bottom of the desk as a footrest, making the desk's set-up as comfortable as possible. Some of the artist furniture, such as those used by the animators, inbetweeners, and clean-up artists, featured drawers and cabinets for the storage of supplies or to keep track of previous sketches.

The Walt Disney Studios was a unique place, where artists worked long, hard hours. But as part of the animation industry, the artists often turned to humour, hobbies, or habits to manage stress and work exhaustion. Kem Weber took this into consideration as well when he designed his pieces. On some desks, such as those used by the animators, a metal cigarette holder was included, preventing a carelessly placed cigarette from lighting the valuable drawings on fire. Some artists adapted the desks to fit their own vices: it was quickly discovered that one of the drawers on the animator's desk was deep enough to hold a fifth of gin or whiskey. Some also realised that the metal handles of the drawers were curved in such a way that they could be used to open a bottle of beer at the end of a long day drawing.

One of the things Kem Weber was most known for in the furniture and design world was the Air Line Chair. First developed in 1929, Weber designed the Air Line Chair to be consumer-friendly: the pieces for the chair were boxed with accompanying instructions for consumer assembly, thus making the design-calibre chair more affordable. Following his typical style of Streamline Moderne, the Air Line Chair was inspired by modern aircraft design with sleek, curved lines reminiscent of motion. The seat was made of leather upholstery, while the chair's two-legged, cantilevered frame was constructed of laminated bows of wood.

While the Air Line Chair had not been a part of the design of the new Walt Disney Studios, Walt was impressed with the implications of the chair. He liked how comfortable it was and the fact that it was relatively lightweight, allowing it to be easily moved during meetings or in order to make room in the small offices of the animators. He was particularly impressed that the seat had a reclining feature, which he believed would be useful during story meetings, as many of his directors and storymen liked to recline or even lie on the floor while they discussed the plot and gags of the films in development. As part of outfitting the studio, Walt ordered two hundred Air Line chairs, which quickly became a coveted piece as the studio expanded.

Walt was a personal and professional beneficiary of the design work of Kem Weber on his series of offices, known as Suite 3H, which were installed on the northeast corner of the third floor of the Animation building. With Walt being extremely busy with his numerous projects, a receptionist and secretary sat outside his offices. Past these desks sat Walt's offices, which included formal and working offices, as well as private apartment space should the studio executive need to pull a late night working.

Within his formal office, Walt would receive any visitors, as well as conduct the official business of the studio. Thus, this room was meant to convey both the formality of an executive and the informality of hospitality. In addition to the heavy desk in the corner, the office had numerous sitting options including a few easy chairs and a sofa. A credenza behind his desk allowed for the display of awards, photographs, and knick-knacks of significance, while bookshelves lined one wall for the display of some of Walt's favourite volumes. One of the highlights of Walt's formal office, however, was a 1914 Knabe grand piano. This piano was modified by Weber to match the Streamline Moderne motif found in the other pieces of art and fixtures in the office suite, and was often used by visiting musicians or, in some cases, was used to accompany those auditioning for major singing parts in upcoming films.

Next door to his formal office was Walt's working office, where he spent the majority of his time. The room featured a smaller desk surrounded by a series of shelves which held scripts for upcoming films and a handful of books that Walt paged through for inspiration on upcoming projects. A small kitchenette was hidden behind sliding panels, allowing for drinks to be served to his work team as they discussed projects. Cupboards were also available to hold snacks, or in the case of his late nights, some of Walt's favourite meals including V-8 Vegetable Juice, Spam, and canned beans and chilli.

The majority of the move from the studio on Hyperion Avenue to the new studio in Burbank began on 26 December 1939 and lasted until 5 January 1940, and was coordinated by Marjorie Luske, wife of supervising animator Hamilton "Ham" Luske. Work was already underway on a number of upcoming films, including *Pinocchio, Fantasia,* and *Bambi*, and as a result, the move happened in stages. A few of the studio's departments moved to the new studio outside of the primary moving window, with the Camera building opening in August 1939 to begin the long process of photographing *Pinocchio*, while the Ink-and-Paint was the last department to move in May 1940 when they had completed their work on *Fantasia*. In fact, on the afternoon before the move, many of the Ink-and-Paint girls brought their supplies, smocks, and department equipment home so that they could bring it to the new studio when they reported for work the next morning.

Not all were keen on Walt's new studio lot. While walking his father through the studio during the early stages of the construction process, Walt was disappointed to find that Elias was less than impressed as he pointed out the excavations and foundations of the structures, explaining how the lot would be organised.

"Walter, what can it be used for?" Elias asked his son. Walt stammered that the campus was a studio for producing his animated shorts and features. Elias repeated his question, "Yes, but what can it be *used* for?" Walt was confused until he realised that his father was asking what practical use the buildings and lot would have should the studio go under and his son needed to sell the complex for capital. To appease his father, Walt suggested that the studio could be turned into a hospital, explaining that operating rooms could potentially be installed on the top floor of the buildings, while individual offices could be turned into hospital rooms. This seemed to reassure the elder Disney.

Walt's father wasn't the only one close to the family-owned company who had criticisms of the new $3.5 million film studio lot. Some within the film industry – including a handful of the studio's own artists – compared the new Burbank studio to a college campus, complaining that it was "too spread-out", too "office-like," and too sterile to inspire Disney's animated films. Others believed that the studio was *too* professional, unlike the seemingly random organisation of the Hyperion lot, and feared that this would take away the informality and camaraderie that the employees had enjoyed in the past.

Luckily this anxiety was in vain: the luxurious upgrade of the studio and the larger workspace provided more opportunities for fun, pranks, and foolishness as many studio employees had the impression there was less a sense of monitoring and supervision. Lunchtime athletics continued, and the prevalence of greenspace encouraged the staff to spend time outdoors during their breaks. Many of the animators in particular spent some time sunbathing, finding the roof of the Animation building the perfect place to get a tan. A call quickly came from St. Joseph's Hospital, located across from the studio on South Buena Vista Street: the nuns who worked at the hospital were both disturbed and amused to find that many of those sunbathing did so in the nude.

Expansion of the studio also meant that more employees were kept on to ensure that the expanded slate of animated shorts and features were completed, leading to the flourishing of new and existing relationships. Studio romances blossomed, particularly between the animators and the Ink-and-Paint girls, who often snuck off to discreet places on the studio lot for a romantic moment. The tunnel between the Animation and Ink-and-Paint buildings was so popular for these couples that it quickly gained the moniker "The Tunnel of Love." Aware of this, Walt often made his way down the stairwell from his office and turned on the light in the tunnel, watching the couples scatter like mice.

Others created new social or affinity groups. For example, animator Ward Kimball, who played trombone, soon learned a handful of his coworkers also played music in their spare time. Looking for a way to relieve the pressure of work deadlines during their lunch break, Kimball and several of these fellow musicians – including Fred Moore and Walt Kelly – would meet up in Moore's office or even the acoustically superior men's bathroom to play the swinging notes of jazz. Soon it was discovered that enough musicians existed at the studio to establish a full band.

Walt's plan to build a state-of-the-art, modern campus that was scientifically organised to maximise the production of animated films was a success. The latest technology, like the multiplane camera, and processes such as the ever-developing Ink-and-Paint department, had dedicated spaces which allowed them to flourish and improve the craft. The Walt Disney Studios was poised to successfully produce animated features and continue innovating to impact the film industry.

In order to ensure that this success was guaranteed, additional capital was required: the studio had a habit of taking all of the income from its films, including *Snow White and the Seven Dwarfs*, and immediately investing the totality into its next project, leaving little money in the bank. With several features in production, the studio had taken out loans, resulting in $4.5 million of debt. Troubles for the studio began shortly after the premiere of *Snow White*, while the studio was still being constructed. War was ramping up in Europe, potentially closing off many nations to Disney films, a market that had provided a good portion of the studio's income on its shorts and *Snow White*.

Roy, being the shrewd businessman that he was, called his younger brother into his office to discuss the studio's finances, a topic that Walt believed hampered his creativity and that of his staff.

"I've got to talk to you, kid. This is serious." Walt knew from his brother's tone that the following discussion would be one in which he would have little say. Roy began to outline the reality of the studio's debt and how, without box office success for the next few films, the Walt Disney Studios would go the way of its predecessors.

"How bad is it?" Walt asked.

"Four-and-a-half million, Walt," Roy responded, his face seeming to grow longer with dread. Walt burst out laughing, reminiscing about how difficult it had been more than a decade prior when banks wouldn't even loan them one thousand dollars. Roy chuckled at his brother's optimism. Coming to an agreement, Walt and Roy decided it was time to open the company to outside investors. The company had originally been incorporated in 1929, issuing ten thousand shares, with Walt and Lillian each getting 30% and Roy getting 40%.

With these new, greater financial burdens, the company was opened to outside investors in 1940, offering four million dollars' worth of non-voting stock, quickly reaching a price of $25 a share due to its success after *Snow White and the Seven Dwarfs*. While Walt, Lillian, Roy, and Edna had several thousand shares set aside for themselves, Walt and Roy also had special plans for 20% of the shares. In the past, the most efficient and talented artists at the studio received a bonus, with some receiving an additional $5000 per year for their work. With this new stock option, the brothers began awarding employees a corresponding number of shares based upon their term of employment. With the nation slowly coming out of the Great Depression and the anticipation that success would continue to smile upon the Walt Disney Studios, Walt and Roy believed that this would be a wonderful incentive to their hardworking employees.

Unfortunately, it did very little to diffuse the storm that was on the horizon.

FANTASOUND

While Walt Disney had been hurt by the comments that undertaking *Snow White and the Seven Dwarfs* was considered a folly, he was still confident that it would be successful, announcing before the film's premiere that several more were in production and would be released on an annual basis. Walt and his story team began to explore a number of different ideas, including those based upon Felix Salten's *Bambi, a Life in the Woods*, JM Barrie's *Peter Pan*, *Alice's Adventures in Wonderland* by Lewis Carroll, *Pinocchio* by Carlo Collodi, and Kenneth Grahame's *The Wind in the Willows*. With the success of *Snow White*, it was soon decided to focus the majority of efforts on developing and ultimately producing treatments of *Pinocchio* and *Bambi,* with the latter planned to be Disney's second animated feature.

Significant effort went into ensuring that the visuals of the two films were as accurate and realistic as possible. *Bambi*, while telling a fictional story from the perspective of woodland creatures who could speak, was intended to depict the characters as lifelike animals rather than anthropomorphised versions of animals like Mickey Mouse, Donald Duck, and Goofy. Extensive study was made of the primary animals featured in the film, such as skunks and rabbits. Two fauns provided by the Maine Development Commission were kept at the studio, with extensive observations made by both the Story department and animators to study their anatomy, behaviour, and movements. Walt insisted that the animals were kept in zoo-like enclosures rather than cages, as animals don't behave naturally when kept in isolated confinement. Italian painter, sculptor, and Chouinard instructor Rico Lebrun was paid to give a series of lectures about animal anatomy and advise the artists by assisting them in creating anatomically-accurate sketches of animal skeletal and muscular systems. When some artists struggled to accurately depict the proportions and lines of a deer, Lebrun suggested that they lightly sketch the animal's skeleton and then draw the animated character overtop. In one particularly memorable lecture, Lebrun sent for the corpse of a faun found along the Angeles Crest, dissecting the dead animal and explaining its musculature to his pupils; many of the animators found themselves feeling ill due to the stench of the mouldering carcass, while the lecturer seemed unfazed.

It was also important to the success of this animated nature film that the environment in which the events took place be as realistic as its characters, yet subdued as the overall tone of the film. For research, the studio sent animator Maurice Day to his native Maine with the film's script to his native Maine, where he and his friend Lester Hall spent several months sketching and photographing various elements of the Mount Katahdin forest. Photo studies were conducted of plants, including hazelnuts, oak trees, and marsh grasses; low angled details, such as pools of water, rotting logs, lichen, and animal tracks; and various locales that could inspire the background scenery of key sequences in the film, such as when Bambi takes his first steps, Thumper's burrow, and the well-known scene of the two friends skating on the frozen forest pond.

Day and Hall's sketches and photographs were brought back to Los Angeles, where they were studied by the layout men, animators, and background artists. One background artist in particular was captivated by the beauty of the Maine landscape: Tyrus Wong. Wong had been born in China in 1910, immigrating with his father to Sacramento, California at nine years old. While in junior high, he received a scholarship to attend the Otis Art Institute of Los Angeles due to his inherent artistic ability, excelling in watercolour and pastel drawing. In 1938, he was hired by Disney as an inspirational artist, and assigned to be part of the *Bambi* unit after Walt saw one of his freelance paintings featuring a stag. Walt was inspired by the atmospheric, almost impressionistic feeling of Wong's work, which often featured motifs inspired by art from the Chinese Song dynasty. Wong produced a number of inspirational watercolour backgrounds for *Bambi*, sacrificing detail for the dynamic atmosphere of the forest: he wanted audiences to feel as though they were more than mere observers, but rather participants of a life spent in the woods alongside the film's characters.

It was soon decided that *Pinocchio* would become the studio's second feature: while his artists had done a great job developing realistic characters and gorgeous settings for *Bambi,* it lacked a cohesive story based upon Salten's novel. In contrast, Walt felt that *Pinocchio*'s story was more straightforward, and while the story team took liberties in diverging from the source material, it was further along in development. Recognising after the success of *Snow White* that lightning never strikes the same place twice, Walt moved the *Pinocchio* unit into the offices next door to Suite 3H so he could keep an eye on production and be as hands-on as possible, giving the team instructions to "crank it out". He often walked past the *Pinocchio* offices on his way to the restroom, bursting in unannounced to get candid glimpses of the work being done, rather than a polished presentation by the team who was expecting him. So frequent were these impromptu visits that the artists blocked the door with a Moviola machine to prevent him from getting in.

Ever one to innovate and embrace progress, Walt wanted *Pinocchio* to be technically superior to its predecessor. The multiplane camera was used more extensively than in *Snow White*, showcasing all that was possible in the first several minutes of the film, as Jiminy Cricket introduced Gepetto's village. The camera was even utilised to simulate the point-of-view of Jiminy as he hopped toward Gepetto's workshop.

Walt also wanted to make good use of the Story department to develop well-rounded characters, which had contributed to the success of *Snow White*. Model sheets of Pinocchio, Gepetto, Jiminy Cricket, and others were provided so that the artists had reference drawings of the characters from all angles, as well as a representation of uniform proportions and different emotions. *Pinocchio* was a unique film, however, and presented challenges to the animators. Marjorie Belcher was once again hired as a live-action reference model for the film's Blue Fairy. Rather than simply performing the motions for her animated character, Belcher was also asked to recite the Blue Fairy's lines to assist animators in accurately drawing the fairy's speaking and facial expressions. However, not all of the characters could utilise a human reference. For example, the film's primary protagonist was a wooden marionette puppet, not a human, and as such needed to be animated differently.

Puppeteer-turned-Disney cameraman Bob Jones offered a solution: why not hire professional sculptors who could create small models of props and characters so the animators could observe them in the real world? Joe Grant, the head of the Story department, thought this was a fantastic idea, and established the Character Model department, hiring a handful of artists to sculpt three-dimensional maquettes, or small, painted models, from clay. Grant joined the effort, crafting a handful of maquettes and firing them in his backyard kiln. An eight-inch-tall Pinocchio marionette was built – complete with strings, crossbar, and hinged limbs – to study how a puppet hung from a puppeteer's hands, how the strings moved, and how the arms and legs of the puppet swung around without much control.

Character maquettes weren't the only things produced by the Character Model department. The team also built many of the items featured in Gepetto's workshop, including several cuckoo clocks, for reference. One model which made the production team especially proud was a miniature gypsy wagon driven by Stromboli as he transported the enslaved Pinocchio from show to show. Bob Jones constructed the miniature gypsy wagon and placed it on a treadmill covered in an uneven surface, to simulate the cobblestone streets depicted in the film. When the treadmill was turned on, the movement of the wagon was filmed on 35 mm film, then printed onto wash off relief cels to be drawn over by the animators and ink-and-paint girls.

Walt also conceived *Pinocchio* to be a "moving illustration", and as such made sure that caricature, realism, and storybook-esque backgrounds were employed. Day trips were taken to the Pacific coast to watch the swelling and crashing waves, to collect seashells, and even enjoy rides on glass-bottomed boats at Catalina Island to provide inspiration for the film's ocean scenes. The studio librarians also conducted abundant research for the artists, with one spending a day at nearby Ocean Park, enjoying "every show [and] every ride…cover[ing] the Midway from beginning to end", accompanied by a studio cameraman to capture every detail as reference for Pleasure Island.

The Story department and its inspirational artists were also called upon to create the European locales and minute details that would help place *Pinocchio* in a particular time and location. Albert Hurter was once again called upon to design the fixtures and furniture of the film, bringing grinning and grotesque faces to objects throughout Gepetto's cottage, as well as providing inspiration for many of the shop's cuckoo clocks. Gustaf Tenggren, who had so successfully helped bring an Old World feel to "The Old Mill" and *Snow White and the Seven Dwarfs,* was once again tapped to bring inspiration to the European-inspired backgrounds of *Pinocchio*. Tenggren had a personal motivation for his work in Disney's second feature film: many of the backgrounds he sketched were based upon small villages in his homeland of Sweden and throughout Bavaria, particularly Rothenburg ob der Tauber.

Pinocchio premiered at New York's Center Theatre on 7 February 1940. While the press and film critics argued that its craftsmanship, articulation of characters, and visual effects "top[ped] the high standard *Snow White*" and that the "[a]nimation is so smooth that cartoon characters carry impression of real persons", the box office results spoke otherwise. The budget for the film was $2.2 million, but with the effort spent on honing special effects, realistic backgrounds, and the extensive use of the multiplane camera, the final amount spent to produce *Pinocchio* totalled nearly $3 million, with only $1 million grossed in ticket sales.

Walt was embarrassed at his film's seeming lack of success. He argued that the film carried too much dialogue and not enough emphasis on music, and vowed that the studio would never again "[sink] all hopes into a single picture." He also believed that what music there was in the film was inferior to the soundtrack of *Snow White*, composed by Frank Churchill, who was not part of *Pinocchio*'s composition team. The Academy of Motion Picture Art and Sciences disagreed with this assessment in 1941, awarding the Walt Disney Studios an Academy Award for Music (Original Score) and Music (Song) for "When You Wish Upon a Star," making this the first time in the history of the Academy Awards that an animated film beat live action contenders.

Pinocchio was not alone in its struggle to achieve box office success in 1940: with the outbreak of war in Europe and the closing of European markets to American-made films, few films made back their expenses in 1940. In fact, the highest grossing film of 1940, *Road to Singapore* starring Bing Crosby, only made $600,000 more than *Pinocchio*, signalling that the studio's newest feature wasn't a total failure after all.

It didn't matter to Walt, though. He believed that a solid soundtrack which helped tell a story was essential to the success of Disney's films. Moving forward, music would support the characters of the animated features, or even become a character in its own right.

As early as the mid-1930s, Walt began toying with the idea of the studio producing a film starring Mickey Mouse. While the public still loved the popular character enough to hold annual celebrations to acknowledge his birthday, his popularity had somewhat waned with the introduction of Donald Duck and Goofy, resulting in the desire to "reintroduce" him. He suggested the idea of featuring Mickey in the title role of "The Sorcerer's

Apprentice", composed by Paul Dukas and conducted by Arturo Toscanini. At nearly ten minutes in length, the orchestral piece would be too long to be a standard two-reel animated short, so it was decided to make Disney's treatment of "The Sorcerer's Apprentice" into a short film with the animation centred around the music, similar to a Silly Symphony.

Good fortune was soon delivered steaming hot on a plate to Walt Disney. One evening, after a long day at work, Walt sat down for a meal at Chasen's, a restaurant located in nearby Beverly Hills. Dining alone, Walt relaxed by watching others dining at the tables and leather booths lining the walls. His eye was drawn to a nearby table, where a tall, skinny man with his hair sticking up all over his head, so blonde that it was nearly white, was sitting alone. The film producer quickly realised that this man was famed conductor of the Philadelphia Orchestra, Leopold Stokowski.

"Mr. Stokowski," Walt called out. The man looked up, curious about the moustachioed man calling his name. Walt extended a hand to another chair at his table. "Why don't we sit together?" Smiling, Stokowski stood up from his table, grabbed his suit coat, and made his way to Walt's table, taking a seat. The two began a lively conversation, with the film executive praising Stokowski's majestic work in the world of music, and the conductor lauding Walt Disney's ability to bring drawings to life on the movie screen. When Walt suggested his plan to create a short film based on Dukas' piece, Stokowski was very excited, and the two began scheming about how such a collaborative project might work. The conversation between the two visionaries lasted three hours.

By the time of this fateful meeting, Leopold Stokowski had experienced quite an illustrious career. A graduate of London's Royal College of Music, Stokowski began conducting a church choir in 1905, earning his first job as a professional orchestral conductor with the Cincinnati Symphony Orchestra in 1909 at the age of twenty-seven, paving the way to several more accomplishments in the world of symphonic music, including orchestrating Tchaikovsky's Piano Concerto No. 1, being appointed the conductor of the prestigious Philadelphia Orchestra, revising classic pieces by noted composers, and helping to bring symphonic music into the popular spotlight by conducting several record albums for the Philadelphia Orchestra. He also had experience composing scores for various Hollywood films, and even starring in films, both as himself and caricatured conductors. For instance, he performed in the Universal film *One Hundred Men and a Girl* which was so successful that it saved Universal from bankruptcy and led to successful sales of recordings of the Philadelphia Orchestra. By the 1930s, Stokowski was so involved in the film industry that he had a home constructed in the Hollywood Hills, spending time on the west coast for days or weeks at a time.

Over the next several weeks after their meeting at Chasen's, Walt was very excited about the prospect of working with the conductor to bring his version of "The Sorcerer's Apprentice" to life. Some of this excitement waned, however, when the conductor suggested that the studio create a new character to serve as the mischievous apprentice, one which could represent the creative, witty, and playful sides of the amalgamation of both Walt and Stokowski. After finding success in this new venture, this new character could be used in any future music-based films the studio might create. Walt insisted that the film feature an existing character in the Disney repertoire, even throwing around the idea of using Dopey from *Snow White and the Seven Dwarfs*.

Walt believed that recasting Dopey as the assistant to a powerful sorcerer rather than working in his gem mine and living in the forest would be inconsistent with his character, resulting in this idea being tossed out in favour of using Mickey Mouse once again. This decision was solidified when animator Fred Moore performed a redesign of Mickey Mouse: Mickey's eyes changed from pie-eyed and black-dot to the more modern white-eyed and black pupiled, while the colour of his face changed from white to flesh-coloured. He also took on a "short[er], chunkier…cuter" appearance, and a more innocent, child-like personality, which fit the narrative of "The Sorcerer's Apprentice" well.

Stokowski arrived back in Hollywood from Philadelphia in January 1938 to conduct the recording of the soundtrack for the animated short film. The first week of his trip was spent at the Hyperion studio, where he sat in on story meetings to provide input on the animation and assist animators in synchronising the film's continuity with a rough track he had sent from Philadelphia several weeks prior.

Recording for "The Sorcerer's Apprentice" was set to begin on Sunday 9 January, taking place at the studio of Selznick International Pictures, which had enough space available for the size of orchestra that Stokowski demanded. Hours were spent before recording began to ensure that the microphones and recording systems were prepared. Each section of the orchestra was isolated within its own specially built bandshell, with an opening facing the conductor; this partitioned arrangement allowed for the best capturing of each section and multichannel recording, which would allow for better recording and mixing for the final soundtrack.

The musicians began arriving late Saturday evening, finding their places within their individual bandshell. As they began to warm up and tune their instruments, a team including Stokowski, Bill Garity, and the heads of the studio's Music department – Leigh Harline and Edward Plumb – adjusted seats and reseated the musicians to ensure the best sound possible. Finally, at midnight on Sunday 9 January, the recording of "The Sorcerer's Apprentice" began. Over the next three hours, Stokowski worked his magic on the conductor's podium, bringing the story of the foolish amateur sorcerer to life, relying upon an abundance of coffee to keep himself and the musicians sharp for their work.

After the recording session was completed and the musicians had dragged themselves home, Garity spent the next several hours mixing and cutting the tracks of each section of the orchestra to create a preliminary recording of the song. The studio technician was less than impressed, calling the gruelling hours of work for a ten-minute symphony "subpar", citing "annoying sounds [coming] from the string section". Stokowski and his musicians would have to return and re-record the entire thing.

Over the next few weeks, artistic production of "The Sorcerer's Apprentice" took place, with Jim Algar directing, Fred Moore as supervising animator, and Bill Tytla, Riley Thomson, Marvin Woodward, Les Clark, Ollie Johnston, Preston Blair, and Grim Natwick assisting. A live action model was needed to provide reference for Mickey dodging flotsam in water, with the studio hiring an athlete from UCLA to jump across boards floating in a swimming pool. The Special Effects department was also called upon to develop realistic representations of water. Ugo D'Orsi singlehandedly completed all of the animation of water throughout the film, even going as far as inking the cels himself to ensure that the animated version adhered to logical laws of physics.

Costs for producing "The Sorcerer's Apprentice" were mounting: the recording process with Stokowski alone cost the Walt Disney Studios $125,000, not to mention all the cost incurred with the actual animation and photography processes. The short film would be too expensive to release on its own: the most expensive Silly Symphony Disney produced was "Mother Goose Goes to Hollywood", which would be released later that year and would cost nearly $70,000, a little more than half of what it was costing to make "The Sorcerer's Apprentice". Not only that, but Walt was advised by Ben Sharpsteen that the short film would not make the studio much, if any, money: as a short film, it would be paired with a full-length feature in the same way as an animated short, only making income off booking fees paid by theatres and any potential merchandising or licensing opportunities.

Walt agreed and asked Stokowski, who was known throughout the studio as "Stoki", to make "The Sorcerer's Apprentice" a part of a larger feature film that would combine classical music with animation. Stokowski agreed, and the film was given the working title *The Concert Feature*. One of the stipulations of producing a full feature centred around symphonies, however, was that it would be accessible and enjoyable for the masses, not something only appreciated by music aficionados.

Before the Story department could plan out the various segments that would make up *The Concert Feature*, the classical music that would make up the film's soundtrack needed to be chosen. Walt was vehement about his dislike of classical music, explaining that he "never liked this stuff…Honest, I just [can't] listen to it." Despite his strong opinion, Lillian enjoyed orchestral music, and so the pair often attended concerts at the Hollywood Bowl. Being forced to partake in these outings still didn't bring him much awareness of the genre, however, and he recognised that he was not expert enough to choose the music for *The Concert Feature.*

A team was created in September to help select the pieces that would be featured in the film: Walt and Stokowski were joined by Dick Huemer and Joe Grant, whose formal education convinced Walt that they would be good at identifying quality music, and Deems Taylor, who served as the music commentator for the radio broadcasts of the New York Philharmonic. As the group listened to hundreds of records over the next several weeks, Grant and Huemer discussed potential story options for each song, particularly looking for what they referred to as "story music," or songs that lent naturally to a particular story or motifs that could be associated with a particular character. Even those working throughout the studio helped in the process: Bob Carr, the studio's Director of Educational Research, made a habit of sending records from his personal collection to Walt's home to provide inspiration for the film's soundtrack.

A number of pieces were chosen, representing a variety of musical moods and genres. As the Story department began to develop narratives and animation styles, ideas ranged from bug balls to indestructible walking broomsticks, from abstraction to dancing hippos, from aerial horses to runaway baby carriages and dancing babies. Compositions that were deemed to be potentially of less interest to audiences or whose animation narrative was weak were tossed out, while the musical composition of some pieces was shortened or rearranged to fit into a feature-length program. After paring down the list of potential songs, eight pieces were chosen: Johann Sebastian Bach's *Toccata and Fugue in D Minor*, selections from *The Nutcracker Suite* by Tchaikovsky, Dukas' *The Sorcerer's Apprentice*, Stravinsky's *Rite of Spring*, *The Pastoral Symphony* by Beethoven, *Dance of the Hours* by Amilcare Ponchielli, *Night on Bald Mountain* by Mussorgsky, and Franz Schubert's *Ave Maria.*

As the film's overarching narrative was developed, it was decided that each song would feature accompanying animation, but portrayed as "designs and pictures and stories that music inspired in the minds and imaginations of a group of artists." The songs would be tied together as a cinematic concert, separated by live-action interstitials featuring Deems Taylor providing commentary on each piece and the silhouettes of Leopold Stokowski and the musicians of the orchestra.

While *The Concert Feature* would be structured as an animated, cinematic concert, its working title seemed bulky and uninspired, certainly un-Disneyesque. Ideas were thrown around by Walt, Stokowski, the Story department, and directors, but *Fantasia*, which was a musical term meaning "a freeform of music", seemed to fit what was envisioned for the film best. Walt particularly liked the name because regardless of the language the film was dubbed in, the title would never have to change: *Fantasia* meant "fantasia" in every language. But he still wasn't quite sure of the title. Would it truly convey the goal and purpose of the film to audiences who might not be educated in musical literacy? Walt wanted to test the name on young families to determine if the film would be something that would be understood and enjoyed by people of all ages and walks of life. Copies of the script were made and sent home with the women of the Ink-and-Paint department for them to read over and share with their husbands and children. A few days later when they reported back to work at the studio, their minds had been made up: *The Concert Feature* would now henceforth be known as *Fantasia.*

Fantasia was going to be something different than its predecessors the Mickey Mouse and Silly Symphonies series, *Snow White and the Seven Dwarfs*, and *Pinocchio*. While those animated features and shorts relied upon gags and bringing a narrative to life, *Fantasia* was meant to bring music appreciation and interpretation to the masses in an artistic way, experimenting to develop new skills and technical advances. As one movie poster described it, *Fantasia* was meant to help audiences "[h]ear the pictures [and s]ee the music."

To maintain the perception that Disney's newest feature was meant to be taken seriously in film, animation, and music circles, an abundance of research was completed by artists and storymen to ensure both realism and lifelike accuracy. For example, the segment based upon *The Nutcracker Suite* featured various flora and fauna, as well as fairies to help reimagine Tchaikovsky's musical narrative. Bianca Majolie and Ethel Kulsar of the Story department ventured onto the studio lot looking for various weeds to model characters after, such as the thistles in "Russian Dance" or the dandelions in "Dance of the Sugar Plum Fairy". Many of the female artists were also tapped to bring "femininity" to the film, including storyboard and concept artist Sylvia Holland, who utilised books from the studio library to design the fairies, sprites, and other fantasy creatures for "Dance of the Sugar Plum Fairies", who were drawn with definite feminine, yet prepubescent, bodies. Likewise, Holland was assigned the task of developing concepts for the centaurettes in *The Pastoral Symphony*, primarily due to her skill in creating realistic horses.

Extensive research was also conducted for the animation accompanying Igor Stravinsky's *The Rite of Spring*. As the ballet's composer originally conceived of his work's story, *The Rite of Spring* was meant to convey the creative, high energy, and at times microscopically violent emergence of spring after a long, bitter winter, featuring pagan symbolism, such as human sacrifice, to bring about the new season. While the Disney production team felt that this narrative might not be accepted by all audiences, they decided to keep the motif of the violence of the ever-changing earth and the life and death of its inhabitants.

After securing personal approval from Stravinsky himself, Walt began to meet with his Story team to develop the narrative for the segment. Listening to the ballet with his team of conceptual artists, the producer exclaimed, "This is marvelous! It would be perfect for prehistoric animals." This was not meant to be a lighthearted depiction of prehistoric beasts as was common in Hollywood at the time, but instead Walt wanted the animation accompanying *The Rite of Spring* to serve as a "scientific document," as though the animators had embarked upon "an expedition back to the earth 6,000,000 years ago."

In order to convey the changing state of the universe from clouds of cosmic dust to the start of single-celled organisms and the emergence of the dinosaurs, the studio researched the current-day paleontological and archaeological findings of the late 1930s, and even conferred with museums and preeminent scientists. In particular, Walt held meetings with naturalist and director of the American Museum of Natural History, Roy Chapman Andrews; evolutionary biologist Julian Huxley; astronomer Edwin Hubble; and Barnum Brown, an American palaeontologist who had earned the nickname "Mr. Bones" after his discovery of the first documented remains of a Tyrannosaurus Rex. Together, the experts met with the Story department to ensure that the depictions of space, evolution, geological history, and prehistoric flora and fauna in Disney's feature were portrayed as realistically as possible according to the research of the times. However, because the orchestration used for *Fantasia* was a mere twenty-two minutes long, many of the geological eras were condensed, inaccurately depicting different dinosaurs living at the same time rather than millions of years apart.

Using much of the scientific research provided by American and British museums and Andrews, Hubble, Huxley, and Brown, *The Rite of Spring* would be the first time most dinosaurs would be seen "in the flesh" and moving in a realistic manner. This sort of depiction of the terrible lizards was new territory for animators who didn't have much frame of reference drawing something so large in both an anatomically realistic and serious manner. Many of the animators were having a difficult time drawing the prehistoric beasts in proper scale compared to their surroundings. Animator Bill Roberts, who co-directed *The Rite of Spring* segment with Paul Satterfield, suggested that the artists "draw a twelve-story building in perspective, convert it into a dinosaur, then animate it." Art direction also instructed the animators to draw from a low camera angle with animation taking place closer to the ground, helping to make the dinosaurs seem even larger.

While there were no adequate reference models for the dinosaurs of *The Rite of Spring* except fossilised skeletons and twelve-story buildings, other segments of *Fantasia* made excellent use of human models to portray non-human characters.

Dance of the Hours reimagined Ponchielli's ballet, using animated hippos, ostriches, elephants and alligators rather than human dancers to portray the struggle between light and dark throughout a day's twenty-four hour period. In its concept, the animal characters of this segment were meant to be caricatures of human dancers, rather than comedic, anthropomorphised animals as in the Mickey Mouse shorts or realistic animals as depicted in *Snow White* and *Bambi.* As a result, the animators sought to understand how human ballerinas with different body types would move and dance. A handful of professional ballet dancers were hired to dance in an enclosed greenspace at the Hyperion studio while animators drew the different poses and sketched the movements of limbs, hair and costumes; film footage was also taken for future reference. Actress Hattie Noel was brought in and asked to wear a tutu to serve as reference for Hyacinth Hippo. The animators were especially curious about how a heavyset individual might go through the motions of ballet, as well as how flesh might stretch and bounce during a dance. They were disappointed to find that Noel had little problem performing the dances, resulting in little successful reference material. Looking for further inspiration, one of the studio secretaries was asked to don a pink ballet outfit and pose as a model for the animators.

A live-action reference model was also needed for the film's *Night on Bald Mountain* segment that served as *Fantasia*'s climax. Actor Bela Lugosi, who was well known for portraying the titular role in the 1931 film *Dracula*, was hired to provide reference material for the larger-than-life demon Chernabog, standing shirtless before the artists for hours, holding poses directed by the artists. A handful of others served as models for Chernabog to give animator Bill Tytla all the material he needed to bring the villainous monster to life. After watching the segment matched to the music and animation completed, Stokowski commented that the *Night on Bald Mountain* segment was his favourite: it was the only piece of the eight chosen segments to live up to his imagination.

Walt wanted *Fantasia* to be something that audiences had never experienced before and would not soon forget. Excited to brainstorm all that could be possible when bringing this new type of film to life, he suggested that part of the film feature three-dimensional effects, be filmed in wide-screen format, and should have moments when scents related to what was on screen were diffused to add more immersion to the experience.

Perhaps more powerfully, Walt wanted *Fantasia* to truly mimic how audience members felt when they were experiencing a true, animated concert performed by a symphony orchestra, one in which the sound was fully dimensional, reverberating, and *alive*. Bill Garity was charged with partnering with RCA to create a special sound system that would "mimic the fullness of the sound of an orchestra lost in the standard theater experience." The studio technician got to work drawing up ideas for this revolutionary system.

Meanwhile, to ensure that this encompassing soundtrack was successful, Stokowski, Walt, Joe Grant and Dick Huemer, travelled to Philadelphia to record the full orchestration of *Fantasia* sans *The Sorcerer's Apprentice*, which had already been recorded during the midnight session at Selznick's studios. The Stokowski-led recording of the Philadelphia Orchestra took place at the Philadelphia Academy of Music, which had been designed with perfect acoustics in mind: the entire performance hall essentially acted as one giant amplifier. A basement below the auditorium was fitted with an oversized sound board, similar to that inside a piano: a solid brick wall stretched beneath the audience seats across which were stringers: when music was played onstage, these stringers vibrated, creating amplified acoustics throughout the performance hall. Scattered throughout this basement was a series of microphones mounted to posts, capturing the specific sounds of their particular theatre location. Twenty-four additional microphones were placed throughout and around the orchestra and performance hall, to record the sound of their own vantage point.

With the recording of the orchestration complete, Stokowski insisted on mixing all the recording tracks of each individual microphone himself to ensure the vision for the film's soundtrack fulfilled the expectations of the Story team, Walt, the directors, and himself. This process allowed for particular portions of the soundtrack to be highlighted, with individual instrument sections increasing or decreasing in volume to highlight a particular melody. For example, while many of the woodwinds tended to be drowned out by the brass and strings in a concert performance of *The Pastoral Symphony*, Stokowski's mixing and editing allowed for this section to be highlighted, bringing new orchestration to Beethoven's piece. Walt was unsure of the conductor's request, explaining that union rules forbade non-union members from mixing final film soundtracks. The conductor was adamant, and the studio circumvented union rules by allowing Luisa Field, Hollywood's first female music editor, to edit Stokowski's tracks to ensure they correctly matched the animation.

Garity's audio playback system, called Fantasound, allowed for a fully stereophonic listening experience. The idea was that several speakers and amplifiers would be placed throughout the movie theatres, to the left and right of the audience, as well as behind and mounted on the front walls and behind the screen. As the animated characters moved across the screen, the audio responded appropriately. To facilitate this, three individual optical soundtracks were printed, allowing for a fuller, more diverse sound, rather than the single, uniform cacophony of a single soundtrack. Each of these three soundtracks would control a particular set of speakers within the theatres: one soundtrack was assigned to speakers on the left side of the audience, one to the right side, and one for those at the front of the theatre and located behind the screen. A fourth track, known as a guide or control track, controlled the volume of the three soundtracks, as well as the fade and balance of the music. For example, in *Ave Maria,* the final segment of the film, the operatic vocalisation begins from the speakers behind the audience. As the music swells, the vocalisation moves to the speakers mounted above the audience before playing on one side of the front wall speakers, creating the auditory illusion that the performer was making her way through the aisles of the theatre.

To test-screen *Fantasia*, a Fantasound system was installed in the studio's theatre, located across the sidewalk from the Animation building. Finding success in their multidimensional audio experience, Garity and the RCA technicians travelled east to begin their installation at New York City's Broadway Theater, where the film's premiere would be held on 13 November 1940. A total of sixty-five speakers were installed at various points throughout the theatre, with three sound horn speakers placed behind the screen to draw immediate attention to the animated action. For example, in *The Rite of Spring*, the sound horns emitted a crashing sound as the Tyrannosaurus Rex appeared on the screen: the noise was so loud, it caused the seats in the theatre to vibrate.

By all appearances the film's premiere wowed its distinguished audience. More than two thousand attended, often breaking out in "spontaneous acclaim and continuous applause." Newspapers and trade journals hailed the achievement of Walt Disney's latest project, with *Time* asserting that "more ears had been saved for Beethoven by 'Fantasia' than by all the symphonic-lecture recitalists in the U.S."*Stage* predicted that within "a few months after the release of this film, barbers, bakers, and taxi drivers throughout the nation will whistle, while they work, random themes from Tchaikovsky, Beethoven, and Bach." The public so anticipated experiencing *Fantasia* that theatre showings were selling out over the first few days. Some theatres even reported that "[a]dditional switchboard help was reported necessary to handle incoming reservation calls."

Historical circumstances of the day were not kind to *Fantasia*. With the outbreak of the Second World War, the entire European market was closed to American films, as were many theatres in Asia and South America. Not only that, but domestic ticket sales dropped: with Americans heavily invested in the patriotic war effort, their bank accounts had priorities *other* than an evening at the movies. As a result, *Fantasia* was considered a box office failure, completely erasing the $1.25 million budget surplus of the Walt Disney Studio and putting them $120,000 in debt. The Academy of Motion Pictures Arts and Sciences was impressed, however: Walt, Bill Garity, and RCA won a special award for their "outstanding contribution to the advancement of the use of sound in motion pictures", while Leopold Stokowski was recognised with a special award for the "unique achievement in the creation of a new form of visualised music". *Fantasia* was also voted by the National Board of Review to be one of the "Ten Best Pictures of 1940", while Walt himself won the Irving G. Thalberg Memorial Award, which recognised him for his "consistently high quality of motion picture production".

The intention was that every major movie house that played *Fantasia* would have a Fantasound system, and there were plans to produce seventy-six individual Fantasound systems. With the outbreak of the Second World War, however, resources were scarce and the willingness to spend an additional $30,000 on outfitting local theatres was a low priority. Smaller theatres throughout the United States would also have difficulty implementing the sound system due to a lack of space: existing projection rooms would have had to be expanded to accommodate the additional sound equipment, and film storage facilities would have had to double in size to hold the additional soundtrack reels. For the larger theatres that could afford to install the new equipment, their business would have to be shuttered for an entire week to accommodate for Fantasound installation, as well as a full week after the end of *Fantasia*'s run, resulting in a loss of potential profits. As a result, few American theatregoers were able to experience Walt's concert feature the way it was intended.

Fantasia truly was revolutionary, both in content and its innovation of multichannel stereophonic sound. Unfortunately, it was perhaps too ahead of its time, with regular use of similar audio systems not being widely implemented until the 1970s. The film was also significant by being the first feature produced by Walt Disney Studios that heavily utilised women outside of the Ink-and-Paint department and that performed by inspirational artists Bianca Majolie, Sylvia Holland, and Ethel Kulsar. For example, Shirley Soderstrom was instrumental in producing model sheets and maquettes of many of the significant characters including the centaurettes and Bacchus in *The Pastoral Symphony.* Viola Anderson held the distinction of being the "first skirted inbetweener," leading the way for four additional women to become assistant animators before the premiere of the film in 1940.

Also significant was the return to the Walt Disney Studios of an artist who was integral to the origin story of the studio and its ensuing fame: Ub Iwerks. While Ub had taken leave from the studio, he still had many friends who continued to work there and with whom he continued to visit. On one occasion, Ub joined Ben Sharpsteen for lunch, during which the Disney employee asked Ub if he would ever consider returning to work at the studio, especially in light of the closure of Iwerks Studio. Ub responded that he would only return if given the option of serving as a "technical problem solver". He had found life in his work on his horizontal multiplane camera, and was unsure of continuing his work as an artist during a time when Hollywood animation was so full of professionally trained artists. Soon after, Walt and Ub met for lunch, and the studio executive accepted his old friend's request. Ub was quickly put to work on a number of projects, including *Fantasia:* he was responsible for finding a way to portray Mickey Mouse shaking hands with Leopold Stokowski, as well as helping Bill Garity develop Fantasound.

In addition to the changing face of his staff, *Fantasia* was also a film that changed the mindset of Walt Disney himself. While he had begrudgingly attended concerts with Lillian in the past, with the completion of *Fantasia*, he found himself to be a new enthusiast of the genre. When asked about the medium of symphonic orchestra, Walt explained that "I can listen to it now. It seems to mean a little more to me…When I heard the music it made pictures in my head…Maybe I can give other people the same thing."

PART 4

WE'VE GOT A JOB TO DO, OR WE'RE SUNK 1941–1959

RELUCTANT WORKERS

As busy as Walt Disney was at his studio, he was still a relatively average American family man. In March 1941, *Ladies' Home Journal* published a profile on "Mr. & Mrs. Disney", highlighting how much he loved and was involved with his family. The article even pointed out that it was Walt's love for Lillian that held him and his work together, explaining that "Mickey would be lost without his Minnie. So would Walt." The article described how much he adored his daughters – Diane who was eight and Sharon who was four at the time of the article – and how he often came home after a long day of work to "roughhouse with [them]." The article went on to describe how, rather than reading to them from a storybook as parents tend to, Walt would "act out scenes from such future projects as *Bambi, Alice in Wonderland,* and *The Birth of Jesus Christ.*"

While things at home painted the picture of a happy family life, the article hinted that tension seemed to be emerging at Walt's studio. As someone who grew up lower-middle class and had experienced financial ruin and bankruptcy several times in his career, the film executive didn't want to seem pretentiously affluent, as he felt it might distance his employees from their boss in a working environment that was known for its informality and tight-knit camaraderie. Walt was proud to say that he drove himself to work every day in his blue coupe, but the article went on to explain that he was embarrassed and "full of apologies when it leaked out that he also has a bigger car in which a chauffeur sometimes drives him around." So worried that he would be viewed as unapproachable, Walt even "cut off his mustache after reading in a magazine that a mustache is a sign of conceit."

Even though he was mindful of how he was perceived on a personal and social basis, Walt still assumed that audiences understood that he did not personally create his studio's animated shorts and features, but rather that he was the producer who worked alongside talented directors and artists. Official studio policy explained that minimising screen credit to individual artists was "calculated to prevent inter-office jealousy rather than a desire on Disney's part to hog the show." Instead, Walt often personally recognised his employees for their hard work through promotions to management positions including director and lead animator, as well as through a system by which bonuses were paid for the amount and quality of footage animated. The studio also prided itself for paying some of the highest studio wages in Hollywood, as well as offering employees paid vacations and creating an internal savings and loans program.

In the months leading up to the premiere of *Snow White and the Seven Dwarfs*, the studio took an attitude of "all hands on deck", increasing artist working hours without an increase in wages. However, Walt and the studio leadership promised some sort of compensation if the feature did well in box office returns. As a result, the hardworking employees overlooked the snub in a pay raise, believing firmly in the work they were doing and looking forward to a lump bonus at the end of 1937 or early 1938.

On 10 May 1938, studio employees found a memo on the bulletin boards across the campus announcing "Walt's Field Day", with the details wittily listed in the form of a story outline often used by the Story department. The adults-only, day-long party would take place at the Lake Norconian Club, a recreational resort property located ninety minutes north of Los Angeles in Norco, California. On 4 June, all Disney personnel and the one guest they were allowed to bring along went to the property to engage in numerous activities, including badminton, horse riding, boating, swimming, volleyball, baseball, and more. The day ended with a catered banquet, followed by a dance led by a hired orchestra, before guests retired to their rooms in the main resort building.

At the conclusion of the evening's festivities, awards were given for the day's athletic contests, followed by a speech from Walt. The executive thanked his staff for all their hard work on *Snow White and the Seven Dwarfs* and explained the upcoming slate for feature animation, before bidding them a good night and leaving the stage. The attendees were confused: where were their bonuses for their excellent work on *Snow White*? Weren't they going to be compensated for all the overtime hours they had worked to ensure the film was completed prior to its

December premiere? Frustrated, many of the employees took advantage of the resort's open bar, resulting in drunken revelry and destruction and many of the single employees retiring to each others' rooms for an evening of inebriated, orgiastic sex.

With tense grumblings echoing throughout the studio over the following weeks, Walt, Roy, and studio lawyer Gunther Lessing finally relented, offering meagre bonuses to the artists. At this point, however, the payout was considered by the employees to be more insulting than rewarding, as many of the bonuses were smaller than they'd received for the animated shorts and had only come after their complaints, rather than out of the executives' goodwill.

Over the next couple years, studio employees continued to be unsatisfied with their work conditions and pay, especially when the studio made slight pay cuts after the financial failures of *Pinocchio* and *Fantasia*. Citing what they believed to be low salaries, the lack of adequate bonuses and compensation for those who had been overworked, and a lack of screen credit on the animated shorts, studio employees attempted to unionise. Around this same time, the Screen Cartoon Guild was attempting to unionise all the studios in Hollywood that produced animation. Disney was their crown jewel: as a studio that *solely* produced animated shorts and had just completed its first animated feature, it had the most potential members and potential due payments to offer the Guild. On the union's Board of Officers was one of Disney's very own: animator Art Babbitt, who had accomplished so much by helping to establish the art classes held at the studio and the partnership with Chouinard, as well as being one of the animators who had helped develop the characters of Donald Duck and Goofy. Once such an integral part of the Walt Disney Studios, Babbitt had several reasons to agitate for changes, including what he considered to be limitations on taking creative licence in his work contrary to instructions from the directors of the animated shorts and the surprisingly low wages of some of the studio's best inbetweeners, cleanup artists and his own assistant animators.

Walt was not pleased with the idea of union activity, especially activity that was encouraged from outside sources like union organiser Herbert K. Sorrell, but knew there was little he could do to stop it. Attempting to appease employees who were part of the Screen Cartoon Guild – who were primarily inbetweeners and assistants at Disney – he raised wages in early 1941, despite the difficult financial circumstances caused by the Great Depression and the war in Europe. His only expectation from members was that all union activity take place off the studio lot: there was too much work to do on the next features.

In a little more than a decade, Walt Disney had made America a fan of animation. The studio had enjoyed an incredible run of incredibly popular projects since "Steamboat Willie" in 1928, including Mickey Mouse shorts, "Three Little Pigs", and *Snow White and the Seven Dwarfs*. Fan mail poured through the gates of the studio, addressed both to Mickey Mouse and Mr. Disney. Several individuals asked to tour the Walt Disney Studio, curious about the process through which Walt's team of artists developed an animated film.

Similarly, in 1938, a theatre manager from Pennsylvania wrote to Walt about a survey he had performed at his theatre: many individuals seated in his audience had no idea how animation was done and were curious to know more.

Walt conceived an idea to create a live-action documentary of sorts to show the different steps in the process. The fact that the film would be live-action meant that it could be produced inexpensively and quickly in a time when the studio was in debt.

Storymen developing the film's narrative decided to play off a real-life inspiration: humourist and actor Robert Benchley pitching an idea for a new animated short to Walt Disney based upon the book *The Reluctant Dragon*. Arriving at the studio, he is assigned an escort, but quickly sneaks away and gets lost on the studio lot. Moving from building to building, he finds himself in a life study sketch class, the maquette studio, the Ink-and-Paint lab, the recording studio (where he meets Clarence Nash and Florence Gill), and the foley studio where sound effects are produced. Demonstrations are also made of the multiplane camera and storyboard process, featuring corresponding animated shorts presented by real Disney animators including Ward Kimball, Fred Moore, Joe Grant and Dick Huemer. At the conclusion of the meeting, Benchley finds Walt in the studio theatre, who invites him to stay for the newest animated Disney short, "The Reluctant Dragon". Disney had beat Benchley to the punch.

Surveyed Americans were not entirely sure what *The Reluctant Dragon* was supposed to be: data collected by George Gallup's Audience Research Institute indicated that only 34% of those polled realised that the film was a feature and not a short or a newsreel, resulting in poor attendance when it released in June 1941. Lucky for the studio, the film accomplished what it set out to do: *The Reluctant Dragon* was a fantastic way to showcase the Walt Disney Studio. It also seemed to portray the studio and its employees as content, peaceful, organised, and enthusiastic, but by this time, like the process of animation itself, this was all an illusion.

Walt Disney loved books. In fact, he often got story ideas for animated shorts and his new slate of features from books. The studio library had become a major dispensary of source material, and new volumes were regularly being added. It was in late 1939 that a book was given to Walt which would lead to the birth of a new Disney character who would become a household name alongside Mickey Mouse and Donald Duck.

Given to him by Kay Kamen, this small book was a story about a baby elephant with oversized ears written by Helen Aberson and Harold Pearl and illustrated by Helen Durney. Rather than a typical children's book, *Dumbo, the Flying Elephant* was presented in a unique, experimental format known as a Roll-a-Book. The text and illustrations of the story were printed on a long scroll of paper which was inserted into a small, handheld box with a square-shaped hole through which each "page" on the scroll could be seen before advancing. Frustrated with the disappointing returns from *Pinocchio*, Walt saw the potential of this new animated project and the opportunity to expand on the story, handing it over to Joe Grant and Dick Huemer to develop.

However, after further consideration, Walt decided he was unsure of the story as the focus of the studio's next project. Grant and Huemer, meanwhile, had fallen in love with the story of Dumbo and were determined not to let their two months of hard work go to waste. Much like a serial novel being released in a newspaper or magazine, the two storymen sent Walt a few pages of their treatment at a time, leaving him hungry for more. After reading the last page, Walt was sold: *Dumbo* would be the next feature after *Fantasia.*

The film was initially meant to be a thirty-minute special, but was expanded to a full-length feature after Walt saw the treatment developed by his storymen. With America anxious about their fate a decade into the Depression and in light of Europe's recent declaration of war, European film markets were closed to American films. The budget to create this new film was limited, only $700,000, and orders were given to complete it for release quickly.

Several of Disney's top artists were assigned to the film, with the goal to make it as "cartoony" as possible, hearkening back to the successful shorts the studio produced in the early 1930s. Bill Tytla, who was known for his excellent work on Grumpy in *Snow White and the Seven Dwarfs*, Stromboli in *Pinocchio*, and Chernabog and the sorcerer in *Fantasia*, was assigned the role as lead animator on the elephant matriarchs and Dumbo himself, modelling the baby elephant on his own two-year-old son. Ward Kimball, the studio musician, had been assigned to animate the anthropomorphised train Casey Jr. and Jim Crow and his pals, while Fred Moore shared his office with a real stork as inspiration for his cartoon counterpart.

The wager made by Joe Grant, Dick Huemer, and Walt Disney paid off when, after *Dumbo*'s premiere on 23 October 1941, it grossed $1.2 million, likely saving the Walt Disney Studios from bankruptcy. Critics agreed with the audiences: they were in love with the flying elephant. Those at the studio were proud to learn that *Time* was planning to feature Dumbo on the cover of its first issue of 1942 as the "Mammal of the Year", even going so far as providing an "official" portrait drawn by one of the studio's top artists. This changed when, on 7 December, the American naval base at Pearl Harbor was bombed by the Japanese, drawing the United States into the Second World War. As a result, the cover featured a portrait of President Franklin D. Roosevelt, flanked by Josef Stalin and Winston Churchill.

Catching wind of the two storymen who developed the characters and plot of *Dumbo*, *Time* also featured an article about those that they considered truly responsible for the adorable baby elephant: Disney storymen Joe Grant and Dick Huemer. Photos showed the two, with Walt in the background, almost forgotten. When he saw the article, the film executive was incensed, believing that it downplayed the importance he played in the development process of films.

Luckily, the recognition his studio once again received from the Academy of Motion Pictures Arts and Sciences seemed to stem his frustration: *Dumbo* was nominated for two Academy Awards, for Best Song ("Baby Mine") and Best Scoring of a Musical Picture for the score written by Oliver Wallace and Frank Churchill, winning the award for the latter. When asked later, Walt claimed that *Dumbo* was his favourite animated film produced by the studio. Unfortunately, it was produced in circumstances that almost destroyed both him and the studio he loved so much.

As artists began arriving to work at the Walt Disney Studios on the morning of 9 January 1941, they found a group of newsboys standing outside the front gate, handing out flyers about the unions to the employees as they drove or walked through the security checkpoint. The flyers also invited the artists to a union meeting on 16 January, which would take place in the auditorium of a local high school.

This didn't sit well with many animators who were close to Walt and who had been a part of the studio since its early days. Tension began to rise, however, when employee behaviour began being tracked, with unit secretaries buzzing employees in and out of their departments and the expectation that they would keep track of working hours. A memo released to studio staff on 6 February complained about the reduced output of the artists, blaming increased union membership and activity among the studio's employees.

Walt believed in his artists. He prided himself on his approachability and the familial atmosphere of his animation studio. He decided that the best way to address any employee frustration was to meet with his staff face-to-face. A meeting was scheduled for 10 February, requesting that all employees attend because Walt planned to address them.

The atmosphere of the studio auditorium and the speech prepared by Walt for this evening was very different from that of the evening he presented his idea for *Snow White* to his team. When almost everyone was settled in their seats, Walt began by reminiscing about the company's past, explaining all the tough times that he and Roy and some of those in attendance had experienced in the 1920s. He explained that with the Great Depression and the outbreak of war, times were tough once again, attributing it to the closed European markets and the indebtedness of the studio to Bank of America for the tune of $2.5 million.

Trying to find common ground with his employees and to prove that he was suffering along with them, he explained that both he and Roy would be taking a pay cut by 75%, and promised that they would take care of the staff by offering pay increases, promotions, vacation time and paid sick leave. He also encouraged the artists to lean upon him and each other in times of struggle and grievance, rather than turning to outside groups with little to no knowledge of the Walt Disney Studios and its operations.

Walt was true to his word: on 24 February, a new pay scale was implemented for the Ink-and-Paint department, offering pay increases in increments of $2 every quarter. He also conceived of a new "bonus plan" for assistant animators and inbetweeners, but the idea was not fully embraced. These attempts to appease his staff were in vain: leaders of the Screen Cartoonist's Guild accused Walt of refusing to negotiate with union leaders and members, citing his statement that his employees cooperate internally rather than with external organisations.

Art Babbitt seemed to be leading the charge on internal Guild activity, talking to his coworkers about the union during company time and encouraging other animators to attend Guild meetings. Various departments continued to make complaints to studio lawyer Gunther Lessing, including unfair treatment, pay cuts and layoffs, and rumours that employees were planning to go on strike began to circulate. There were also complaints by many of the more experienced male artists that Walt had turned to hiring women and less experienced artists in order to reduce studio costs, resulting in the layoff of many people with more skill and experience.

Studio executives began to panic: several studio security guards were given the authority as deputised members of the Burbank Police to use force to stop any violence that broke out, while Walt threatened to close the studio in case violent disruptions occurred. Looking for a source of unrest with whom they could negotiate or villainise if necessary, Lessing blamed Art Babbitt, who had been in leadership with the Screen Cartoonist's Guild and was actively discussing the union throughout the studio.

On 20 May, a notice was delivered to twenty-four artists stating that they would be unemployed as of 5:30 that afternoon, offering two weeks' severance pay. Of this group, seventeen were members of the Guild. Walt assured the group, however, that their layoff was not a result of their union activity, but rather an unfortunate "circumstance beyond the control of this studio", citing the financial and political turmoil plaguing the world.

Art Babbitt was incensed over the continuing injustice that he believed Disney's executive team was employing against its employees. A meeting at Los Angeles' Roosevelt Hotel was called on the evening of 22 May, where they discussed the possibility of striking against the Walt Disney Studios. Four days later, on 26 May, a vote was cast at the Roosevelt: out of the 319 Guild members in attendance, only four voted not to strike, and so a strike was duly scheduled to begin two days later on 28 May.

Walt caught wind of the Guild's plans and in response called a meeting for the entire staff on 27 May, where he promised that in the event of a strike, the studio would remain open. He encouraged any staff interested in joining a union to do so, vowing that he, Roy and Lessing would be willing to negotiate with any collective bargaining offered by the unions. Shortly thereafter, while Babbitt was enjoying lunch in the studio restaurant, he was given an envelope notifying him that he was no longer employed by the Walt Disney Studios, effective immediately.

As studio employees began to arrive to work on the morning of 28 May, a crowd of nearly five hundred – primarily inbetweeners, assistants, and members of the Ink-and-Paint department – were gathered outside the front gate, many of them holding picket signs bearing the faces of Disney's beloved characters "complaining" about Disney's work conditions, the studio's apparent antagonism against union activity, and low pay. Many in the group hurled insults at those who refused to strike and were reporting to work, calling many of them out by name. They had a job to do, however, as production was continuing on several features including *Dumbo, Bambi,* and *The Reluctant Dragon*. The strike, led by Babbitt, would last nine gruelling weeks.

Walt felt betrayed. He had counted on his staff: they had been through difficult times together and sometimes spent more time together at work than they spent at home with their families. The artists had played together, eaten meals together, laughed and played pranks on each other, and everyone was on a first name basis, with Walt right there alongside them, not as a dictator but as a colleague. Reluctantly, he recognised what was best for his studio moving forward and decided to ensure that events like this wouldn't happen again once the strike was resolved. Photographers were hired to take pictures of each striker, with the portraits hung in Walt's office. Several of his loyal employees were called in to help identify the strikers, with Walt offering them a glass of Harvey's Bristol Cream to demonstrate that he felt they were all equals and enduring this challenge together. He promised that those who decided to continue working on *Dumbo* and the shorts would be protected by the authorities and studio security as they crossed the picket line. The fear was that if work did not continue on the latest feature, the bank would pull its funding, foreclosing on the studio lot and its assets.

The studio wasn't the only place that the strikers agitated: they had also convinced some to picket outside theatres playing *Fantasia* and the most recent shorts, to educate the public on Disney's unfair practices and encourage the boycott of films. Herbert Sorrell also encouraged striking at Technicolor, which still processed Disney's films, shutting production down. As a result, processing of *The Reluctant Dragon* was held up for several weeks. Many of the signs that the strikers carried, both outside the studio and the theatres showing Disney films, featured the animated dragon from *The Reluctant Dragon*, hoping to damage the film's success. Strikers even paraded up and down the sidewalk of the Pantages and RKO Hillstreet theatres on the evening of the Hollywood premiere of *The Reluctant Dragon.*

At times, the tactics of some Disney strikers became unreasonable and even violent. Gunther Lessing was hung in effigy. Non-strikers' cars were vandalised, with air let out of the tires and paint scraped off using screwdrivers. Many of the female artists arriving at work felt threatened and insulted by those who they had once considered friends when the strikers told them that they "should be home having babies" rather than reporting to their job, while others were insulted about their looks or physical appearance.

In one particular instance, Walt was driving past the strikers, when Babbitt called over the bullhorn to him: "Walt Disney, you ought to be ashamed!" The studio executive, who had endured weeks of strike, reassuring frightened employees still coming to work at the risk of their feelings, reputations, and physical wellbeing, and the stress of meeting film deadlines with only a skeleton crew, slammed on his brakes and threw his car into park. Throwing open his door, Walt leaped out and turned to face Babbitt, fists clenched and ready to fight.

He then stomped over to his previous employee. "You dirty son of a bitch!" he yelled. Those nearby knew that this could get violent quickly, and grabbed the strike leader by the arms, pulling him away to safety. After fuming for a moment while the strikers stood at a distance laughing, Walt spun on his heel, climbed back into his car, and sped away.

Things were becoming desperate for the Walt Disney Studios, especially after the United States government offered the studio the opportunity to develop films as part of the Good Neighbor program. A number of mediators and arbitrators were brought in to negotiate a settlement between the Guild members and the studio executives, but time after time one of the parties rejected the terms of settlement.

Roy, who saw how serious things were getting due to his job handling company finances, contacted the United States Conciliation office for official federal arbitration.

Within a week of meetings commencing between the Walt Disney Studios and members of the Screen Cartoonist's Guild, arbitrated by James Dewey, the strike was called off on 30 July 1941, the strikers were reinstated as employees of the studio, and a new union contract was offered on 2 August. Unfortunately for the studio, the strikers had won everything they demanded and more: the Walt Disney Studios would be a closed shop requiring all employees to join the union, all low-level employees would receive a raise, reasonable working hours were outlined with overtime pay offered if necessary, female and male employees would be paid equally, strikers would receive back pay, and Art Babbitt would be rehired without fear of further disciplinary action due to union and strike activities. Screen credit for artists was also mentioned, but the particular details would be negotiated at a later time.

Over the next few weeks, relationships at the studio remained tense. Word got around that layoffs were on the horizon and that those that participated in the strike would be the first to go. A list was compiled of those marked for lay off and handed over to James Dewey for consideration. The list was also sent to the Guild. Neither were pleased with the list, and it was returned to studio executives to revise. After the new list completed, it was once again vetted by Dewey and the union, who approved of the dismissal of the 263 listed employees.

Art Babbitt was not one who found himself on the street as a result of this new round of layoffs. That didn't mean that life at the studio for the master animator was easy though. In his absence, Babbitt's office had been given away to another artist, as well as his amenities, equipment, and Kem Weber-designed furniture. Finding it unfair to vacate an artist from Babbitt's old office who had been loyal during the strike, studio leadership found a smaller, less equipped office for Babbitt to move into. The strike leader demanded that his benefits as a head animator and tenured employee be fully reinstated, but his requests fell on deaf ears. Over the next few years, he also found that the directors of the features and shorts were giving him work typically performed by assistants, and that the amount of work he had been given to complete became less and less until his assignments stopped altogether. Eventually, he found that much of his time was spent sitting in his cramped office with nothing to do.

After complaining several times about his lack of work, he received notification that he had once again lost his job. Convinced this was vengeance over his role in the strike, he petitioned the National Labor Relations Board to file a lawsuit on his behalf with the Ninth Circuit of the United States Court of Appeals. The studio argued that, after a prolonged absence due to the strike, Babbitt had lost his confidence and his animation was not as good as it had once been. The US Court of Appeals ruled in his favour, and Babbitt was once again rehired. However, over the next several weeks, it became obvious that the studio's assertion about the quality of his animation was actually true. The studio offered him a large cash settlement if he agreed to resign from his position. After fighting injustice at the Walt Disney Studios for five years, the artist who had given life and personality to Donald Duck and Goofy, who had helped create the villainous intricacies of the Big Bad Wolf and helped start the Disney art training program, accepted the studio's offer and resigned from his position on 16 January 1947.

Walt Disney was exhausted, stressed, disappointed, and felt like he could no longer trust anyone at his studio. However, while the strikers had technically won and received everything they had demanded, Walt had still saved his studio, which gave him a burst of motivation. But it wasn't only his studio that had needed saving: after the US government came knocking at the front gates, he realised he was needed to help save the world.

GOOD NEIGHBORS

With world war breaking out in the eastern hemisphere during the late 1930s, America was in a very interesting position regarding its place in the conflict. Some argued that the United States should remain isolated and not interfere, explaining that after the loss of young life in the First World War, America would be better off minding its own business: after all, the war in Europe didn't involve the U.S. Instead of choosing sides and spending money and resources on the aggressors, it simply made more sense to build up the nation's own defences in preparation for the war making its way to America's shores.

While it vowed not to get involved, America was still fearful about the spread of fascism across Europe, perpetuated by the takeover of Italy by Benito Mussolini and the land grab of Nazi Germany under the rule of Adolf Hitler. This aggressive political ideology went against everything that American democracy stood for, and there was genuine fear that fascism could infiltrate American politics and society. Thus, it became necessary for the United States to win over its neighbours and demonstrate the merits of democracy (or at least the danger of Nazism) to the other nations situated in the western hemisphere.

While presidents Calvin Coolidge and Herbert Hoover had worked hard to reconcile the strained relationships between the United States and the Central and South American nations that had resulted from decades of American imperialism and intervention, President Franklin Roosevelt recognised the importance of working with their southern neighbours in the dark days of the Great Depression and the beginning of the Second World War. Roosevelt understood how vital it was to sell the democratic, capitalist American way of life to the people of Latin America to prevent any kind of allegiance or interest in the fascist ways of the Axis Powers. Diplomacy thus required that the United States not only had to prove how appealing its government, economics, and culture were, but they also needed to change their own prejudiced perception of the people and cultures outside their borders.

In his first inaugural address on 4 March 1933, Franklin Roosevelt outlined his stance on foreign policy: the United States would be dedicated "to the policy of the good neighbor – the neighbor who resolutely respects himself and, because he does so, respects the rights of others." Over the next several years, Roosevelt would make good on this pledge through various diplomatic and political moves to honour the interests and self-determination of several Latin American nations including Cuba, Nicaragua, and Argentina.

Politics alone wouldn't change the hearts and minds of the people of the western hemisphere. In fact, the American government more often than not reinforced the authority of dictators. In 1940, the government established the Office of the Coordinator of Inter-American Affairs to showcase the merits of American commercialism and culture and its place in the other cultures of the hemisphere. In addition to sending American celebrities on goodwill tours of Latin America, the federal government encouraged Hollywood to venture into Central and South America to search for "untapped foreign markets" and identify source material for films that could be attractive to both citizens of the United States and the other nations of the western hemisphere, resulting in nearly every American film studio producing "Latin-themed neighbourly films".

Studios were also encouraged to seek out and employ more Latin American singers, dancers, and actors to star in these new films to prove that the United States saw the value in the cultures they were trying to reach. While the films of the past had traditionally depicted America's Spanish-speaking neighbours as variously slow-witted, exotic, villainous, and seductive, the CIAA's Motion Picture Division instead asked filmmakers to portray characters in a "non-offensive" way, as modern, civilised, and fun-loving, and even went so far as to create the Production Code Administration to enforce expectations and pull any film that was deemed offensive or inauthentically or unfairly portrayed Latin America and its inhabitants.

To ensure that any money spent throughout a film's production schedule wasn't wasted, studios established research departments to study cultural customs, practices, costumes, dancers and music. Native speakers were hired to train actors and actresses, as well as ensure that Spanish and Portuguese dialogue was accurate. Specialists were retained to provide books, magazines, and photographs to assist in the design and planning of films, and some studios even sent expeditions on tour throughout the Caribbean, Central, and South America.

With the European markets closed to many American films due to the war, the Walt Disney Studios began looking for new opportunities to replace this lost income. In 1941, Gunther Lessing introduced Walt to John Hay Whitney, director of the CIAA's Motion Picture Division. Whitney told him about the other studios throughout Hollywood that were conducting goodwill tours of Latin America and hinted that Walt should personally engage in a goodwill tour of his own. When Walt expressed reluctance, Whitney suggested that the producer bring along a handful of his artists for the purpose of gathering material for future features and shorts. After a conversation with Nelson Rockefeller, the Coordinator for Latin American Affairs, who explained that the State Department would agree to reimburse the studio for up to $70,000 in travelling expenses and guarantee up to $50,000 per film produced as a result of a goodwill tour, Walt was sold.

The Latin American nations seemed ripe for an economic and cultural exchange with the Walt Disney Studios. American films, often dubbed into Spanish or Portuguese, often did relatively well in Central and South America, and because the United States had the most successful animation studios, American shorts were beloved in the southern hemisphere. Mickey Mouse and Donald Duck were particular favourites, taking on Latin-inspired personalities and even having Spanish translations of their names: Mickey was known as El Ratón Miguelito, while Donald was called El Pato Donald.

Throughout the summer of 1941, Walt began to compile a list of studio artists and employees who would join him on this combination goodwill tour-research trip to Latin America: director Norm Ferguson; assistant animator Frank Thomas; Storymen Bill Cottrell, Ted Sears, and Webb Smith; inspirational sketch artists Jack Miller, James Bordrero, and husband and wife team Lee and Mary Blair; film editor Larry Lansburgh; art director Herb Ryman and his wife Janet; composer Charles Wolcott; Jack Cutting, animator and head of the studio's Foreign Department; story researcher John Rose; publicist Janet Martin; and Lillian Disney and Hazel Sewell. Collectively, the team became known as 'El Grupo', a nickname they heartily embraced throughout their two-month journey south.

On 17 August, the group departed Los Angeles, bound for Brazil, where they studied native wildlife at the Belem Zoo, watched and danced the Samba, and studied the architecture of regions including Rio de Janeiro and Bahia. While in Brazil, Walt attended the Brazilian premiere of *Fantasia* and engaged in diplomatic activities, such as sharing dinner with Brazil's president Getúlio Vargas. From there, El Grupo made their way to Argentina, making the Alvear Palace Hotel of Buenos Aires their temporary studio for the duration of their time in the country. When their time in Argentina was done, the group split up, with some making their way to Santiago, Chile and the nearby Andes Mountains, while others went to Northern Argentina or La Paz, Bolivia and Lake Titicaca.

A relative newcomer to the Walt Disney Studio was Mary Blair, a watercolour artist and cel painter, who had followed her inbetweener husband Lee from Harman-Ising Studio to Disney in 1940. Her unique take on colour and impressionistic watercolour paintings caught the attention of Disney executives, who placed her in the Story department as a concept artist. When El Grupo was organised, Mary was chosen to join for the purpose of capturing the mood, movement, colours, and spirit of Latin cultures in her sketches, paintings, and pastels. The young artist quickly found herself surrounded by a kaleidoscopic variety of senses; exotic locales including marketplaces, beaches, and gardens; and interacting with the unique characters of the fishermen, artisans, artists, dancers, and gauchos.

Looking for inspiration for new characters, many members of the Story department surrounded themselves with the flora and fauna of Central and South America, taking in bullfights and riding llamas in the Andes. Jack Miller spent time with Brazil's green parrots, developing the character of José Carioca, friend and tour guide of Donald Duck in the features that emerged from El Grupo's trip. James Bordrero, also of the Story department, was invited to participate in a condor hunt and would combine elements of several South American birds for the wacky Aracuan Bird.

In addition to the individual pieces of concept art, sketches, and paintings produced on the trip, El Grupo made musical recordings of local musicians as reference for Disney's musical team. Walt and his artists also recorded several reels of 16-mm colour film of different locales, performers, animals, and more as visual reference for the artists back in Los Angeles when production on the subsequent projects began.

The contract they had with the Office for the Coordinator of Inter-American Affairs initially called for twelve one-reel short cartoons resulting from Disney's Good Neighbor trip. For the sake of scheduling and production, Walt and his team of directors realised it would be best to produce and release the shorts in groups of four. However, it was quickly decided that it would make more financial sense for the studio, and better stewardship of the government's stipend, to combine the individual shorts into longer feature films. These films, which would be a collection of shorts organised around a central theme or narrative with animated interstitials, would become known as a "package film", due to the fact that they were several films "packaged" into a single feature.

The first of the Latin American package films was the forty-two minute long *Saludos Amigos*, which featured Donald Duck's travelogue to Lake Titicaca; the story of Pedro, a young mailplane assigned the task of transporting the mail across the Andes; an animated short featuring Goofy out of his element as a gaucho in the Argentinean pampas; and "Aquarela do Brasil," a musical short featuring Donald Duck and José Carioca dancing the Samba through well-known locations throughout Brazil. The film was completed less than a year after El Grupo's trip south. True to its purpose of entertaining and wooing the Latin American nations to the concept of Pan-Americanism, *Saludos Amigos* first premiered in Rio de Janeiro on 24 August 1942, soon followed by a premiere in Buenos Aires on 6 October, before its American opening in Boston on 6 February 1943. While the film did not win any Oscars at the 1943 Academy Awards, despite receiving three nominations, it had widespread success throughout South America: theatres sold out for six months, breaking all ticket sales records across the continent. Latin American critics praised Disney's efforts: Buenos Aires' *La Prensa* described *Saludos Amigos* as "show[ing] Disney's ability in catching our customs and music."

Another Disney feature premiered outside American borders a few days before *Saludos Amigos*. After several years in development and production, *Bambi* premiered in London on 8 August 1942, with a domestic opening at New York City's Radio City Music Hall on 13 August. Walt had been unsure of an animated film with lifelike animal characters and so hosted a special preview for 700 young people between the ages of 18 and 26. The audience overwhelmingly approved of the film: according to one article, "Disney discovered he had turned out a perfect picture 'for young people in love!'"

Film critics praised *Bambi* for its narrative and artistic accomplishment. An October 1942 article in *Modern Screen* described *Bambi* as "pure Disney…a world delightful, natural and real as only Disney can create." In spite of the film's lack of human depiction, reviewer Zachary Gold found himself still drawn into the story: "If, before the final fadeout," he wrote, "you find yourself wishing you were born a deer, a rabbit or even a skunk, that's only fair tribute to the Disney magic." Gold even attributed the work of Disney as being the reason behind human anatomical development: "[Humans] evolved eyes back in the days when the world was still evolving, because someone had a suspicion Disney was coming."

Not all critics believed that the studio's experiment in a realistic animated world panned out. One reviewer for the *New York Times* argued that Walt had come close to destroying his successful run of animated films. Even Walt's eldest daughter, Diane, complained about the fate of Bambi's mother at the hands of hunters.

Unfortunately, despite the six years of work that Disney's artists had poured into *Bambi*, it did not earn as much as Walt and Roy had hoped. The Second World War's effect on international markets, as well as Americans' frugality due to the war effort, prevented Disney's newest feature from performing as well as it should have done during its initial release. However, after a few months, ticket sales picked up earning *Bambi* $2.95 million, approximately one-third the amount grossed by *Snow White and the Seven Dwarfs*.

While nominated for three categories in the 1943 Academy Awards, the Academy ultimately agreed with the negative reviews: *Bambi* would be Disney's first full-length animated feature to not win a single Oscar at the Academy Awards.

The second film to come out of El Grupo's Good Neighbor tour was referred to throughout the studio by the title *Surprise Package*: this alluded to the fact that this new film would be a package film similar to its predecessor, but was also a reference to the film's overarching storyline: while celebrating his birthday, Donald Duck receives a series of surprise birthday gifts from his friends in Central and South America. The film's title soon changed to *The Three Caballeros,* taking its name from the catchy song in the film's second half. *The Three Caballeros* would primarily focus on the culture of Mexico, with some animated segments highlighting other nations of the southern hemisphere:

"The Cold-Blooded Penguin," narrated by Sterling Holloway, followed an Antarctic penguin who fled to the Galapagos Islands; "The Flying Gauchito" served as a memoir piece of a young Uruguayan boy who discovered a flying donkey; José Carioca returned to take Donald Duck on a tour of a beloved Brazilian region in "Baía;" and the two birds were joined by Mexican rooster Panchito who educates them on Mexican traditions throughout the remainder of the film.

The art team for *The Three Caballeros* focused on the role that emotion, colour and music plays in Mexican and South American culture. Mary Blair was brought in to provide colour and art direction for the film, and made an additional trip to Mexico in 1942 for research purposes. She also proved several concept sketches, especially highlighting the juxtaposition of bright colours against black backgrounds. Some of her sketches were used as still images to help tell the story of a Mexican Christmas tradition in the "Las Posadas" sequence.

Newcomer Panchito, a Mexican rooster dressed as a vaquero, brought high energy to the film, which was particularly showcased in the titular song "The Three Caballeros". Later in the film, Panchito teaches Donald and José about the tradition of the piñata, which is often shaped like animals and fantastic creatures and is filled with candy and toys. To bring energy and zaniness to these scenes, animator Ward Kimball was assigned the sequences and given free rein to animate from his imagination, regardless of whether it adhered to past animation styles or philosophies of the Walt Disney Studios. Kimball was also musically inclined, having formed his own studio-wide musical groups including the Hungry 5 and Hugajeedy 8, and was given many of the sequences where José danced the Samba and Donald *attempted* to dance with the live-action actors and actresses.

As the studio began planning *Saludos Amigos* and its sequel-of-sorts *The Three Caballeros*, Walt and his directors received bad news from Roy: the financial problems plaguing the studio as a result of the war would prevent the Good Neighbor films from being fully animated. To save money, they decided that live action footage would be used as filler. In *Saludos Amigos*, actual footage from El Grupo's trip to South and Central America was used to help tell the story of the film's production. In some cases, such as the scene where El Grupo is seen boarding their plane to depart to Brazil, footage was staged as no recording was made while on the trip. While *The Three Caballeros* would have animated interstitials to link the four animated shorts together in a cohesive narrative, a different solution needed to be identified to include the live action footage.

It was decided that the studio would try to utilise an updated method of an old technique to bring live action footage to *The Three Caballeros*: much like Walt Disney's first foray into animation with the Alice Comedies, live actors and actresses would find themselves in an animated world interacting with animated props and characters. Unfortunately, the process that was used in Disney's Alice Comedies was outdated and took a long time and a lot of money to create. Walt turned to Ub Iwerks, whose talent he felt was being wasted in the Checking department, to come up with a new process to make the combination of live action Technicolor and animation quicker, cheaper, and more believable.

Two solutions were developed to bring people into the animated world of Donald, José, and Panchito. The first process involved close-up shots of the live actors and actresses. In order to create animated depth with the human actor in the foreground, initial animation was completed and then rear projected onto a screen behind them. For example, as Aurora Miranda danced and sang "Os Quindins de Yayá" through the cartoon streets of Baía, animated footage of Donald and José Carioca can be seen dimly projected behind her.

The Three Caballeros also featured scenes where the animated characters interacted with a live-action world, such as when Donald played a blindfolded game of hide-and-seek with several girls in bathing suits on a simulated beach set up in the studio's parking lot. Ub, who had been promoted to head of Disney's Optical Printing department, worked to improve upon the travelling matte process, allowing animation to be overlaid onto live action footage. In Donald's hide-and-seek scene, for example, the actresses were filmed chasing and running away from an imaginary cartoon character. After printing the live action footage, a Donald-shaped matte was placed over each frame as a placeholder for where its animated counterpart would be. Donald Duck was then animated on cels, with separate photography taken. The film was then fed into Ub's specially-created optical printer, which combined the two strips of film, followed by the photography of each frame to create a single strip of film showing the animated Donald Duck taunting the sunbathing girls. The astonishing success of this process revolutionised Disney's ability to combine the two mediums of live action and animation, which would later be used in subsequent Disney films including *Song of the South, Fun and Fancy Free*, and *Mary Poppins*.

With the completion of *The Three Caballeros*, the studio began production on a third Good Neighbor package film, which would feature segments highlighting the culture of Mexico, Brazil, and Cuba. Additional research trips were taken, with Mary Blair and Fred Moore travelling to Cuba in 1943 and 1944. Production was halted, however, after *The Three Caballeros* failed to be a box office or critical success, breaking the studio's contract with the Coordinator for Inter-American Affairs for twelve short films. Walt and the CIAA weren't too concerned with this breach of contract, however as by then the studio was too busy fighting the Axis Powers.

While the Second World War had been raging in Europe since 1939, the United States spent the first couple years trying to convince itself that it would not get involved, preferring to isolate itself rather than intervene in a conflict that didn't involve them. However, as the tide seemed to turn toward an Axis victory, the perspective of America began to change as they increasingly started to support their allies rather than continue to take an attitude of nonintervention.

Hollywood was one of the first bastions to promote antifascist rhetoric, officially beginning as early as 1940. It was in this year that the Motion Picture Committee Cooperating for National Defense was established, which helped to plan war-related features and shorts for the various studios, as well as handle distribution of the films throughout the United States. These live action features and animated shorts tended to focus on war or military-related themes and included films like Charlie Chaplin's *The Great Dictator*, which satirised Hitler and Nazi Germany; *The Fighting 69th* starring James Cagney, a historical piece about a soldier during the First World War; and Warner Bros.' animated short "Rhapsody in Rivets," which had patriotic and retaliatory undertones.

Walt Disney considered himself to be a patriotic American, and was once quoted as saying that "[i]f you could see close in my eyes, the American flag is waving in both of them and up my spine is growing this red, white and blue stripe." He felt so strongly about supporting his nation that as a teenager during the First World War, he had tried several times to enlist despite being too young. He eventually found a way around the government's rules by joining the American Red Cross because they accepted seventeen-year-old recruits, and even then forged his age as he was actually just sixteen.

Thus, while America began to mobilise as the clouds of war gathered on the horizon, Walt decided to offer the services of his studio artists in creating insignia for the United States armed forces. In February 1941, a studio-wide Insignia Design contest began, resulting in more than one thousand entries for the United States Army, Navy and Air Force. Nearly five hundred Disney-designed insignia wcrc approved and would consequently be found everywhere: on the sides of aeroplanes, as lapel pins, and on patches for aviation jackets. Many of Disney's animated characters were featured, including Donald Duck, Max Hare, Pluto, Flower, Jiminy Cricket and Bambi, with many of the winning designs created by studio artists Hank Porter and Roy Williams. Dumbo served as the mascot of Fresno, California's 2nd Reconnaissance Squadron, while Pete, dressed as a pirate and straddling an aeroplane, served as a symbol of the Fighting Squadron 422, also known as the "Flying Buccaneers". A cartoon mosquito riding a torpedo served as the visual representation of Squadron Three's Motor Torpedo Boats. Studio musicians even pitched in, composing the "official theme music" for the Beechcraft Aircraft Company, as well as a new bee character to serve as the company's wartime mascot.

The studio also produced drawings for various wartime agencies in order to boost soldier morale. For example, Fred Moore, who was renowned throughout the studio for his sensuous drawings of the female figure, particularly the centaurettes in *Fantasia*, drew pictures of nude pin-up girls. Mickey Mouse was featured in several propaganda posters. A February 1943 advertisement titled "So You Won't Run, eh, Adolf!" showed Mickey, Goofy and Donald accompanied by the British lion, the Russian bear, and the Chinese dragon as they surrounded a cowering Hitler. Hank Porter drew an illustration for the front of a program of the Masquers Servicemen's Morale Corps featuring Mickey, Minnie and Donald saluting a flag while the faces of smiling servicemen look on, while another image showed Mickey dressed in the uniform of the Aircraft Warning Service, preparing to report upon suspicious activity.

Early 1941 also brought Disney the opportunity to support the war on-screen when the studio found itself receiving commissions for training films to instruct employees of various government agencies, factory workers, and those serving in the armed forces. For instance, in April

1941, the Commissioner of the National Board of Canada approached the studio to produce a short documentary for the country's Department of National Defence. The Canadian government was pleased with Disney's "Stop that Tank!" and requested four additional propaganda shorts to encourage citizens to purchase bonds to support the war effort. These animated shorts featured popular characters from the Silly Symphonies and features, including the Three Little Pigs, the Seven Dwarfs, Donald Duck, Mickey Mouse and his band from "The Band Concert", and Pinocchio and Gepetto.

Early on, Walt had resolved that he would produce any wartime shorts at-cost, essentially making no profit off the studio's work while it did its patriotic duty during the war. As a result, many shorts – the four Canadian bond shorts in particular – recycled animation from the previous shorts and features, or in some cases, re-released abbreviated shorts that had been modified to fit the wartime message. For example, Canada's "The Thrifty Pig" retold the story of 1933's "Three Little Pigs". Much of the original animation was reused, but some of the art was changed, giving the Big Bad Wolf a hat and armband, both sporting the Nazi swastika. Another of the Canadian bond films, "7 Wise Dwarfs", featured the beloved characters digging in their gem mine and singing "Heigh Ho" as they leave work at the end of the day. Rather than the background being one of forests and waterfalls as seen in the original film, Ottawa's Parchment Hill is seen in the distance. The dwarves arrive in town, where they exchange their bags of gems for war savings bonds, thus doing their part to support Canada's war effort.

Disney's war films became domestic after the Lockheed Aircraft Company, located a couple miles from the Walt Disney Studios, asked the studio to produce a training film for employees called "Four Methods of Flush Riveting". The film featured no plot or gags, but was instead an animated instruction of how to rivet two pieces of metal together, accompanied by narration. Walt was more than happy to oblige: in an article in *The Public Opinion Quarterly*, he explained that training films like this "[sped] up learning, increas[ed] retention, and compel[ed] interest", aiding in the learning process, but also recognising that films like his could not "replace the textbook, the laboratory, or the lecture." A survey was conducted with two control groups: one group who simply read a training manual for several weeks to complete their jobs and another group who viewed a training film about the same topic a single time. The results were striking: those who viewed the training film performed better than their counterparts by 20 per cent.

Additional training films were produced by the studio during the war, particularly for the different divisions of the armed forces. The American Navy in particular was a beneficiary: Ub Iwerks helped develop a series of shorts to help servicemen identify different enemy aircraft and warships, with the studio producing several at-cost that were released within ninety days of receiving the contract. To save time and money, many shortcuts were used, such as using models, stills and cutouts rather than taking time to fully animate scenes like those in the studio's feature films. Walt didn't mind: he wasn't in it for the money anyway.

Late 1941 was particularly difficult for Walt Disney's emotional and mental state. While Walt was in Buenos Aires for a portion of the Goodwill Tour, Elias Disney's health had begun to deteriorate. He had been vomiting repeatedly without many other symptoms other than being exhausted and in bed. After a few days, the family doctor made a home visit and ordered that Elias be transported to the hospital for examination. It was discovered that the elder Disney was suffering from a bowel obstruction, and surgery was successfully performed. Unfortunately, his condition continued to deteriorate over the next few days with the onset of pneumonia and a dangerously high temperature. The attending doctor was discouraged by Elias' health, declaring his condition "hopeless". Walt and Roy's father succumbed to his illness, passing away on 13 September. Elias was buried in the Great Mausoleum alongside his wife, Flora. Walt was the sole member of his immediate family not in attendance at the funeral due to his trip to South America.

As 1941 drew to a close, things didn't seem to get any easier. Early in December, Walt was enjoying a quiet Sunday at home with his family, a rare morning away from the studio, and was relaxing while the radio played quietly in the background when suddenly, at around 11 o'clock, a news brief interrupted and announced that the Japanese had attacked the United States. Walt's mind began spinning, and as he considered how this might cause the pace of the studio's wartime projects to increase he received a phone call from the studio.

On the line was the manager of the studio's facilities, who told him that the Army had rolled up to the front gate of the studio, demanding admittance. Knowing that Walt was quite possessive of his company's property and assets, he insisted on calling his boss before allowing the Army to enter.

"Go ahead, call him if you want," the commanding officer said. "We're moving in anyhow." In the midst of the phone conversation with the studio executive, seven hundred soldiers began marching through the studio gates, moving military supplies and weapons into the studio, mustering in the common spaces until given instruction by their superiors. Walt hopped into his car and drove to the studio, prepared to meet with Army commanders to discover how his studio could best serve its nation.

He soon learned that the studio would be used as a makeshift base for the Army, specifically to protect nearby aircraft manufacturers including Lockheed and Douglas. Animators were kicked out of their offices in exchange for workspace and sleeping arrangements for the soldiers. Anti-aircraft gear and machine-shop trucks were brought into the studio, with the soundstage being used to house many of the larger pieces of equipment for protection in case of an airstrike. Sheds around the studio became storage for artillery, including three million rounds of ammunition. Even Lockheed utilised space at the studio, taking over offices on the first floor of the Animation building. Studio employees had mixed opinions about the soldiers who now called the campus home: while they obviously resented being kicked out of their offices so the soldiers had makeshift barracks, they nonetheless welcomed many military personnel into the culture of Disney, inviting them to participate in the lunchtime softball games and dances with the Ink-and-Paint girls on the studio's soundstage.

The studio and its staff had been drafted to fight the war against the Axis in the matter of moments. In addition to continuing production on upcoming shorts and features including *Bambi* and the Good Neighbor films, they were expected to produce the Navy's training films, educational shorts, and animated propaganda to be shown to civilians in theatres. The freedom and familiarity of the studio was sacrificed in exchange for national safety, with armed guards standing post at the studio gates, asking for identification from each individual passing through, including Walt Disney himself.

Several artists and staff members from the Walt Disney Studios made greater sacrifices toward the war effort by becoming active participants in domestic security or enlisting to fight. Many studio artists were commissioned by the Army's 604th Engineer Camouflage Battalion to design patterns that would hide factories, such as those owned by Consolidated, North American, and Northrop, from enemy airmen. Other artists were tasked with constructing miniature towns and neighbourhoods, complete with scale model homes, cars, streetlights, clotheslines and trees, on top of aeroplane factories like Lockheed and Boeing along America's west coast. Some artists were also given the job of creating a slide film to explain the history and value of camouflage. Animator Roy Williams did his part to protect the important work happening at the studio by volunteering his time to serve as an air raid warden, not only for the city of Burbank, but also on the roofs of the studio, helmeted and with binoculars in hand. Late in the war, concept artist James Bodrero joined the USO, travelling around the country entertaining troops by performing live sketches, as well as drawing caricatures and Disney characters on the military's tanks, jeeps, cannons and aeroplanes. Story and layout man Dick Kelsey was commissioned by the Marines to build scale models of Pacific islands for strategic purposes. So significant was his work to the military that he was given the status of officer, ultimately becoming a Major, and receiving a commendation from General Douglas MacArthur himself.

Some studio employees answered the call to serve by taking up arms in the name of freedom. Roy Disney, in particular, proudly called the studio "an organization of veterans", after reflecting upon a service flag that hung on studio grounds covered in 165 service stars, including two gold stars signifying that a serviceman had given his life for the cause. Roy himself had served in the First World War alongside others including Perce Pearce, Ben Sharpsteen, and Jack King.

The artists at the Walt Disney Studios were seen as an essential part of helping the United States win the war, and as a result, many of them were eligible for draft deferments. Some, however, chose to enlist to do their part, with many writing letters back to their friends working on propaganda films in southern California. Over the course of the war, numerous studio employees served in the armed forces, including Frank Thomas and Wolfgang "Wooly" Reitherman. Not everyone made it back, however. In 1943, word came from Colonel and Mrs. E James of London that their son, Animator Gerry James, a pilot in the Royal Air Force, had gone missing while on a mission. Shortly after receiving the letter, his coworkers at Disney were dismayed to learn that his body had been discovered on Holland's shores. More bad news arrived when it was announced that Johnnie Leighton, Jr. of the studio's New York office had been killed while fighting on the Alaskan front.

Many of Disney's female employees found themselves receiving promotions within the filmmaking process: with many of the male animators and technicians either enlisted or serving in other off-campus capacities, several talented women were promoted to be assistant animators and inbetweeners. To ensure the best were chosen, they were tested with footage featuring Donald falling off a cliff only to be saved by bouncing when he hit the ground. The footage was screened by the directorial staff, and the female artists were assigned accordingly. Some women also filled in as technicians, serving in the Camera, Background, and Cutting departments. Many were surprised when they were forced to sign an oath of loyalty, promising to maintain secrecy and confidentiality about the shorts they worked on as by taking these assignments they were now accountable to the various branches of the U.S. military, the Federal Bureau of Investigation, and the federal government.

Animation studios like Disney played a crucial role in providing instruction and motivation to those in the armed forces and wartime industries during the Second World War. Perhaps more important, however, was capturing the hearts and minds of the citizen populace and convincing them that this was a righteous war and so they should support the war effort in any way possible. In what seemed to be a practice isolated to the American film industry, Warner Bros., Universal, MGM, Disney and Columbia each released war-related propaganda shorts, while studios without animation divisions distributed cartoons, such as the Fleischers creating shorts for Paramount.

Rather than trying to persuade American filmgoers through content and instruction alone, animated propaganda shorts also carried a strong, distinctly patriotic attitude that was meant to inspire ordinary Americans with bravery, boldness, and a desire to fight the war at home. While the content itself could be seen as boring, such as the purchasing of war bonds, the merits of rationing or the importance of immunisation, crass humour and exaggeration were employed to hold audiences' attention. Subconscious symbolism was also used to create feelings of excitement or dread: for instance, many of Disney's shorts during the Second World War used the theme from Beethoven's "Symphony No. 5" to evoke the danger of the Axis Powers. Astute viewers would notice a musical phrase corresponding with the "three dots and a dash" of the morse code representing the letter V. Thus, this tune in the Disney shorts symbolised America's impending victory against its enemies.

Disney's propaganda shorts began being released for general audiences in late 1941, with many of them featuring Donald Duck, whose humorous antics and big temper entertained viewers who often felt the darkness of war on a daily basis, while Mickey Mouse was perceived by both the studio and audiences as a peacemaker. There was also a concern at the studio that using Mickey Mouse, the most important piece of capital at the Walt Disney Studios, could be risky should the Allies lose the war. While Walt maintained that Mickey was "retired for the duration" of the conflict, the Animation department continued to produce shorts in the Mickey Mouse series showing the mouse as an American everyman to encourage audiences and give them a sense of normality as they watched him going golfing, battling a whirlwind while raking leaves, enjoying a birthday party, and taking an expedition to South America with Pluto to photograph armadillos, a short which resulted from El Grupo's Good Neighbor trip.

There were two main categories of general release propaganda shorts produced by Disney during the Second World War. The first, known as homefront propaganda, was meant to entertain audiences while educating them about how they could contribute to or support the war effort. The second was hard propaganda, which was meant to insult or demonise the enemy through an exaggerated or stereotypical portrayal, in order to convince Americans why they should support aggression against the Axis armies.

As 1942 began, 93% of the studio's production was propaganda and training films, most of which was produced at-cost which resulted in no profit to the studio; Disney significantly outpaced the industry average, of which 44% of animated shorts were war-related. The studio's homefront propaganda covered a variety of subjects including rationing ("Out of the Frying Pan and Into the Firing Line"), encouraging the farmers of America to continue their efforts supporting the war ("Food Will Win the War"), and asking Americans to approach the war rationally rather than acting on their feelings ("Reason and Emotion").

In some cases, Disney received special commissions to produce shorts by particular American government agencies. In mid-December 1941, Walt was called to Washington DC for a meeting with Secretary of the Treasury Henry Morganthau Jr. and Guy Helvering, Commissioner of the Internal Revenue Service. Accompanied by Joe Grant and Dick Huemer, Walt listened as Morganthau proposed a short to persuade Americans to file their taxes, which would help support the government during the war. Walt and his storymen accepted the assignment, but were startled to learn that they only had three months to produce the entire short from start to finish.

Grant and Huemer began work on the new IRS short immediately upon returning to California, submitting the initial story treatment to Morganthau two days later on 20 December. The short, called "The New Spirit", would feature Donald Duck learning how to quickly and correctly fill out his income tax form, concluding with a montage of what Americans' tax money was going towards: factory-manufactured munitions, aeroplanes, battleships and tanks. While the Treasury secretary approved of the short's narrative, he insisted that the cartoon use an original character rather than Donald. Walt, who understood the appeal of using a recognisable character in getting audiences' attention, insisted that Donald would have to stay in the film if the studio were to produce the short. Morganthau relented.

The entire production of the short "The New Spirit", took a mere four weeks from start to finish, rather than the standard six months it typically took to produce an average Disney short. As the short was developed in partnership with the Department of Treasury, the government provided prints of the film to approximately 12,000 theatres for free so that as many Americans as possible were encouraged to file their taxes. The short was not only very popular with audiences but also successfully imparted its message: data from Gallup polls showed that though the film premiered nearly three months prior to the tax deadline, 37% of Americans filed their taxes immediately after seeing the film. The government was so impressed, especially afterthe Academy of Motion Pictures Arts and Sciences nominated the short for Best Documentary, that it ordered a sequel to the film to be released the following year: "The Spirit of '43."

The Walt Disney Studios also produced entertaining animated shorts to improve the wartime morale of both soldiers and civilians. Many of these shorts were meant to justify the war and encourage Americans to laugh in the face of the Axis. Several cartoons featuring Donald Duck as an Army private made audiences laugh as their favourite duck made bumbling mistakes, such as destroying a Japanese air force base by rerouting a river, painting a tank with invisible paint, or accidentally bayonetting his drill sergeant. Other shorts were more serious such as "Education for Death" which featured an innocent German boy who was brainwashed into an evil, fascist, brutal killing machine, only to meet his own untimely death.

One short in particular brought the Walt Disney Studios great praise during the Second World War: "Der Fuhrer's Face". Walt and his team initially came up with an idea for a cartoon in which Donald Duck experienced life in "Naziland", which included extreme food shortages, the expectation that all Germans read Adolf Hitler's *Mein Kampf*, being overworked in munitions factories, and excessive saluting at the chancellor's photograph. To drive home the point of how absurd fascist Germany was, Walt wanted an equally ridiculous song to accompany the picture.

Walt approached one of his composers, Oliver Wallace, with a request: "Ollie, I want a serious song, *but it's got to be funny.*" He went on to explain that the song was meant to be sung by the German people in the film, who considered their song to be reverent to the state, when actually it was found ridiculous by democratic nations. Wallace went home and lay on the couch, frustrated because he didn't quite understand the assignment. His wife walked in and suggested that rather than being lazy, he ride his bike with her to the store. On the way, as Wallace later explained, "[t]he music came to me in one flash. It nearly knocked me off my bicycle." Opening his mouth in surprise at this burst of creativity, he was stunned to find lyrics begin to emit from his lips, sung loudly and in a German accent, much to his wife's embarrassment as this impromptu performance took place in the middle of the street. As she began laughing it off, asking him who wrote the absurd song he was singing, he yelled back to her that he was in the process of writing it, and became so distracted by the shock of the song and the conversation with his wife that he nearly rode his bike into a truck. The following day, Wallace pulled Walt aside and began singing the newly composed song. Walt began laughing. "That'll do, Ollie," he said.

"Der Fuhrer's Face" became animated gold. It rallied American audiences against a common enemy, bringing them together through laughter and giving them reason not to take Hitler and his Nazi state seriously. Adolf Hitler himself was reportedly furious about the film and burned every copy that he and his enforcers could get their hands on, demonstrating how powerful the short and Wallace's song were in boosting morale and diminishing Germany's intimidation. The short was smuggled into Europe, particularly the nations under German influence, as an effort to turn the repressed citizenry against their oppressors. The film also achieved critical success, winning an Academy Award for Short Subject (Cartoon) in 1943.

In the months following the attack on Pearl Harbor, things appeared grim for the United States forces in the Pacific. The Japanese military had taken possession of dozens of strategic islands, and an American victory seemed unlikely. In May 1942, Major Alexander de Seversky published *Victory Through Air Power*, a book about how the United States could utilise aviation to win the war, citing the long-range bombing strategy employed by General Billy Mitchell during the First World War as evidence. The book quickly became a bestseller and became part of the general American cultural awareness.

Nonetheless, many were sceptical of de Seversky's assertion that air power – not amphibious or land-based invasion – would win the war. After reading the book, Walt felt that turning de Seversky's book into a full-length motion picture rather than a nine-minute short would have the greatest impact in convincing Americans of the merits of aviation during wartime, particularly if they combined emotion-provoking visuals with a dramatic score. Curious about whether a film adaptation of de Seversky's book would be successful, Walt once again commissioned Gallup's Audience Research Institute. Data demonstrated that approximately twenty million people had heard of de Seversky and his theories, and at least five million had read the entirety or condensed version of his work. Walt felt so strongly about contributing this ideology to the war effort, that he committed to finance the film himself, rather than relying upon government commissions or dipping into the studio's budget.

Victory Through Air Power would not be story-driven and full of gags like the studio's previous features. Instead, its only goal was to persuade and inspire audiences. After a short segment at the beginning of the film explaining the history of flight using traditional Disney animation and a smattering of gags, the rest of the film became more serious, using symbolism, montages of munitions and wartime machines coming off factory assembly lines, live action footage of both Billy Mitchell and

Major de Seversky, and animated diagrams showing potential strategy and manoeuvres against the enemy.

All of the creative resources available at the Walt Disney Studios were employed to create this next feature. As with previous features, this project led to the development of new effects, including one developed by Ub utilising the cutout silhouettes of aircrafts moved incrementally across a background as both a cost-saving measure and a way to ensure realism and consistency of aircraft. The Walt Disney Studios also took the opportunity to hone their skills at live-action cinematography, particularly in the segments featuring de Seversky's monologue. In fact, partially due to the work done on *Victory Through Air Power*, approximately 50% of the studio's footage shot in 1943 was live action.

Some of the studio's best story artists were employed to plan the film: inspirational sketch artist Sylvia Holland was tasked with storyboarding the feature, while her colleagues James Bodrero and Retta Scott provided concept sketches. So many of these initial drawings featured diagrams and maps of the proposed military ideology that Scott took to calling the film "Victory Through Arrow Power".

Victory Through Air Power was distributed by United Artists and released to the general public in July 1943, receiving positive reviews. *The Film Daily* wrote that "Disney does superb job with film version of Seversky book; Timely pic[ture] deserves wide audience...[it is] an achievement fully worthy of [Walt Disney's] name...Every person seriously interested in victory against the Axis owes it to himself to see the film." *The New York Times* also praised the use of visuals to depict de Seversky's argument to the layman.

While the feature was geared towards the general public, many in positions of power or decision-making screened it as well. For example, both President Franklin Roosevelt and Winston Churchill were convinced of Seversky's assertion that air power was superior after viewing the Disney film. While America's long-range bombing had begun several weeks before, the film's premise only gave Roosevelt more resolve as the war moved forward.

The success of Disney's animated documentary created new opportunities for the studio, which were especially welcome at a time when there were fewer opportunities due to the closure of foreign film markets. Various organisations and agencies reached out, requesting that the studio produce educational films about how healthy and informed

Americans would better guarantee an Allied victory. Documentary shorts were produced covering a variety of topics including venereal disease, chemical warfare, and immunisation.

One joint commission that Disney received came from the Public Health Service and Pan American Sanitary Bureau requesting a short discussing the correlation between mosquitoes and malaria. The film, "The Winged Scourge", used dramatic music, symbolism, and hyperbole to stress the seriousness of eradicating malaria through the control of mosquitoes. For example, as the short opens, an announcer describes the mosquito as "Public Enemy No. 1", reading from a poster that they are wanted dead or alive. A four-minute segment shows how the mosquito can transmit the disease, using limited animation and still drawings. As the camera pulls back, audiences discover that the seven dwarfs are also screening the instructional film. The narrator explains how the mosquito population can be controlled, and the dwarfs take his advice by cutting swamp grass, spreading oil or pesticides on top of standing water to kill larvae, and digging trenches to drain stagnant pools, all to the tune of "Whistle While You Work".

In planning "The Winged Scourge", Walt wanted to use the dwarfs to "stress how simple it is [to eliminate mosquitoes]. If you make it look like a tremendous job, they'll say, hell, I'll take the mosquitoes. When they go about it, it oughtn't be any trouble at all." When asked what angle the film could take to motivate civilians during wartime, Walt explained that they could "play up [the] loss of time and the inconvenience of disability" in a time when every worker and every minute were necessary to defeat the Axis. While little data is available regarding the direct impact of this Disney short, within a few years malaria was eradicated from the United States, showing that the film helped to educate Americans.

As one of Hollywood's preeminent film studios, the features and shorts of the Walt Disney Studios had surpassed their founder's earlier goal of entertaining audiences through story, gags, and accompanying music. Since the introduction of Mickey Mouse, Walt and his artists had been cultural influencers. But with the coming of war, Disney had taken on a new role, one which played an integral part in uniting hemispheres, bringing down empires, boosting the morale of soldiers and civilians alike, helping to advance military theory, and saving lives. Animation was no longer an entertaining art form: it had been elevated to a serious medium which impacted the entire world.

WIDER VISTAS

Between the animators' strike of 1941 and the significant and challenging work of the Good Neighbor program and the Second World War, Walt Disney became a changed man, particularly in regards to how he managed his studio and approached his employees. The close camaraderie that had characterised the Walt Disney Studios was not only impacted by the larger staff resulting from production of the features and the scope of the new Burbank campus, but the strike had introduced an atmosphere of paranoia and distrust between staff members while the contributions toward international diplomacy created a highly competitive and cutthroat environment. In other words, work at the Walt Disney Studios had gone from being fun, friendly and cooperative to an environment marked by prevailing seriousness, high standards, and competition.

The shift in this atmosphere was partially a result of Walt's own beliefs about the studio and its work. During the strike, he had felt personally attacked and betrayed by those he had once admired and had close personal relationships with, including Art Babbitt and Bill Tytla. With the advent of features, work focused more on story and technical advances, rather than gags, resulting in less hilarity throughout the studio, and as a result, Walt became more focused on artistic excellence. In fact, he was so stringent on the quality of the animation produced by his artists that some referred to him as "Der Fuhrer" throughout the 1940s.

Walt was still incredibly involved in all projects that the studio produced, especially the features. While he had a trusted team of directors who provided their vision to individual sequences and scenes, entire film plots were vetted by Walt, who was considered Producer at the studio. His high expectations often led to the cutting of entire sequences from the final print of a film, with the justification that they did not add to the narrative's continuity, much to the frustration of those who had spent months working on the animation. He was also known to get frustrated during Story meetings and while reviewing the Dailies when the work did not live up to his standards or someone disagreed with him. The artists quickly learned how to discern when Walt was approaching their offices to check on their work: his approach was particularly recognisable due to his heavy-footed walk and wracking cough. Employees would look at each other and mutter a coded warning: "Man is in the forest", a reference to the warning given to Bambi by his mother.

Those who were closer to him, such as Jack Kinney and Ward Kimball, saw Walt for what he really was: rather than being a harsh taskmaster, they perceived him as "dedicated" and "driven". Oftentimes, his most trusted artists viewed their boss as simply "one of them", "another person" who worked at the studio, rather than an executive who was higher up in the hierarchy. He often made jokes while in casual conversation with those around him, many of which were perceived as being "rural" in nature, often referencing outhouses, bedpans, cow udders, and farts.

Despite his high professional expectations and the fact that his professional career was such a large part of his life, Walt often participated in social engagements. He spent time watching and participating in various sporting events, including baseball, polo and horse racing. He and Lillian also enjoyed the occasional dinner at a local restaurant or concert at the Hollywood Bowl, often with the Hollywood elite or members of his staff. Walt also took occasional trips with close friends, including a trip to Chicago and Dearborn, Michigan with artist Ward Kimball.

Most evenings, however, Walt preferred to spend time at home with his family. Diane and Sharon adored their father, who, as much as possible, often went out of his way to leave work at the studio so he could be with his family. By the early 1950s, Diane had enrolled at the University of Southern California, while Sharon conducted her studies as a sophomore in high school. While their relationship with their father was different to how it had been during their childhood, they later recalled how he would play games and swim with them in the family pool. One of their favourite games was one they called "Old Witch": Walt would act like a scary hag and hide somewhere in the house. The girls would slowly walk through the house, looking for their father, and were always startled when he would jump out from behind a door or curtain and yell.

Walt took every opportunity he could to dote on the girls. Regardless of what was happening at the studio, he made sure that he attended every recital, performance, event, or outing that Diane and Sharon had, often sitting towards the front with a smile on his face. In addition to being physically present, he also gave the girls gifts to demonstrate his affection. In one instance, he came home from the studio with a goat; unfortunately Lillian wouldn't allow it into the house, so Walt, furious, stalked out of the house, goat in tow, back to the studio for the night. He was also incredibly patient with his daughters: when Diane wrecked the family car when she was learning to drive, Walt was very gracious, and simply purchased another car to ease the anxiety of his regretful daughter.

As America and Hollywood returned to a sense of normalcy with the end of the Second World War, the focus at the Walt Disney Studios shifted from wartime projects back to what Walt referred to as "good entertainment projects". The Story department found itself particularly busy, developing concepts for a number of new features including *Peter Pan, Don Quixote, Robinson Crusoe, Alice in Wonderland*, and a film adaptation of Kenneth Grahame's *The Wind in the Willows*.

Meanwhile, many of the artists who had left their jobs in filmmaking behind to serve their country were welcomed back, sending the Ink-and-Paint girls and other women who had worked as animators and camera operators back to their jobs in their own segregated department.

Studio executives knew that most of Europe would spend the next several years rebuilding after the conclusion of the war and that enjoying a movie would therefore not be a priority for European survivors, resulting in the limited nature of film markets of Europe, if not closed to Hollywood altogether. Fewer dollars were available to invest on larger full-length projects and the studio needed a quick and easy way to make money after the challenges of having a low income during the war while they produced their commissioned work at-cost. They also realised they had found some success in the Western Hemisphere with the Good Neighbor films, so it was decided that the studio would continue to produce package films. Each of these projects would serve as a collection of shorts or featurettes combined with interstitials to connect together around a central theme.

During the initial planning for *Fantasia*, Walt had suggested that the studio could re-release the film on a regular basis but with new symphonic pieces and animation. After the film didn't do as well as hoped and the Second World War shifted the focus of the features division, many of the ideas for subsequent segments were shelved. However, no good idea ever really died at Disney, and many of the songs and concepts set aside found their way into the new package films, such as *Make Mine Music* and *Melody Time*, including Debussy's "Clair de Lune" and a jazzy interpretation of Rimsky-Korsakov's "Flight of the Bumblebee". More modern tunes as well as Disney-written compositions such as "Once Upon a Wintertime", "Casey at the Bat", and Joyce Kilmer's poem "Trees" were included as well.

As Disney and the European film markets began to recover in the late 1940s, the studio also produced a handful of compilation films that paired longer stories with more developed plots that were too short to be features and too long to be in previous package films as individual shorts. The first, *Fun and Fancy Free*, is narrated by a curious Jiminy Cricket who enjoys a vinyl retelling of Sinclair Lewis' "Bongo" and listens to the tale of "Mickey and the Beanstalk" as told by ventriloquist Edgar Bergen and his puppets, Charlie McCarthy and Mortimer Snerd. The second compilation film, *The Adventures of Ichabod and Mr. Toad*, focused on great literature and featured stories from Grahame's *The Wind in the Willows*, with inspiration taken from A.A. Milne's stage adaptation of *Toad of Toad Hall*, and Washington Irving's short story, "The Legend of Sleepy Hollow". Both films attracted mostly positive critical reviews, bringing audiences comedic retellings of stories they knew, narrated by celebrities of the day alongside classic Disney animation.

While few advances in animation occurred as a result of work on the postwar package films, *Fun and Fancy Free* in particular had some significant impact on the development of both narrative and characters at Disney moving forward. For example, one of the early treatments developed for the "Mickey and the Beanstalk" segment was initially written by director Thornton Francis "T." Hee and story writer Bill Cottrell as a satire on the process of making a film at the Walt Disney Studios, leading to a later practice of using satire and caricature more heavily in the studio's feature films, shorts and other projects. "Mickey and the Beanstalk" was also a significant moment in the studio's history because it was the first project where Mickey Mouse was not voiced by Walt Disney. Instead, Jimmy MacDonald, who invented and helped record many of the sound effects for the studio's features and shorts, took on the role of Mickey Mouse, which he played until the mid-1970s. The film also utilised animated characters including Jiminy Cricket and Willie the Giant interacting with live action characters and elements.

The Walt Disney Studios had been so focused on its features and wartime efforts throughout the late 1930s and 1940s that they began to lose touch with their shorts division. While Disney was using moving drawings to fight the Axis, other animation studios surpassed the Walt Disney Studios. In fact, "Der Fuhrer's Face", released in 1943, was the last Academy Award that Disney would win until 1954 when the studio netted four Oscars. Recognising they were no longer the most prominent animation studio and needing to make some additional income, the studio took on the task of producing a number of commissioned educational shorts and short subject featurettes. Several public health shorts were produced for various Latin American countries and agencies, while some corporations hired the studio to create shorts to both educate the public and serve as subversive advertising, as in the example of the studio producing the 1946 short film, "The Story of Menstruation" for Kotex.

Some of the studio's educational short films were made to be shown in public schools, combining Disney's animated humour with legitimate educational concepts. The 1959 featurette "Donald in Mathmagic Land" features Donald's journey through a fantasy land where he learns how maths can be found in everyday life, including artwork, nature, music, everyday inventions, and even popular athletic and recreational activities. The animated short film went on to win an Oscar for Best Documentary (Short Subject) in that year's Academy Awards. Some educational shorts were released for general audiences. The early 1950s brought a few music-themed animated specials, including "Melody" and "Toot, Whistle, Plunk and Boom", which were released to theatres and taught audiences about the history of music and the way instruments make different musical sounds.

In the same way that Disney artists used the Silly Symphonies to experiment with animation in the 1930s, the animated shorts and short films of the late 1940s and 1950s helped hone the technical craft of animated film as well. A handful of animators began to dabble in the popular 3D films of the 1950s, trying their hand in the 1953 shorts "Melody" and "Working for Peanuts". However, while the studio was relatively successful at creating a few 3D animated shorts, they would simply remain a successful experiment. The studio also dabbled with stop-motion animation, using small dolls in "Noah's Ark" akin to those used in the Rankin/Bass Christmas specials, while characters made of coloured paper were arranged and rearranged for "A Symposium on Popular Songs".

The postwar years also brought an opportunity for unique collaborations to the Walt Disney Studios. Walt, who, by nature of his work had many prominent friends, was constantly entertaining and showing musicians and architects, politicians and diplomats, movie stars and artists around his studio. One friend in particular, surrealist Salvador Dalí, was impressed with the studio's craft, gushing that animation had the potential to "enhance art". The filmmaker and the artist began talking and agreed to collaborate on an animated short using the talent of Disney's animators and the surrealism of Dalí. The world renown artist moved his equipment into the studio, where he spent time sketching and painting. A number of meetings took place with artist John Hench, where the envisioned short was storyboarded. Work began on the short, but with a mere fifteen seconds of animation completed, Walt and Dalí parted ways in 1946 due to "differences in vision". However, they remained friends, often dreaming about potential projects together.

After generating the studio a moderate amount of income from their package films, educational shorts, and commissioned films, Walt once again turned to full-length features. Ever one to push the boundary of animation and filmmaking, and recognising how expensive it was to produce a fully animated feature, he began to explore the idea of producing live action films that would use animated sequences to help drive the narrative: animation remained the studio's bread and butter, however, and as such, Walt was hesitant to produce a fully live-action film.

As early as the 1930s, Walt had considered producing a film based upon the stories of Joel Chandler Harris, most famously the fables and folktales narrated by the fictional Uncle Remus about the foolishly heroic Br'er Rabbit, his cunning adversary Br'er Fox, and the slow-witted Br'er Bear. After some negotiating, Walt was able to secure the rights to Harris' stories for $10,000 in 1939 with production commencing in 1944. A story was crafted around the character of a young boy who spends time in the company of a recently liberated slave, Uncle Remus, who dispenses wisdom through his tales.

Walt was insistent that the character of Uncle Remus should be live action, choosing actor James Baskett to fill the role and also provide the voice for Br'er Fox. To research the film's styling, Mary Blair took a ten-day trip to Atlanta and the rural areas outside the city, providing concept sketches and collaborating with Claude Coats for colour sampling to provide art direction for the film.

While the majority of the film was live action with animated sequences to depict Uncle Remus' stories, a few scenes required Remus to enter into the animated world and interact with the cartoon forest characters. Rather than utilise the rear projection method implemented for *The Three Caballeros*, a forty-five metre cyclorama mural was painted to serve as a colourful, animated background for the live-action Baskett. To help guide Baskett's gaze, a stick was held to represent the animated character, later covered by the animated cel in the editing process.

While planning and producing what would become *Song of the South*, Walt and his Story and Directorial teams realised that the source material could present some challenges, as it took place in the post-Civil War south and dealt with the issues of race. The studio wanted to ensure that this newest film was not only faithful to Harris' stories but also sensitive to the issues portrayed as well as the actors and audiences who belonged to minority groups. To help avoid controversy, the studio hired a number of experts to provide accuracy, including African American actor and composer Clarence Muse who wrote the music for the film.

Unfortunately, many in the early civil rights communities were not thrilled with *Song of the South*. Both the Urban League and the National Association for the Advancement of Colored People (NAACP) lambasted the film as distorting the truth about an "idyllic master-slave relationship", arguing that Uncle Remus and his cohorts living on the plantation were too friendly with the whites that had previously owned them. *Time* agreed with the civil rights organisation, commenting that the film would "enrage all educated Negroes, and a number of damn yankees".

Film critics, for the most part, overlooked the racial controversy, especially after its success at the box office. *Song of the South* was nominated for a handful of Academy Awards, including Music (Scoring of a Musical Picture) and Music (Song), with "Zip-A-Dee-Doo-Dah" winning the Best Song award for 1948.

Walt was incensed that James Baskett was denied entry to the premiere of the film in Atlanta due to the active segregation of public facilities in the south. This, in spite of many critics adoring his performance as Uncle Remus. As a sort of recompense, Walt petitioned the Academy of Motion Pictures Arts and Sciences to give Baskett a Special Award for his role in *Song of the South*, which he received at the Academy Awards of 1948.

The studio attempted another film that utilised animated sequences shortly after *Song of the South. So Dear to My Heart*, which was about a small-town, midwestern boy raising a black lamb in anticipation of the county fair, premiered in late 1948. The project was especially dear to Walt Disney's heart as he certainly related to the situations depicted in the film, having spent many of his formative years in rural Missouri, living and working on a farm for Elias. Looking to depict these homey, small-town feelings in a visual way, Disney put Mary Blair to work, who, after conducting a research trip to the farming communities of Indiana, did many conceptual sketches and designed concepts for the costumes of the live actors. Her concept art, in particular, was described as distinct and based upon quilting patterns commonly found in middle American farming communities. When production began, however, Walt made an important distinction from *Song of the South*: the animation featured in *So Dear to My Heart* would be used to simply enhance the film: animated sequences would be used to highlight the imagination of the film's protagonist, rather than become an important plot element or bring animated characters into a live action world.

While *Song of the South* and *So Dear to My Heart* were fun interludes for the Walt Disney Studio, they didn't make the money Walt and Roy needed to help the studio rebuild after the war. The brothers realised that their studio required a blockbuster: something that was "classic Disney", with great songs and artistic excellence and beauty that would lift hearts. Walt and his team looked over the concepts in development, but few seemed to be what the studio needed at that time, which was something that "audiences can relate to". Recalling that it was a fairy tale that had brought such success to the Walt Disney Studios in 1937, and that they were often a part of cultural literacy, he decided that the next animated feature would also be a fairy tale.

Joe Grant and Dick Huemer began writing the initial treatment for *Cinderella* in 1943. Over the next few years, work continued in fits and spurts, with storyboarding taking place in the mid-1940s. Shortly thereafter, the overall plot of the film was set and production could officially begin. At the same time, the Story department began providing conceptual sketches and colour keying to determine what the overall look, mood and tone of Disney's newest fairy tale would be, with Mary Blair once again leading the way. While she had traditionally provided concepts for previous films, Blair was given a more significant role in the planning of *Cinderella:* she was assigned the responsibility of staging each sequence, determining what the focal point, general composition, and movement and flow of each scene should be.

Cinderella was essentially a fresh start for Disney's full-length animated features: a reboot of sorts. As a result, Walt wanted the film to be believable enough to elicit audience buy-in and emotional responses while also providing humour and delight, as was the case for *Snow White and the Seven Dwarfs.* Thus the film would combine both realistic serious characters, such as Cinderella and Lady Tremaine, and those who were caricatured, such as the stepsisters, Fairy Godmother and Grand Duke.

To ensure the realistic, lifelike accuracy of both movement and human anatomy, Disney decided once again to use live reference models to assist animators. Unlike *Snow White*, however, the decision was made that the models would act out the entirety of *Cinderella* on the studio's soundstage in full costume. From there, animators gained an extensive amount of footage from which to draw from, particularly accurate movements of the ladies' ballgowns and the regal poise of Cinderella herself. This process of finalising and shooting the live action footage of the entire film before animating also saved animators time and money: by the time animating began, all sequences and scenes had been decided upon, and nothing that the artists drew would be cut from the final film. This process would change how Disney produced its animated features throughout the 1950s, hiring models, actors and actresses to perform the film in live action for animated reference for films including *Peter Pan* and *Alice in Wonderland.*

The vocal talent and music of *Cinderella* was memorable and made a significant impact upon the film as well. The talent cast to voice the characters fit the characters well. Eleanor Audley, who not only acted in the live action footage as Lady Tremaine, also served as a visual reference for the girl's evil stepmother and provided the villainess's voice. Verna Felton, who had acted and provided voices for motherly characters in both film and radio became the Fairy Godmother, while

Ilene Woods, similar to Adriana Caselotti, was chosen as the voice of the princess on the merit of her singing voice.

Walt and his team decided that music should be a very important part of this newest feature: songs, particularly those sung by the characters, would be once again used to help convey the film's narrative, much in the way of *Snow White and the Seven Dwarfs*. As a result, some of entertainment's best songwriters and composers were hired to contribute to the film, including Oliver Wallace, Paul Smith, and Tin Pan Alley songwriters Al Hoffman, Jerry Livingston, and Mack David.

While the Walt Disney Studios had been relatively respected in the film community, critical press, and opinions of everyday Americans since the release of *Snow White and the Seven Dwarfs,* the Good Neighbor films, package films, and live action-animated combination films hadn't done as well as Walt had hoped. Inspired by Gallup's Audience Research Institute, the studio began a process of offering private screenings of film rough cuts to subsections of its employees that matched the demographics of America's general filmgoing population. Known as the "noncritical group", these audiences were not professional animators but instead had maintenance and custodial jobs or were inbetweeners, Ink-and-Paint girls, and technicians. From 1945 until the mid-1950s, every film and short produced by the Walt Disney Studios was previewed by these test audiences, who were asked specific, pointed questions about what they liked or disliked, which gags worked and which didn't, and whether there were sequences that they found uninteresting or confusing. Results were typed up and submitted to the film's directors for review so that appropriate changes could be made to improve the film before its premiere.

Cinderella became an instant film classic upon its release in 1950 to American audiences, grossing $4 million in its first release. The film won several awards, including three Oscars and the Golden Bear at the Berlin Film Festival of 1951. After surviving a World War, Disney had returned to its roots of fairy tales and literature, proving that the animated feature was still relevant.

Much like *Cinderella,* conceptual work on the studio's next two films began several years earlier, with their origins reaching back into the early days of Disney entertainment. As early as 1931, Walt Disney had considered a film adaptation of *Alice's Adventures in Wonderland,* with *The New Yorker* printing an interview where mention was made of the story being used as inspiration for an animated short. Walt had been interested in the fantastical adventures of Alice and her friends since the advent of the Disney Brothers Studio in 1923 with Walt's first short, "Alice's Wonderland", featuring a live action girl entering an animated world.

It wasn't until the late 1930s and into the 1940s that Walt Disney began to seriously consider *Alice in Wonderland* as a potential feature, meeting with storymen Bill Cottrell and T. Hee to develop a treatment. Early sketches took inspiration from the drawings by John Tenniel: after acquiring rights to Tenniel's work, Disney modified the characters, putting the studio's own spin on the classic illustrations.

Unfortunately, the Carroll stories were long and featured nonsensical events, making it difficult to establish a continuity for an animated film. Several treatments were written, including some by Joseph Wood Krutch, Robert L Fontaine, and Aldous Huxley. Unfortunately, none of these were sufficient for Walt, who ultimately assigned thirteen writers and several directors to hash out the final treatment. Joe Grant and Dick Huemer were also ordered to work on straightening the narrative continuity out for the film.

It was decided that, much like *Cinderella*, live action models would be hired to act out the entirety of *Alice in Wonderland* as reference for the animators. Several of the actors and actresses who lent their voices to the film served as their own live reference models, including Kathryn Beaumont as Alice, Jerry Colonna as the March Hare, and Ed Wynn, who improvised many of his lines, as the Mad Hatter.

Walt was interested in making *Alice in Wonderland* as visually zany as the novels. Mary Blair was once again assigned to provide concepts and colour keying for the film, sketching ideas for leaf patterns, film settings, props, and characters, as well as highlighting characters in both primary and secondary colours against a usually muted background. Ward Kimball, who was often given free rein in his animating of chaotic scenes including the titular sequence for *The Three Caballeros*, animated Alice's attendance at the Mad Tea Party.

An incredible amount of work went into the production of *Alice in Wonderland*, with nearly seventy thousand individual drawings taking fifty thousand working hours, with a cost to the studio of approximately $4 million. Walt considered it to be his greatest masterpiece to date. He was particularly hopeful that the people of Britain, from where author Lewis Carroll originated, would accept the film, explaining in a 31 May 1951 interview with the *Kinematograph Weekly* that "[i]n many respects this is a British film – and I hope you in Britain will enjoy it." To help drive the point home, the film's premiere took place at London's Leicester Square Theatre on 26 July 1951.

The general reaction, particularly from the British, to *Alice in Wonderland* seemed to contradict Walt's belief that the film was his masterpiece. William Whitebait of *New Statesman* wrote that the studio's "idea [of Alice] is all chocolate-box and music-hall; and anything more remote from the original – indeed idiotically at odds with it – would be very hard to imagine…This million-pound ineptitude deserves nothing but boos, and I wish cinema audiences were in the habit of according them." It was also noticed that the name of the author, Lewis Carroll, was misspelt in the film's title card, communicating to the British that the studio and its executive had a lack of respect to the film's source material. While the film was able to snag an Oscar for Oliver Wallace's scoring, the reviews and ticket returns told the ultimate truth: *Alice in Wonderland* only earned a total of $2.4 million in its initial release, posting a significant loss to the studio. Walt couldn't lie to himself or the public anymore: he later said that Carroll's *Alice in Wonderland* was "a classic we couldn't tamper with". He believed that the source material focused more on gags and doubted that "anything without heart is good or will last. To me humor involves both laughter and tears."

Walt must have been feeling particularly nostalgic in the late 1940s and early 1950s. Not only was his studio in the process of producing a feature-length version of the first short they had released, but he also initiated production on the animated version of a story that had been an integral part of his life since childhood: *Peter Pan*. Walt first experienced J.M. Barrie's play in 1913 as a young man living in Marceline, Missouri. Spellbound by the tale of the boy who wouldn't grow up, young Walt eagerly accepted the role of Peter Pan when his school decided to put on the play as their annual drama, convincing Roy to build a hoist to assist him in 'flying' across the stage.

Walt's desire to make a feature-length animated film based on *Peter Pan* began after the success of *Snow White and the Seven Dwarfs*, when he stated that it would be the next film to go into production. Much to Walt's delight, the studio acquired the rights to the play for a mere £5,000 in 1939. He decided to hold off, however, until he and his team had honed the narrative and developed the necessary techniques and special effects to effectively depict the story he loved so much. He soon put the best members of his Story department to work, including Dorothy Ann Blank, Joe Grant, Bill Cottrell, and Bianca Majolie. Production halted, however, after the attack on Pearl Harbor in December 1941, and did not resume until after the successful release of *Cinderella* in 1950.

Other experts across the studio were utilised as well. Mary Blair was joined by Claude Coats, John Hench, and Don DaGradi to develop the colour and styling for the film, while Al Dempster and newcomer Eyvind Earl designed the 934 backgrounds that made their way into the final film. Some of the studio's best animators, including Frank Thomas, Ollie Johnston, Ward Kimball, and Woolie Reitherman, brought the characters to life. So important was this film, that Walt entrusted some of the most significant work to those who had been with the studio from the beginning: Hamilton Luske and Wilfred Jackson, who served as directors.

As with *Cinderella* and *Alice in Wonderland*, it was decided to film *Peter Pan* in live action to provide reference to animators as well as save time and money by finalising the entire story and its sequences prior to animating. Walt controversially broke precedent by deciding that the role of Peter Pan would not be filled by a woman but rather a boy – Bobby Driscoll. As a result, the live action model for Peter was held by Roland Dupree. Some of the reference models were portrayed by the actors and actresses who would depict the characters, including Hans Conreid as Captain Hook and Mr. Darling and Kathryn Beaumont as Wendy. Despite having experience as a reference model, Beaumont's talents were stretched when she found herself being strapped into a harness and filmed flying across the studio's soundstage to provide reference for how a girl with curls and wearing a nightgown might look as she flew across London.

Peter Pan was completed before its premiere in February 1953, and was significantly more successful than its predecessor, grossing $6 million domestically with an additional amount of nearly $3 million at international markets. Once again reviewers in Britain felt a sense of proprietary pride in the source material being adapted by an American studio: one critic wrote that "[h]aving mutilated *Alice in Wonderland,* [Walt Disney] now murders *Peter Pan*, and I hate the assumed innocence with which he does it." Writer Paul Holt critiqued the film in *The Daily Herald* by saying that "in place of childhood dreaming there is strip-cartoon violence and constant hints at sex." A reviewer for *Newsweek* described *Peter Pan* as "infinitely more…a perfect subject for Walt Disney's magic pot of cinematic paints [than *Alice in Wonderland*]...the time has come, in the opinion of many people who have gotten around to growing up, when Barrie's determinedly elfin whimsies could benefit from a healthy dose of Disney's broad comedy. This has happened without any loss to the play's perennial charm. The result is Barrie and Disney at their best."

While *Alice in Wonderland* had not performed well, the animated features of the early 1950s brought with them a widespread success of Disney's animated features that the studio had not experienced since *Snow White and the Seven Dwarfs* and *Dumbo*. While *Cinderella, Alice in Wonderland,* and *Peter Pan* did little to technologically advance the craft of animation, they were an opportunity for the studio to reset after several years of producing limited animation to save money during the Second World War, and also to produce a feature-length film with a fully fleshed out narrative, unlike the Good Neighbor, Package and Special Films of the 1940s. The three films did, however, help the Walt Disney Studios to establish its own personal style of animation, which would follow it during the second half of the twentieth century, primarily through the use of colour, layouts, and styling as perfected by artists including Mary Blair and Claude Coats. The practice of filming the entire film in live action to provide a full reference also helped hone the skills of the animators to bring life and realism to the medium in a whole new way.

Hollywood in the 1950s found itself challenged by a new adversary: the television. Entertainment including concerts, sporting events, and short-format serials were now being beamed into the households of consumers lucky enough to own a television set. While the initial investment was pricey, potential audiences chose to have free daily original entertainment in the comfort and informality of their own home instead of the ticketed upholstered seats of darkened theatres. Filmmakers realised that they needed to develop new technology and gimmicks to stay relevant.

Film in the first half of the twentieth century simply made audiences casual observers. As filmmaking techniques and technology advanced in the late 1940s and early 1950s, the focus became to make audiences feel that they were participants in a film, that the epic, fantastic, or horrifying events taking place on-screen didn't merely happen on a two-dimensional plane, but rather were a part of our world, making the theatre a truly immersive experience. Several filmmakers, including Disney, tinkered with three-dimensional films, but the effect often wasn't very successful. Instead, the goal became to make the individual theatregoer feel like the film existed solely for their enjoyment, that they were at the literal centre of the action.

In 1952, film producer Mike Todd released the film *This is Cinerama* at New York City's Broadway Theatre. The show began by describing the history of film, going as far as describing the technical specifications of film, particularly highlighting monotone sound and aspect ratio, or the height and width of the projected area of a film, which had traditionally been 1.37:1 since cinema began in the late 1800s. Suddenly, as the film's narrator announced the words "This is Cinerama!" the screen expanded to a new aspect ratio hitherto unseen by American audiences: 2.85:1, which would be later known as "widescreen". To demonstrate the merits of this new Cinerama aspect ratio, the film was a series of vignettes including a first-person view of a ride on the Atom Smasher roller coaster, a view of Niagara Falls, and a Spanish bullfight. Several scenes also demonstrated Cinerama's implementation of stereophonic sound, including scenes from Cypress Gardens and an assortment of pieces sung by the Mormon Tabernacle Choir.

Todd's groundbreaking film combined several existing film technologies, as well as ushering in the development of new processes. In filming the footage for *This is Cinerama*, three separate cameras were used to create a panorama effect when played back on individual film projectors. Existing movie screens, however, were not large enough to accommodate for the new aspect ratio, resulting in the construction of a large curved screen (three times the length of a standard movie theatre screen), covering a total of 146°. A new process of magnetic sound film was also developed, allowing for stereophonic sound in an industry previously dominated by monophonic, or single-channel, sound.

While *This is Cinerama* was revolutionary, it was not a technology that could be feasibly utilised by the major film studios or theatres around the nation. The fact that each projector had its own strip of film synchronised to the others posed the possibility of one strip failing, effectively ruining the film and its effects.

Fascinated by the idea, 20th Century Fox reached out to Professor Henri Chrétien of France, who had developed a process he called "Anamorphoscope" in the 1920s. This process eliminated the need for three separate cameras, strips of films, and projectors to produce a widescreen film, instead utilising a special lens, called a "hypergonar", which, when affixed to a film camera, distorted the image to create the illusion of a widescreen, or panoramic, image. This allowed for the image to be "squeezed" onto a standard 35mm filmstrip; when the filmstrip was fed through a normal projector with its own affixed hypergonar anamorphic lens, the image was stretched out, creating the widescreen effect.

After acquiring permission to use Chrétien's Anamorphoscope process and his hypergonar lenses and renaming it CinemaScope, 20th Century Fox shot the entirety of their upcoming film, *The Robe*, in this new widescreen format which measured an aspect ratio of 2.55:1. To compete with 20th Century Fox, other studios began developing their own versions of widescreen technology, including Paramount's VistaVision.

Darryl F. Zanuck, a director at 20th Century Fox, believed that CinemaScope would be perfect for animated shorts and films. Generously, 20th Century Fox decided to open the use of CinemaScope to all studios, contrary to the regular practice of making the newest filmmaking technology proprietary. Walt Disney, ever one desiring to push the envelope to technologically revolutionise the medium of animation and take his studio to the next level, quickly put Ward Kimball on the job, asking one of his favourite artists and directors at the studio to determine the feasibility of producing animation in a new aspect ratio. Kimball soon found that larger celluloid would need to be used, resulting in adjustments being made to the desks of animators and the artists of the Ink-and-Paint department.

A number of animated shorts were put into development at the Walt Disney Studios to test out CinemaScope, including "Toot, Whistle, Plunk, and Boom", "Grand Canyonscope", and "Chips Ahoy". In fact, after "Toot, Whistle, Plunk and Boom" won an Academy Award, Walt partially attributed the accolade to the studio's successful use of the new technology. Work immediately began on developing an animated feature, hoping to draw audiences to the latest Disney film using this new process.

A project called *Happy Dan, the Whistling Dog, and Miss Patsy, the Beautiful Spaniel* had been in the conceptual stage at the studio since 1937. Joe Grant had initially written an original treatment based upon a springer spaniel owned by his family named Lady Nell the Second. He had become inspired after watching his daughter Carol play with the dog, sketching the two of them together and imagining what types of adventures Lady Nell might have when her owners weren't around. Some of Grant's inspiration came from a highland terrier who lived next door, as well as a haughty aunt who owned mischievous twin Siamese cats.

In one of his visits to the Story department in 1939, Walt came across some of Grant's inspirational sketches and began asking questions about Lady Nell. He quickly decided that the idea had merit, and Grant was joined by Mary Blair and Jack Miller to begin developing additional concept sketches and write the first draft of a script. Work moved slowly over the next two years, with the studio's work during the Second World War putting the project on hold until 1943.

Unfortunately, Walt was less than impressed with what his Story writers had come up with and it wasn't long until he came across some new material that could help spice up the adventures of the springer spaniel, now known as Miss Patsy. After reading the short story "Happy Dan, the Cynical Dog" in a 1945 issue of *Cosmopolitan*, Walt decided it was just the foil Miss Patsy needed, and he purchased the rights to the source material.

Work commenced in the Story department to combine the tale of Happy Dan with the prim and proper Miss Patsy, with the plan to turn the story into a featurette, renamed *Lady and the Tramp.* It soon became obvious that the animated Special could be turned into a full-length feature, and adjustments were made to the story to accommodate this. The decision was also made to film *Lady and the Tramp* in CinemaScope. While producing animated shorts and Specials in CinemaScope had not posed much of a challenge to the animators, producing an animated feature using the new widescreen technology was uncharted territory. The nature of the wider aspect ratio made the depiction of characters in close-up more difficult, resulting in few close-up shots in the film. It also made group shots harder, resulting in the artists responsible for laying out scenes to adjust character spacing to prevent large gaps of space void of characters. The larger aspect ratio also tended to produce a graininess to the image due to the image being expanded and stretched out when photographed. Unsure of how successful his use of CinemaScope would be, Walt also had a print of the film photographed in standard ratio as well.

Disney's distributor at the time, RKO, demanded that Disney change the name of the film due to the song "The Lady is a Tramp", which served as a commentary on the distasteful practices of society women. However, Walt insisted that the name chosen for the film would remain despite his distributor's demands as he wasn't worried about what they thought. In 1953, the Walt Disney Studios had created its own distribution company, Buena Vista Film Distribution Company, Inc., after RKO refused to distribute the studio's first live-action nature documentary, *The Living Desert.* It simply made sense to Walt and Roy to move the distribution of their upcoming animated films, including *Lady and the Tramp*, to their in-house distribution company, rather than entertain a conflict with RKO.

The relative success of *Lady and the Tramp* convinced Walt that it was worth making additional features in the widescreen format. Technology for producing films with greater aspect ratio had progressed since production had begun on *Lady and the Tramp*, with immediate benefits to the medium of animation. Walt was particularly impressed with Technirama, the new process developed by Technicolor, whom the studio had previously partnered with in experimenting with colour animation in "Flowers and Trees". Filmmakers enjoyed Technirama's higher quality, particularly in the depiction of colour, which was less grainy than CinemaScope's process. Part of this new technology was due to Technirama utilising a pair of curved mirrors, situated similarly to the structure of a periscope, to increase the size of the image and maintain the quality of the colourised picture, rather than projecting three separate film strips on a wide screen using an anamorphic lens. Technirama also put the entire film on a single strip of 35mm film, rather than CinemaScope's three strips. However, rather than the frames on the strip of film being oriented vertically, Technirama oriented the frames horizontally to allow for a wider image on the strip itself, helping to expand the image in lieu of an anamorphic lens.

Recognising the technical superiority of Technirama over CinemaScope, Walt decided to utilise the new process for his next animated feature: *Sleeping Beauty*. Initial conceptual artwork was completed by artist Eyvind Earle, who modelled his paintings on paintings and tapestries from the Renaissance. Walt, who was impressed by Earle's work, believed that it would be best shown in higher definition widescreen, with the bright reds, greens and blues portrayed in glorious Technicolor. He thought this beautiful and grand film deserved an image of crisp sharpness and panoramic grandeur. Walt was particularly impressed by the epic films of the mid-1950s that were making use of the experimental 70mm film strips and commissioned Technicolor to utilise the technology for *Sleeping Beauty*.

Technicolor had recently advanced their Technirama process by printing films on 70mm strip and running it through special projectors that could accommodate the increase in film stock. This allowed for the still image to be "unsqueezed", as well as allowing for a magnetic soundtrack to be printed on the strip itself, rather than as a separate strip that needed to be printed, stored, and threaded through a camera. This process, known as Super Technirama 70, not only projected the films using the Technirama process, but photographed the films in Technirama as well, using a special anamorphic lens on the camera itself. Walt was especially proud that *Sleeping Beauty* was not only photographed using the Technirama process, but that it was also the first film of any sort photographed using the Super Technirama 70 technique.

Sleeping Beauty was an artistic undertaking. Not only did the studio have to adjust to preparing the film for the Super Technirama 70 format, but the multiplane camera was also heavily used. Several special effects were utilised, particularly in the final battle between Maleficent and Prince Phillip, and the Ink-and-Paint girls were put to work to produce and apply the bright colours and intense shadows prevalent throughout the film. After six years of hard work, *Sleeping Beauty* premiered on 29 January 1959. Unfortunately, the critics and audiences were not impressed by the story, artistic styling, or technical advancements of the latest Disney fairy tale, with the studio losing nearly a million dollars due to poor ticket sales. Walt was disappointed, but used the film's poor performance to determine that perhaps American audiences favoured more modern stories and were not as intrigued by fairy tales and princess stories as they once were. It would be the last animated fairy tale to be produced by the Walt Disney Studios in Walt's lifetime.

With the production and release of *Sleeping Beauty,* Walt Disney and his studio had come full circle. The Walt Disney Studios had enjoyed many high points over its thirty-one years since the "birth" of Mickey Mouse in "Steamboat Willie". From early on, music had been an integral part to the Disney shorts, and the features were no different: the Disney version of *Sleeping Beauty* heavily utilised themes and pieces from Tchaikovsky's ballet to help drive the story. The Story department had brought believable life to a handful of pencil lines through the development of personality animation in "The Three Little Pigs", continuing this trend when depicting the curious Aurora; her caretakers, the Good Fairies; and the vengeful Maleficent. Walt himself had taken a risk when he proposed a feature-length animated film, one that prioritised story over gags. While those in the industry deemed him a fool, Walt had proved them wrong, helping to produce nearly twenty films that were either fully animated or had animated segments.

The Walt Disney Studios also made several technological innovations that helped to advance the craft of animation. The multiplane camera achieved the seemingly impossible task of adding realistic depth to a two-dimensional drawing, beginning with "The Old Mill", and then used consistently, including in *Sleeping Beauty.* Processes had been used to bring live action actors into the animated world and animated characters into the real world. The studio had helped usher colour into the theatres when it produced the very first colour animated film, "Flowers and Trees", with the help of Technicolor. Now, nearly three decades later, Disney was again pioneering another of Technicolor's technical advances, Super Technirama 70, providing a panoramic view in rich colours.

Walt Disney and his studio didn't and wouldn't stop there: he had wider vistas just ahead.

EPILOGUE

It was a beautiful Saturday morning. The sun was shining in a bright blue California sky. Walt Disney sat with the morning newspaper, enjoying the quiet before the sounds of Diane and Sharon waking up and making their way into the kitchen of the new family house located at 355 North Carolwood Drive, west of Los Angeles.

Walt loved Saturday mornings: some of his favourite memories were of those, nearly a decade before, when Diane and Sharon were very young. He remembered how the girls would practically run into the kitchen, bouncing with excitement about the plans their father had for the day. Even now, after the girls finished their breakfast and got dressed, they would enjoy the weekly holiday that the family called "Daddy's Day", where the girls got to spend time alone with their adoring father away from the pressures and busyness of the film studio.

On this particular Saturday morning, the girls excitedly chattered with their father as they skipped and scurried outside to the shiny family car. Walt, ever the gentleman, held the car door open and put the top down so his daughters could enjoy the warm breeze and sunlight as they drove beneath the towering palm trees to one of their favourite places: Griffith Park.

Walt could hardly contain his smile as he gingerly navigated the steep and twisting roads of the Holmby Hills neighbourhood. The girls were practically talking over each other, simultaneously telling their father and sister about their week. A few minutes later, the trio arrived at the sprawling park situated on the side of the Santa Monica Mountains. The girls wondered what activities they would enjoy at the park this time: horseback riding? The zoo? Searching for the park's diverse variety of birds as they hiked along the trails? They cheered in delight when the car turned down a road which terminated in a parking lot near a red-and-white tent-like structure.

The girls practically jumped out of the car before it had come to a stop and began running toward the round building. Walt chuckled to himself as he locked the car and began following his daughters. As he got closer, the sound of calliope music wafted on the breeze from a merry-go-round situated inside the red-and-white pavilion. The calls of "Daddy!" seemed to rise and fall as Diane and Sharon came into view and disappeared with the spinning of the carousel.

Walt sat down on a green bench a few feet away from the merry-go-round and watched with delight as the girls enjoyed several rides, hopping off their horse at the conclusion of each one and racing to choose a different mount before the spinning commenced again. Looking around at the park, with its tall trees, leaves blowing in the wind, the sound of joyful music and laughing children in his ears, Walt Disney found himself grateful for the opportunity to spend time with his daughters, having fun together.

Suddenly, everything around him seemed to fade away. The colours of the blue sky, bright green trees, warm sunlight, and the kaleidoscopic merry-go-round became dull, while the sounds of the carousel became secondary to thoughts that began to swirl in his mind. Thoughts of something different, something new, something for parents and kids to enjoy *together*. Immediately, he heard a thought, as though audible, as it came to the forefront of his mind:

> "There should be a place…"

Appendix

LIST OF DISNEY'S ACADEMY AWARDS AND NOMINATIONS FOR ANIMATED SHORTS AND FEATURES

1932	Won	"Flowers and Trees"
	Nominated	"Mickey's Orphans"
	Honorary Award	Creation of Mickey Mouse
1933	Won	"The Three Little Pigs"
	Nominated	"Building a Building"
1934	Won	"The Tortoise and the Hare"
1935	Won	"Three Orphan Kittens"
	Nominated	"Who Killed Cock Robin?"
1936	Won	"The Country Cousin"
1937	Won	"The Old Mill"
1938	Won	"Ferdinand the Bull"
	Nominated	"Brave Little Tailor"
	Nominated	"Good Scouts"
	Nominated	"Mother Goose Goes Hollywood"
	Technical Award	Design and application of the multiplane camera
1939	Won	"The Ugly Duckling"
	Nominated	"The Pointer"
	Honorary Award	Snow White and the Seven Dwarfs
1941	Won	"Lend a Paw"
	Won	"Der Fuhrer's Face"

	Won	Pinocchio, Best Score
	Won	Pinocchio, "When You Wish Upon a Star"
	Nominated	"Truant Officer Donald"
1942	Won	Dumbo, Best Score
	Nominated	"The Grain That Built a Hemisphere"
	Nominated	"The New Spirit"
	Honorary Award	"...for the advancement of sound in motion pictures…[in] Fantasia"
	Honorary Award	Irving G. Thalberg Memorial Award
1943	Nominated	"Reason and Emotion"
1944	Nominated	"How to Play Football"
1945	Nominated	"Donald's Crime"
1946	Nominated	"Squatter's Rights"
1947	Nominated	"Chip an' Dale"
	Nominated	"Pluto's Blue Note"
1948	Won	Song of the South, "Zip-a-Dee-Doo-Dah"
	Nominated	"Mickey and the Seal"
	Nominated	"Tea for Two Hundred"
	Honorary Award	James Baskett in Song of the South for his portrayal of Uncle Remus
1949	Nominated	"Toy Tinkers"
1950	Honorary Award	Bobby Driscoll, outstanding juvenile actor of 1949, So Dear to My Heart
1951	Nominated	"Lambert the Sheepish Lion"
1953	Won	"Toot, Whistle, Plunk and Boom"
	Nominated	"Rugged Bear"
	Nominated	"Ben and Me"
1954	Nominated	"Pigs is Pigs"
1955	Nominated	"No Hunting"

BIBLIOGRAPHY

"2000 Acclaim 'Fantasia' at Premiere." *The Bulletin.* Vol. 3 No. 5. November 1940.

"Air Conditioning in Walt Disney Studios: Comprehensive Temperature Control by Johnson." *Architect and Engineer* (January 1941): 5.

Bailey, Adrian. *Walt Disney's World of Fantasy*. New York: Gallery Books, 1982.

Barton, Craig D. "1933- Three Pigs, One Wolf, and a Storyteller." Communerdy. February 9, 2022. https://www.communerdy.com/1933-three-pigs-one-wolf-and-a-storyteller.

Bernardi, Daniel, ed. *Classic Hollywood, Classic Whiteness.* Minneapolis, MN: University of Minnesota Press, 2001.

Bertolaccini, Bri. "Snow White and the Seven Dwarfs Honorary Academy Award." The Walt Disney Family Museum. February 23, 2023. https://www.waltdisney.org/blog/snow-white-and-seven-dwarfs-honorary-academy-awardr.

"The Big Bad Wolf." *Fortune*, November 1934, 88-148.

Bossert, David A. *Kem Weber: Mid-Century Furniture Designs for the Disney Studios*. Valencia, CA: Old Mill Press, 2020.

Bossert, Dave. "Walt Disney Classified: The Layout Manual, Part 3 – The 11 Field Crane." Cartoon Research. February 17, 2020.

Bragdon, Claude. "Mickey Mouse and What He Means." Straws in the Wind. *Scribner's*, July 1934, 40-43.

Brockway, Robert W. "The Masks of Mickey Mouse: Symbol of a Generation." *Journal of Popular Culture* 22, no. 4 (1989): 25-34.

Broggie, Michael. *Walt Disney's Railroad Story*. Pasadena, CA: Pentrex, 1997.

The Bulletin. Vol. 1 No. 4. January 1939.

Canemaker, John. *The Art and Flair of Mary Blair*. New York: Disney Editions, 2003.

Canemaker, John. *Two Guys Named Joe: Master Animation Storytellers Joe Grant and Joe Ranft*. New York: Disney Editions, 2010.

Clague, Mark. "Playing in 'Toon: Walt Disney's 'Fantasia' (1940) and the Imagineering of Classical Music." *American Music* 22, no. 1 (2004): 91-109.

Culhane, John. *Walt Disney's Fantasia*. New York: Harry N. Abrams, Inc., 1983.

Chasins, Abram. *Leopold Stokowski: A Profile*. New York: Hawthorn Books, Inc., 1979.

Chavez, Tizoc. ""The One Bright Spot": Presidential Personal Diplomacy and the Good Neighbor Policy." *Presidential Studies Quarterly* 51, no. 2 (June 2021): 290-326.

Crafton, Donald. "Infectious Laughter: Cartoons' Cure for the Depression." In *Funny Pictures: Animation and Comedy in Studio-Era Hollywood*, edited by Daniel I. Goldmark and Charles Keil, 69-92. N.p.: University of California Press, 2011.

Culhane, Shamus. *Talking Animals and Other People*. New York: St. Martin's Press, 1986.

Danks, Adrian. "Huffing and Puffing About Three Little Pigs." Senses of Cinema. Last modified November, 2003. http://archive.sensesofcinema.com/contents/cteq/03/29/3_little_pigs.html.

Deem, Jack, David Starnes, and James Ziegler. "The Influence of Early Life Experiences on Later Life Behaviors: An Examination of the Life of Walt Disney." *Journal of Behavioral and Applied Management* 23, no. 2 (2023): 114-21.

Disney Miller, Diane. *The Story of Walt Disney*. New York: Dell, 1956.

"Disney Legends: Tyrus Wong." Walt Disney Archives. https://d23.com/walt-disney-legend/tyrus-wong/.

"Disney Productions Occupy New Home." *Architect and Engineer* (October 1940): 58.

"Disney's 'Fantasia' is Really Revolutionary." *American Cinematographer* (December 1940).

"Disney Goes South." *The Montgomery Advertiser*, September 2, 1941.

Disney, Roy E., Daniel H. Disney, and Charles E. Disney. "Flora Call Disney." Find a Grave. March 9, 2000. https://www.findagrave.com/memorial/8807/flora-disney.

Disney, Walt. 1940. Art of Animation. US Patent 2,201,689. Filed September 1, 1936, and issued May 21, 1940.

Disney, Walt. "Mickey as Professor." *Film and Radio Guide* XII, no. 2 (1945): 26-28.

"Disney's New Burbank Studio First to be Wholly Air Conditioned; Install GE Plant." *Film Daily* (March 6, 1940).

Dispatch from Disney's. 1943.

Donald, Ralph. "Hollywood and Washington." *Hollywood Enlists!: Propaganda Films of World War II*. Lanham, MD: Rowman & Littlefield Publishers, 2017.

"The Evolution of Mickey Mouse." *Motion Picture Daily* (June 20, 1931): 7.

"'Fantasia' Sound: Its Processes and Their Portent." *Better Theatres* 141, no. 7 (November 16, 1940).

Finch, Christopher. *The Art of Walt Disney: From Mickey Mouse to the Magic Kingdoms*. New York: Harry N. Abrams, Inc., 1975.

Finch, Christopher. *Walt Disney's America*. New York: Abbeville Press, Inc., 1978.

"First Mickey Convention Big Success." *Motion Picture Daily* (June 20, 1931): 12.

Flueckiger, Barbara. Timeline of Historical Film Colors. 2012. www.filmcolors.org.

Friedman, Jake S. *The Disney Revolt: the Great Labor War of Animation's Golden Age*. Chicago: Chicago Review Press, 2022.

Gabler, Neal. *Walt Disney: The Triumph of the American Imagination*. New York: Vintage, 2006.

"'Get Film Good-Neighbor Ideas in South America', Disney Advises." *Motion Picture Herald* (October 25, 1941): 29.

Ghez, Didier. *Disney's Grand Tour: Walt and Roy's European Vacation, Summer 1935*. Theme Park Press, 2014.

Ghez, Didier. *They Drew as They Pleased: The Hidden Art of Disney's Golden Age, the 1930s*. San Francisco: Chronicle Books, 2015.

Ghez, Didier. *They Drew as They Pleased: The Hidden Art of Disney's Late Golden Age, the 1940s Part Two*. San Francisco: Chronicle Books, 2017.

Ghez, Didier. *They Drew as They Pleased: The Hidden Art of Disney's Musical Years, the 1940s Part One*. San Francisco: Chronicle Books, 2016.

"Gleanings from Studios." *New York Times*, September 25, 1932.

Glover, Erin. "Opening Night, 1937: 'Snow White and the Seven Dwarfs' Premieres at Carthay Circle Theatre." Disney Parks Blog. December 21, 2011.

Gold, Zachary. "Movie Reviews: Bambi." *Modern Screen* (October 1942): 6-8.

Graff, Cory. "How Hollywood Set Designers Hid America's WWII Aircraft Factories." *Popular Mechanics*, November 2020, 52-57

Green, Amy B., and Howard E. GGreen. *Remembering Walt: Favorite Memories of Walt Disney*. New York: Disney Editions, 1999.

Hahn, Don, and Tracey Miller-Zarneke. *Before Ever After: The Lost Lectures of Walt Disney's Animation Studio*. Los Angeles: Disney Editions, 2015.

Hart, Martin B. The American WideScreen Museum. 2015. https://www.widescreenmuseum.com/.

H Brothers. "New York City Weather in 1929." Extreme Weather Watch. https://www.extremeweatherwatch.com/cities/new-york/year-1929.

Hickman, Walter D. "Mickey Mouse Movies Have Own Theme Song." *The Indianapolis Times*, August 8, 1933.

Higgins, Scott. *Harnessing the Technicolor Rainbow: Color Design in the 1930s*. Austin: University of Texas Press, 2007.

Higgins, Scott. "Technology and Aesthetics: Technicolor Cinematography and Design in the Late 1930s." *Film History* 11 (1999): 55-76. JSTOR.

Holliss, Richard, and Brian Sibley. *The Disney Studio Story*. New York: Crown Publishers, Inc., 1988.

Holliss, Richard, and Brian Sibley. *Walt Disney's Snow White and the Seven Dwarfs & the Making of the Classic Film*. New York: Hyperion, 1987.

"Inkers-Painters Move Monday." *The Bulletin*. Vol. 2 No. 36. May 1940.

Iwerks, Don. *Walt Disney's Ultimate Inventor: The Genius of Ub Iwerks*. Los Angeles: Disney Editions, 2019.

Iwerks, Leslie, and John Kenworthy. *The Hand Behind the Mouse*. New York: Disney Editions, 2001.

Jaeger, Luke. "The Fleischer Studios' 'Setback' Camera vs. Disney Realism." animationstudies 2.0. May 7, 2013. https://blog.animationstudies.org/?p=233.

Johnson, Mindy. *Ink & Paint: The Women of Walt Disney's Animation*. Los Angeles: Disney Editions, 2017.

Kaufman, JB, and David Gerstein. *Walt Disney's Mickey Mouse: The Ultimate History*, edited by Daniel Kothenschulte, Cologne, Germany: Taschen, 2020.

Kinney, Jack. *Walt Disney and Assorted Other Characters*. New York: Harmony Books, 1988.

Kiste, Andrew S. *The Early Life of Walt Disney*. Barnsley, U.K.: White Owl, 2021.

Kothenschulte, Daniel, ed. *The Walt Disney Film Archives: The Animated Movies 1921-1968*. Taschen, 2020.

Kothenschulte, Daniel, ed. *Walt Disney's Mickey Mouse: The Ultimate History*. Taschen, 2018.

Lesjak, David. "Foundation of an Empire." The Walt Disney Family Museum. July 6, 2012. https://www.waltdisney.org/blog/foundation-empire.

Levine, Lawrence. "The Folklore of Industrial Society: Popular Culture and its Audiences." *Unpredictable Past: Explorations in American Cultural History*. New York: Oxford University Press, 1993.

Levine, Lawrence. "American Culture and the Great Depression." *Unpredictable Past: Explorations in American Cultural History*. New York: Oxford University Press, 1993.

Maltin, Leonard. *Of Mice and Magic: A History of American Animated Cartoons*. New York: McGraw-Hill Book Company, 1980.

Mann, Arthur. "Mickey Mouse's Financial Career." *Harper's Magazine*, May 1934, 714-21.

Marchand, Roland. "Advertising in Overalls: Parables and Visual Clichés of the Depression." *Advertising in the American Dream: Making Way for Modernity*. Berkeley, CA: University of California Press, 1985.

"The March of Time Newsreels." HBO Archives. https://web.archive.org/web/20100924101524/https://www.hboarchives.com/marchoftime/MOT-Newsreels-Synopsis.pdf.

Martin, Janet. "Librarian to Walt Disney." *Wilson Library Bulletin*, December 1939. 292-93. https://www.dix-project.net/document/misc-magazines_1939-12_librarian-to-walt-disney.

Merritt, Russell, and J.B. Kaufman. *Walt Disney's Silly Symphonies: A Companion to the Classic Cartoon Series*. Glendale, CA: Disney Editions, 2016.

"Mickey Mouse Clubs Cover Nation." *Motion Picture Daily* (June 20, 1931): 8.

"Mickey Mouse's Miraculous Move Monkey-shines." *The Literary Digest* (August 9, 1930): 36-37.

Mines, Harry. "Disney's 'Snow White' an Unforgettable Novelty." *Daily News* (Los Angeles), December 22, 1937. 20.

Mintz, Steven. "Coming of Age in the Great Depression." *Huck's Raft: A History of American Childhood.* Cambridge, CA: Belknap Press, 2004.

"Mr. & Mrs. Disney." *Ladies' Home Journal*, March 1941.

Moos, Caleb. "The Multiplane Camera." Medium. July 3, 2019.

"Multiplane Educator Guide." The Walt Disney Family Museum. https://www.waltdisney.org/sites/default/files/MultiplaneGuide CurriculumPacket_Final.pdf.

Neupert, Richard. """We're Happy When We're Sad": Comedy, Gags, and 1930s Cartoon Narration." In *Funny Pictures: Animation and Comedy in Studio-Era Hollywood*, edited by Daniel I. Goldmark and Charles Keil, 93-108. N.p.: University of California Press, 2011.

Nowicki, Brenda. "The Live Action Cinderella You've Never Seen." If the Glass Slipper Fits...Then Wear It. July 1, 2016. https://iftheglassslipperfitsblog.wordpress.com/2016/07/01/the-live-action-cinderella-youve-never-seen/.

Ohmer, Susan. "Laughter by Numbers: the Science of Comedy at the Walt Disney Studio." In *Funny Pictures: Animation and Comedy in Studio-Era Hollywood*, edited by Daniel I. Goldmark and Charles Keil, 109-26. N.p.: University of California Press, 2011.

Parra, Gabriella. "The Mouse and the Maker: How Walt Disney Made Some Noise for the Animation Industry." StMU Research Scholars. March 25, 2022. https://stmuscholars.org/the-mouse-and-the-maker-how-walt-disney-made-some-noise-for-the-animation-industry/.

Parry, Florence F. "Silly Symphony Rated High Art." *The Pittsburgh Press*, August 25, 1935.

Pautz, Michelle C. "The Decline in Average Weekly Cinema Attendance, 1930-2000." *Political Science Faculty Publications* (2002). https://ecommons.udayton.edu/cgi/viewcontent.cgi?article=1023&context=pol_fac_pub#:~:text=In%201930%20(the%20earliest%20year,U.S.%20Statistical%20Abstract).

Peri, Don. *Working with Walt: Interviews with Disney Artists*. Jackson, MS: University Press of Mississippi, 2008.

"The Personalities Behind the Laughs." *Motion Picture Daily* (June 20, 1931): 9.

Pierce, Todd J. *The Life and Times of Ward Kimball: Maverick of Disney Animation*. Jackson, MS: University Press of Mississippi, 2019.

"Pinocchio is Alive!" *Electrical West* 85, no. 1 (July 1940).

"Promoting Flight." Charles Lindbergh House and Museum. https://www.mnhs.org/lindbergh/learn/aviation/promoting.

Rauchway, Eric. *The Great Depression & The New Deal: A Very Short Introduction*. New York: Oxford University Press, 2008.

RCA Institutes, Inc. *Sound Heads Used with Standard Motion Picture Projectors*. 3rd ed. Vol. 58. https://www.worldradiohistory.com/Archive-Courses/RCA-1932/RCA-58-03-Projector-Sound-Heads.pdf.

Reid, Jane. "An Interview with Ray Pointer: Part Three." Fleischer Studios. https://www.fleischerstudios.com/ray3.html.

"Reviews of the New Films: "Victory Through Air Power"." *The Film Daily*, July 8, 1943.

Rivkin, Allen. "The Hollywood Letter." *Free World* (May 1946): 62-64.

"Saludos Amigos." *The Austin American*, August 7, 1943.

Schallert, Edwin. ""Snow White" Already Nominated Winner." *The Los Angeles Times*, December 26, 1937. 33.

Scheuer, Philip K. "Town Called Hollywood." *The Los Angeles Times*, December 26, 1937. 33.

"Screen Notes." *New York Times*, September 30, 1931.

Seastrom, Lucas. "Flowers and Trees at 90: Disney's First Color Movie." Walt Disney Family Museum. October 17, 2022.

"The Shakespeare Bridge: Franklin Avenue Bridge." Los Angeles Explorers Guild. Last modified November 15, 2021. https://losangelesexplorersguild.com/2021/11/15/shakespeare-bridge-franklin-avenue-bridge/.

Shortsleeve, Kevin. "The Wonderful World of the Depression: Disney, Despotism, and the 1930s. Or, Why Disney Scares Us." *The Lion and the Unicorn* (2004): 1-30.

Shull, Michael S., and David E. Wilt. *Doing Their Bit: Wartime American Animated Short Films, 1939-1945*. Jefferson, NC: McFarland & Company, Inc. Publishers, 1987.

Sibley, Brian. "With a Smile and a Song: Adriana Caselotti." *Animator Magazine* (1987): 22-23. https://www.animatormag.com/archive/1987/issue-21/issue-21-page-22/.

"Silly Symphony Secrets." *The Daily Telegraph* (London), November 3, 1934.

Sklar, Robert. *Movie-Made America: A Cultural History of American Movies*. New York: Vintage Books, 1994.

"Snow White Cottages." Atlas Obscura. https://www.atlasobscura.com/places/snow-white-cottages.

Spatz, Libby. "The Making of a Mickey Mouse Doll in 1930s Style." D23. June 11, 2013. https://d23.com/mc-calls-mickey-minnie-plush-dolls-1930/.

"The Story of Legendary Asian American Artist, Tyrus Wong." Asian Community Development Corporation. July 15, 2019. https://asiancdc.org/blog/2019/7/8/tyrus-wong.

Stull, William. "Fantasound – Disney's New Sound System." *American Cinematographer* (February 1941).

Suite 3H: The Offices of Walt Disney. Burbank, California: Walt Disney Archives.

Thomas, Bob. *Walt Disney: An American Original*. New York: Simon and Schuster, 1976.

Thompson, Kristin, and David Bordwell. *Film History: An Introduction*. 2nd ed. New York: McGraw-Hill, 2003.

Tillman, Nola T. "Charles Lindbergh and the First Solo Atlantic Flight." Space.com. June 11, 2019. https://www.space.com/16677-charles-lindbergh.html.

"To Discover the Real Bambi, Walt Disney Goes to Maine." New England Historical Society. 2022. https://newenglandhistoricalsociety.com/to-discover-the-real-bambi-walt-disney-goes-to-maine/.

Top Disney. "Walt Disney and Saint Joseph's Day." Top Disney. https://topdisneyblog.com/walt-disney-and-saint-josephs-day.

"Walt Disney: Great Teacher." *Fortune*, August 1942, 90-95.

Welky, David. *Everything Was Better in America: Print Culture in the Great Depression*. Urbana, IL: University of Illinois Press, 2008.

Wilson, B.F. "The Lowdown on Mickey Mouse." *Modern Screen* (March 1934).

Woolf, SJ. "Walt Disney Tells Us What Makes Him Happy." *New York Times*, July 10, 1938.

Young, Robert L. "They Have Named Club Mickey Mouse." *The Chicago Defender*, September 19, 1931.